enVision Mathematics
Common Core

Volume 1 Topics 1-8

Authors

Randall I. Charles
Professor Emeritus
Department of Mathematics
San Jose State University
San Jose, California

Jennifer Bay-Williams
Professor of Mathematics Education
College of Education and Human
Development
University of Louisville
Louisville, Kentucky

Robert Q. Berry, III
Professor of Mathematics Education
Department of Curriculum,
Instruction and Special Education
University of Virginia
Charlottesville, Virginia

Janet H. Caldwell
Professor Emerita
Department of Mathematics
Rowan University
Glassboro, New Jersey

Zachary Champagne
Assistant in Research
Florida Center for Research in Science,
Technology, Engineering, and
Mathematics (FCR-STEM)
Jacksonville, Florida

Juanita Copley
Professor Emerita, College of Education
University of Houston
Houston, Texas

Warren Crown
Professor Emeritus of Mathematics
Education
Graduate School of Education
Rutgers University
New Brunswick, New Jersey

Francis (Skip) Fennell
Professor Emeritus of
Education and Graduate and
Professional Studies
McDaniel College
Westminster, Maryland

Karen Karp
Professor of Mathematics Education
School of Education
Johns Hopkins University
Baltimore, Maryland

Stuart J. Murphy
Visual Learning Specialist
Boston, Massachusetts

Jane F. Schielack
Professor Emerita
Department of Mathematics
Texas A&M University
College Station, Texas

Jennifer M. Suh
Associate Professor for
Mathematics Education
George Mason University
Fairfax, Virginia

Jonathan A. Wray
Mathematics Supervisor
Howard County Public Schools
Ellicott City, Maryland

SAVVAS
LEARNING COMPANY

Mathematicians

Roger Howe
Professor of Mathematics
Yale University
New Haven, Connecticut

Gary Lippman
Professor of Mathematics and
Computer Science
California State University, East Bay
Hayward, California

ELL Consultants

Janice R. Corona
Independent Education Consultant
Dallas, Texas

Jim Cummins
Professor
The University of Toronto
Toronto, Canada

Reviewers

Katina Arnold
Teacher
Liberty Public School District
Kansas City, Missouri

Christy Bennett
Elementary Math and Science
Specialist
DeSoto County Schools
Hernando, Mississippi

Shauna Bostick
Elementary Math Specialist
Lee County School District
Tupelo, Mississippi

Samantha Brant
Teacher
Platte County School District
Platte City, Missouri

Jamie Clark
Elementary Math Coach
Allegany County Public Schools
Cumberland, Maryland

Shauna Gardner
Math and Science Instructional Coach
DeSoto County Schools
Hernando, Mississippi

Kathy Graham
Educational Consultant
Twin Falls, Idaho

Andrea Hamilton
K-5 Math Specialist
Lake Forest School District
Felton, Delaware

Susan Hankins
Instructional Coach
Tupelo Public School District
Tupelo, Mississippi

Barb Jamison
Teacher
Excelsior Springs School District
Excelsior Springs, Missouri

Pam Jones
Elementary Math Coach
Lake Region School District
Bridgton, Maine

Sherri Kane
Secondary Mathematics
Curriculum Specialist
Lee's Summit R7 School District
Lee's Summit, Missouri

Jessica Leonard
ESOL Teacher
Volusia County Schools
DeLand, Florida

Jill K. Milton
Elementary Math Coordinator
Norwood Public Schools
Norwood, Massachusetts

Jamie Pickett
Teacher
Platte County School District
Kansas City, Missouri

Mandy Schall
Math Coach
Allegany County Public Schools
Cumberland, Maryland

Marjorie Stevens
Math Consultant
Utica Community Schools
Shelby Township, Michigan

Shyree Stevenson
ELL Teacher
Penns Grove-Carneys Point
Regional School District
Penns Grove, New Jersey

Kayla Stone
Teacher
Excelsior Springs School District
Excelsior Springs, Missouri

Sara Sultan
PD Academic Trainer, Math
Tucson Unified School District
Tucson, Arizona

Angela Waltrup
Elementary Math Content Specialist
Washington County Public Schools
Hagerstown, Maryland

ISBN-13: 978-0-13-495466-0
ISBN-10: 0-13-495466-1
9 2022

You'll be using these digital resources throughout the year!

Digital Resources

Go to SavvasRealize.com

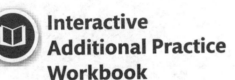 **Interactive Student Edition**
Access online or offline.

 **Visual Learning**
Interact with visual learning animations.

 Activity
Solve a problem and share your thinking.

 **Interactive Additional Practice Workbook**
Access online or offline.

Videos
Watch Math Practices Animations, Another Look Videos, and clips to support 3-Act Math.

 Practice Buddy
Do interactive practice online.

Math Tools
Explore math with digital tools.

 Games
Play math games to help you learn.

 Glossary
Read and listen in English and Spanish.

Assessment
Show what you've learned.

SAVVAS realize™ Everything you need for math anytime, anywhere

Contents

Digital Resources at SavvasRealize.com

And remember your Interactive Student Edition is available at SavvasRealize.com!

SavvasRealize.com

You can use numbers to show the number of objects.

4

TOPIC 1
Numbers 0 to 5

Contents

There are more tennis balls than footballs when you compare.

TOPIC 2
Compare Numbers 0 to 5

SavvasRealize.com

You can use counters to show how many.

TOPIC 3
Numbers 6 to 10

Contents

There is a greater number of red fish than purple fish.

TOPIC 4
Compare Numbers 0 to 10

The animals are classified into a category of animals with hair and a category of animals without hair.

Hair   NO Hair

TOPIC 5
Classify and Count Data

Contents

You can use addition to show joining groups.

___ and ___ is ___.

TOPIC 6
Understand Addition

This shows 5 − 2 = 3.

TOPIC 7
Understand Subtraction

Contents

You can write equations to show parts of numbers.

$$8 = 2 + 6$$

TOPIC 8
More Addition and Subtraction

Dear Families,

The standards on the following pages describe the math that students will learn this year.

DOMAIN K.CC
COUNTING AND CARDINALITY

MAJOR CLUSTER K.OA.A
Know number names and the count sequence.

K.CC.A.1 Count to 100 by ones and by tens.

K.CC.A.2 Count forward beginning from a given number within the known sequence (instead of having to begin at 1).

K.CC.A.3 Write numbers from 0 to 20. Represent a number of objects with a written numeral 0–20 (with 0 representing a count of no objects).

MAJOR CLUSTER K.CC.B
Count to tell the number of objects.

K.CC.B.4 Understand the relationship between numbers and quantities; connect counting to cardinality.

K.CC.B.4a When counting objects, say the number names in the standard order, pairing each object with one and only one number name and each number name with one and only one object.

K.CC.B.4b Understand that the last number name said tells the number of objects counted. The number of objects is the same regardless of their arrangement or the order in which they were counted.

K.CC.B.4c Understand that each successive number name refers to a quantity that is one larger.

K.CC.B.5 Count to answer "how many?" questions about as many as 20 things arranged in a line, a rectangular array, or a circle, or as many as 10 things in a scattered configuration; given a number from 1–20, count out that many objects.

Common Core Standards

MAJOR CLUSTER K.CC.C
Compare numbers.

K.CC.C.6 Identify whether the number of objects in one group is greater than, less than, or equal to the number of objects in another group, e.g., by using matching and counting strategies.[1]

K.CC.C.7 Compare two numbers between 1 and 10 presented as written numerals.

DOMAIN K.OA
OPERATIONS AND ALGEBRAIC THINKING

MAJOR CLUSTER K.OA.A
Understand addition as putting together and adding to, and understand subtraction as taking apart and taking from.

K.OA.A.1 Represent addition and subtraction with objects, fingers, mental images, drawings[2], sounds (e.g., claps), acting out situations, verbal explanations, expressions, or equations.

K.OA.A.2 Solve addition and subtraction word problems, and add and subtract within 10, e.g., by using objects or drawings to represent the problem ([1]Students are not required to independently read the word problems.)

K.OA.A.3 Decompose numbers less than or equal to 10 into pairs in more than one way, e.g., by using objects or drawings, and record each decomposition by a drawing or equation (e.g., $5 = 2 + 3$ and $5 = 4 + 1$).

K.OA.A.4 For any number from 1 to 9, find the number that makes 10 when added to the given number, e.g., by using objects or drawings, and record the answer with a drawing or equation.

K.OA.A.5 Fluently add and subtract within 5.

DOMAIN K.NBT
NUMBER AND OPERATIONS IN BASE TEN

MAJOR CLUSTER K.NBT.A
Work with numbers 11–19 to gain foundations for place value.

K.NBT.A.1 Compose and decompose numbers from 11 to 19 into ten ones and some further ones, e.g., by using objects or drawings, and record each composition or decomposition by a drawing or equation (e.g., $18 = 10 + 8$); understand that these numbers are composed of ten ones and one, two, three, four, five, six, seven, eight, or nine ones.

DOMAIN K.MD
MEASUREMENT AND DATA

ADDITIONAL CLUSTER K.MD.A
Describe and compare measurable attributes.

K.MD.A.1 Describe measurable attributes of objects, such as length or weight. Describe several measurable attributes of a single object.

K.MD.A.2 Directly compare two objects with a measurable attribute in common, to see which object has "more of"/"less of" the attribute, and describe the difference. *For example, directly compare the heights of two children and describe one child as taller/shorter.*

SUPPORTING CLUSTER K.MD.B
Classify objects and count the number of objects in each category.

K.MD.B.3 Classify objects into given categories; count the numbers of objects in each category and sort the categories by count.[3]

Common Core Standards

DOMAIN K.G
GEOMETRY

ADDITIONAL CLUSTER K.G.A
Identify and describe shapes (squares, circles, triangles, rectangles, hexagons, cubes, cones, cylinders, and spheres).

K.G.A.1 Describe objects in the environment using names of shapes, and describe the relative positions of these objects using terms such as *above, below, beside, in front of, behind,* and *next to.*

K.G.A.2 Correctly name shapes regardless of their orientations or overall size.

K.G.A.3 Identify shapes as two-dimensional (lying in a plane, "flat") or three-dimensional ("solid").

SUPPORTING CLUSTER K.G.B
Analyze, compare, create, and compose shapes.

K.G.B.4 Analyze and compare two- and three-dimensional shapes, in different sizes and orientations, using informal language to describe their similarities, differences, parts (e.g., number of sides and vertices/"corners") and other attributes (e.g., having sides of equal length).

K.G.B.5 Model shapes in the world by building shapes from components (e.g., sticks and clay balls) and drawing shapes.

K.G.B.6 Compose simple shapes to form larger shapes. *For example, "Can you join these two triangles with full sides touching to make a rectangle?"*

[1]Include groups with up to ten objects.
[2]Drawings need not show details, but should show the mathematics in the problem. (This applies wherever drawings are mentioned on the Standards.)

[3]Limit category counts to be less than or equal to 10.

MATHEMATICAL PRACTICES

MP.1 Make sense of problems and persevere in solving them.

MP.2 Reason abstractly and quantitatively.

MP.3 Construct viable arguments and critique the reasoning of others.

MP.4 Model with mathematics.

MP.5 Use appropriate tools strategically.

MP.6 Attend to precision.

MP.7 Look for and make use of structure.

MP.8 Look for and express regularity in repeated reasoning.

Math Practices and Problem Solving Handbook

The **Math Practices and Problem Solving Handbook** is available at SavvasRealize.com.

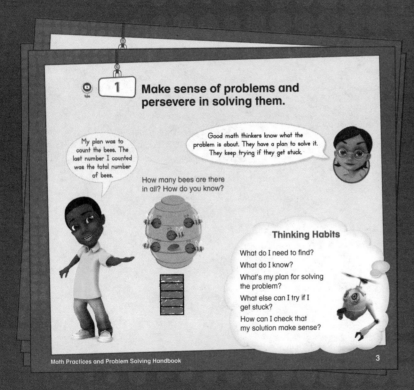

Math Practices

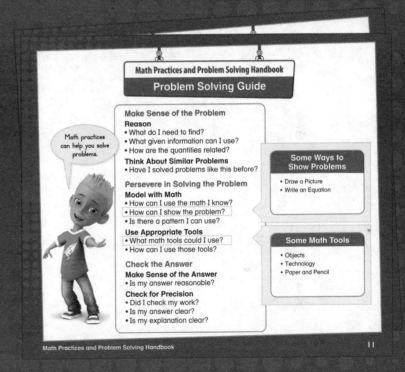

Problem Solving Guide
Problem Solving Recording Sheet

TOPIC
1

Numbers 0 to 5

Essential Question: How can numbers from 0 to 5 be counted, read, and written?

Digital Resources

Interactive Student Edition · Activity · Visual Learning · Video · Practice

Assessment · Games · Tools · Glossary

It rains on some days. It is sunny on other days.

Rain

enVision STEM Project: Weather Changes

Directions Read the character speech bubbles to students. **Find Out!** Have students pay attention to the daily weather changes. Say: *The weather changes from day to day. Talk to friends and relatives about the weather. Ask them to help you record the number of sunny days and rainy days from Monday to Friday.* **Journal: Make a Poster** Have students make a poster of the weather information they collected. Have them draw suns for the number of sunny days and clouds with raindrops for the number of rainy days. Then have students write the numbers to tell how many.

Name _____

Review What You Know

1

2

3

4

5

6

Directions Have students: **1** draw a circle around the animal that is on the right; **2** draw a circle around the animal that is on the left; **3** draw a circle around the animal that is green; **4**–**6** draw a line from each object in the top row to an object in the bottom row.

2 two

Topic 1

Name _____

A

B

C

Directions Say: *You will choose one of these projects. Look at picture **A**. Think about this question: What would animals say if they could talk? If you choose Project A, you will create funny animal characters and tell a story. Look at picture **B**. Think about this question: Does your favorite sport or game use a ball? If you choose Project B, you will make a poster of different balls that are used in sports and games. Look at picture **C**. Think about this question: What would you want to show on a license plate? If you choose Project C, you will create a license plate for your bike.*

3-ACT MATH PREVIEW

Set the Table

Video

Who's hungry?

Directions Read the robot's speech bubble to students. **Generate Interest** Ask students if they have ever set the table. Say: *Who sets the table before meals? What chores are you responsible for at home?* Have them share stories about responsibilities and rules around the house.

I can ...
model with math to count to solve a problem.

© **Mathematical Practices** MP.4
Also MP.1, MP.6
Content Standards K.CC.B.4b
Also K.CC.A.3, K.CC.B.4a,
K.CC.B.4c, K.CC.B.5

Solve & Share

Name _____

Activity

Directions Have students place 2 counters in the nest on the workmat. Say: *Peeps the bird found these worms for her babies. Draw a circle around the colored box that shows how many worms Peeps found. Tell how you know you are correct.*

I can ...
count 1, 2, and 3 objects.

© **Content Standards** K.CC.B.4a
Also K.CC.B.5
Mathematical Practices MP.2, MP.3, and MP.5

⭐ Guided Practice

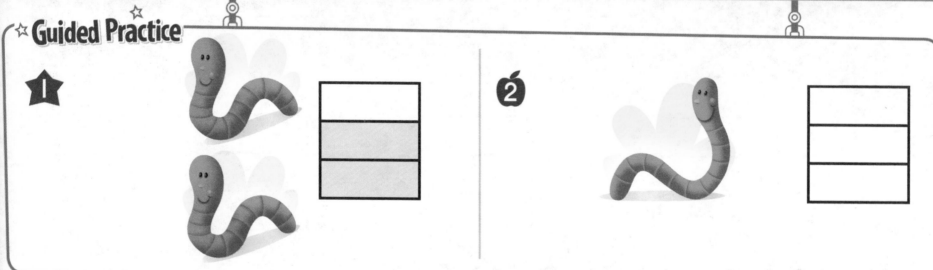

Directions ⭐ and ❷ Have students color a box as they count each worm to show how many.

Name ______________________________

3

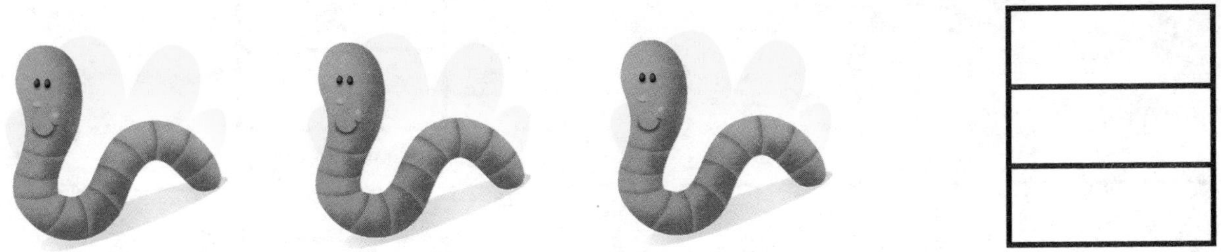

4

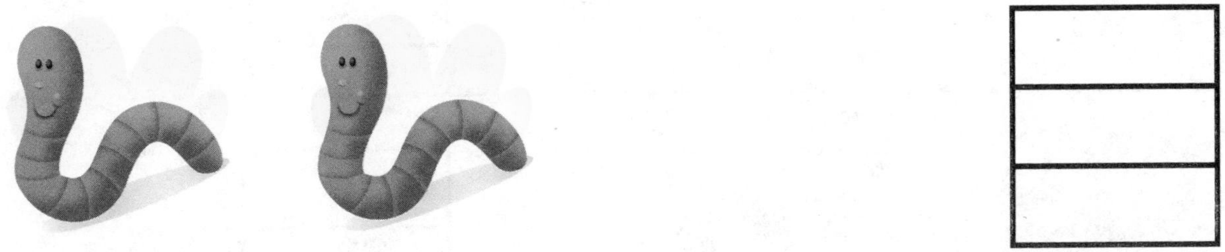

5

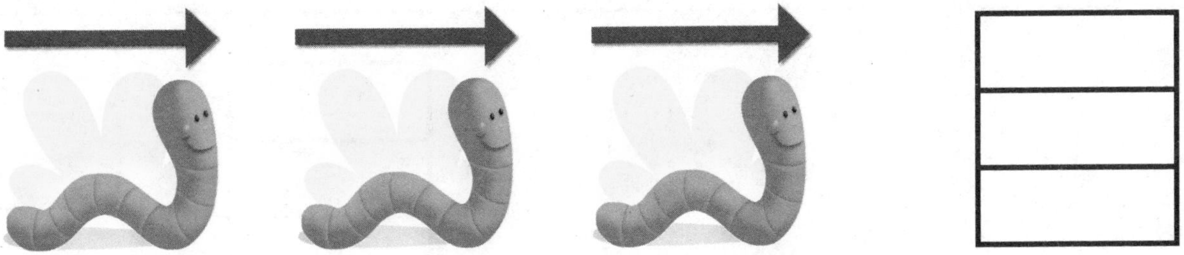

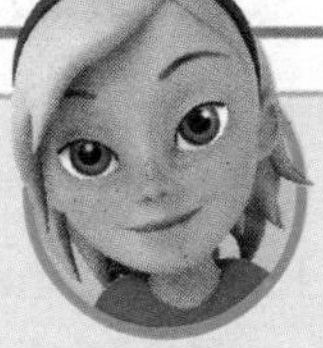

Directions 3 and 4 Have students color a box as they count each worm to show how many. 5 **Vocabulary** Have students **count** the worms, and color a box as they count each worm aloud.

Independent Practice

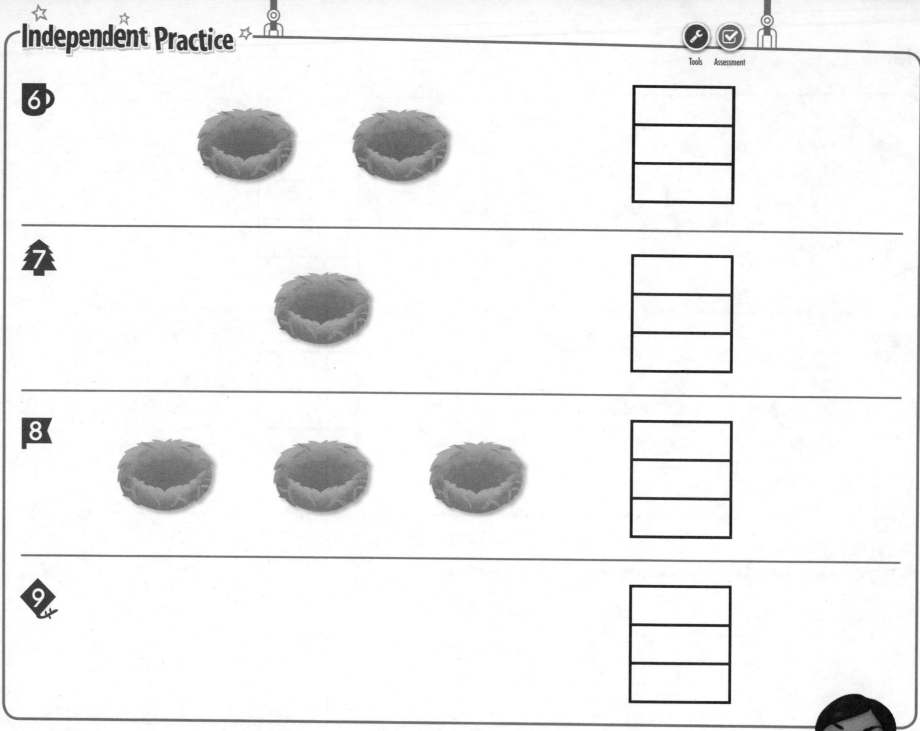

Directions 6–8 Have students color a box as they count each nest to show how many. ✦ **Higher Order Thinking** Have students draw 1, 2, or 3 nests, and then color a box as they draw each nest to show how many.

8 eight

Topic 1 | Lesson 1

Solve & Share

Name _____

Activity

Lesson 1-2
Recognize
1, 2, and 3
in Different
Arrangements

Directions Say: *Redbird and Bluebird each have 2 babies. Redbird and Bluebird get worms for their babies and put them in their nests. Bluebird's worms moved around in the nest. Show and count how many worms with your counters. Color the boxes to show the worms in each nest. Tell how you know you are correct.*

I can ...
count groups of 1, 2, and 3 objects shown in different ways.

© **Content Standards** K.CC.B.4b
Also K.CC.B.5
Mathematical Practices MP.2,
MP.3, and MP.4

Visual Learning Bridge

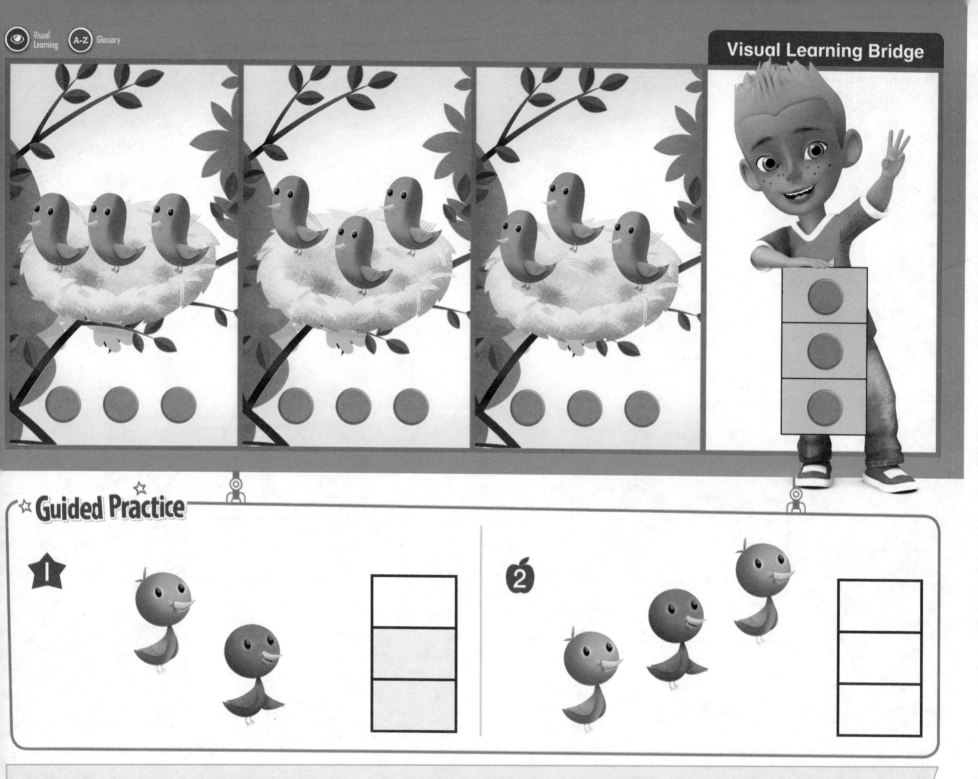

☆ Guided Practice

1

2

Directions ⭐ and 🍎 Have students count each bird, and then color the boxes to show how many.

Topic 1 | Lesson 2

Name ______________________________

3

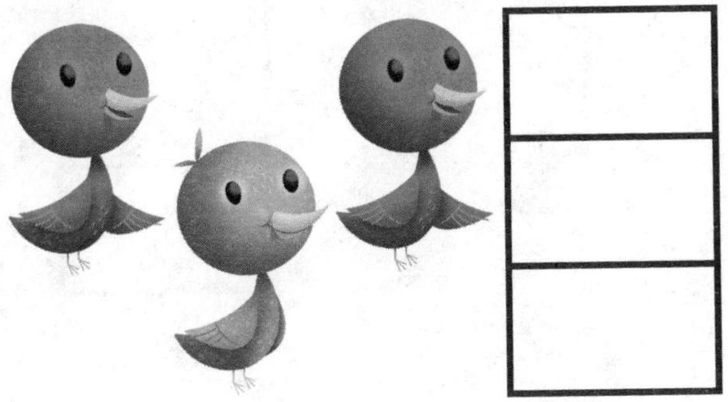

4

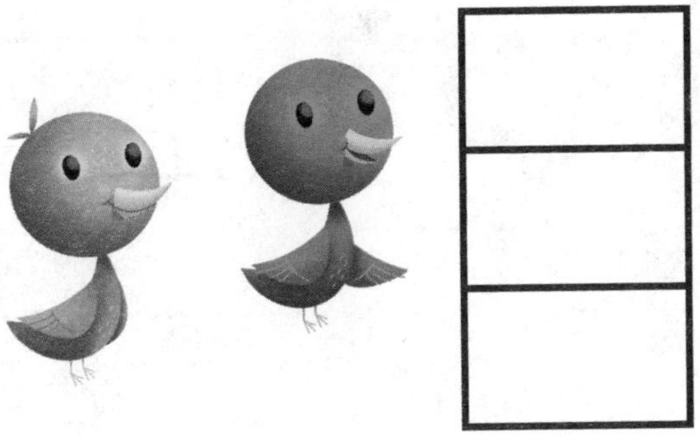

5

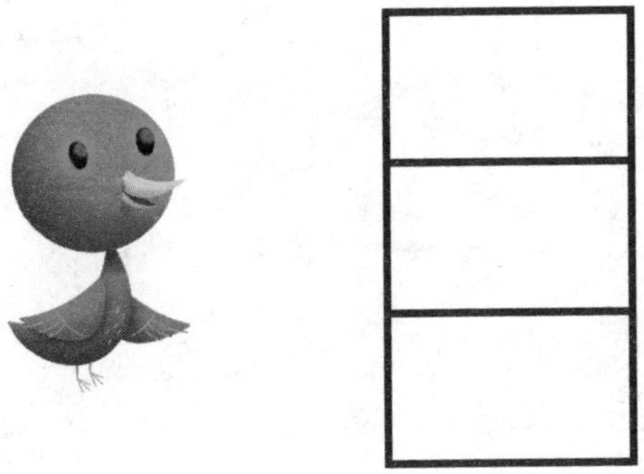

6

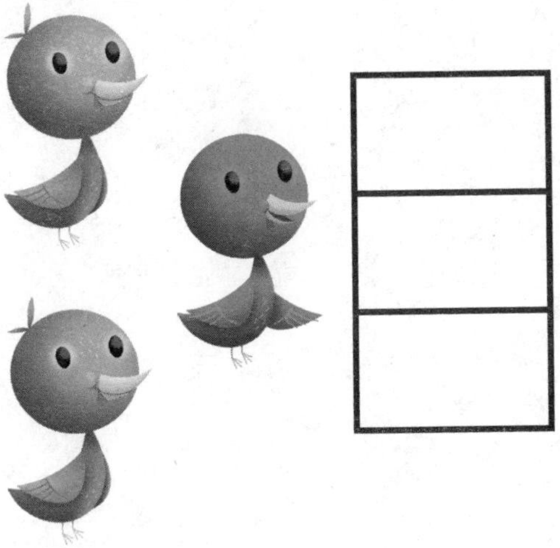

7

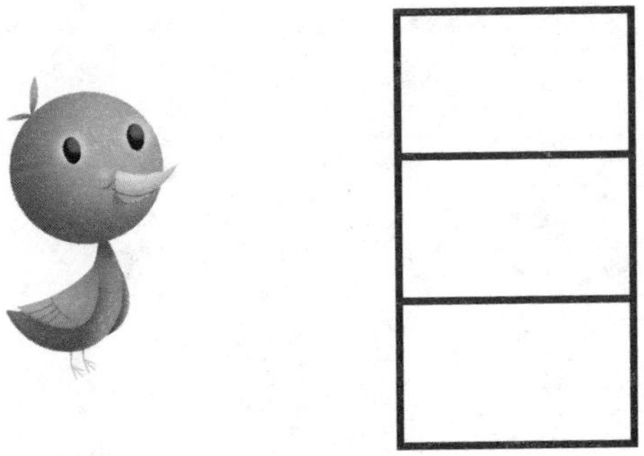

8

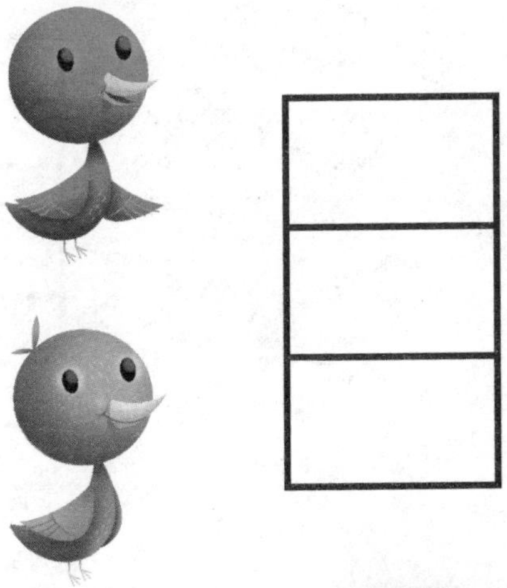

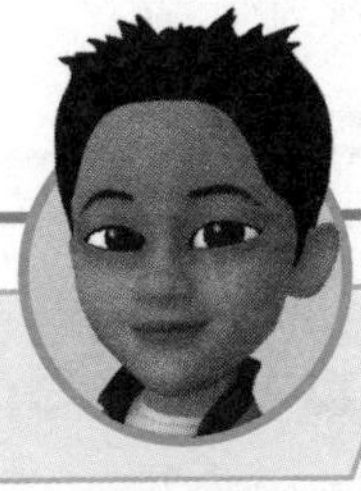

Directions 3–8 Have students count each bird, and then color the boxes to show how many.

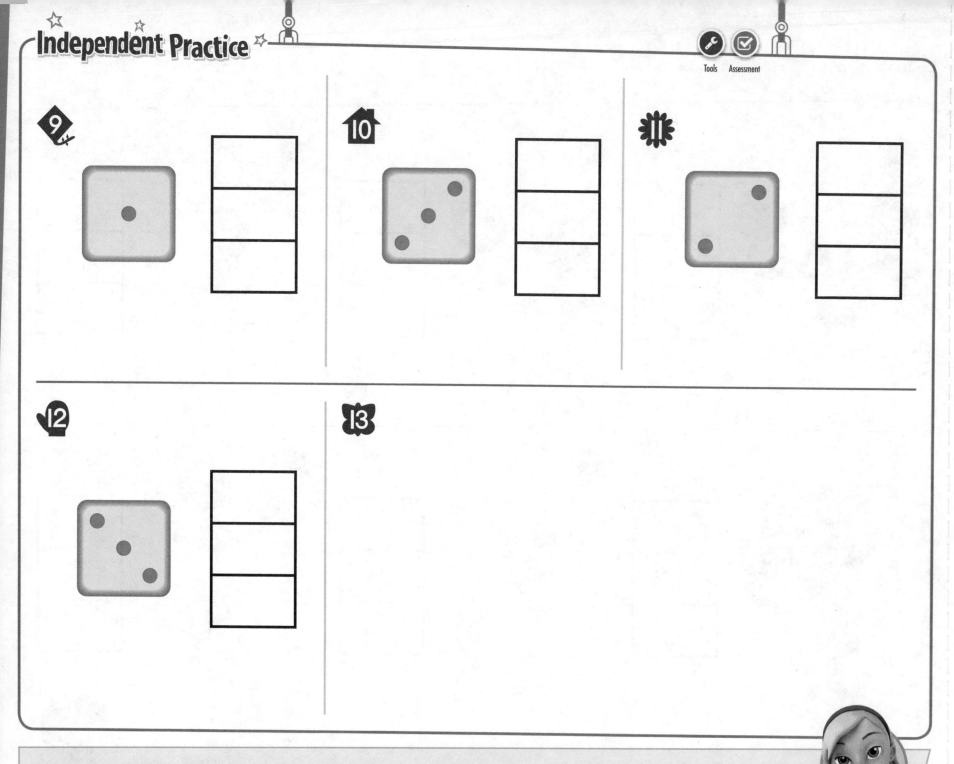

9

10

11

12

13

Directions 9—12 Have students count the dots, and then color the boxes to show how many.
13 **Higher Order Thinking** Have students draw 2 counters, and then draw 2 counters in a different way.

12 twelve

Topic 1 | Lesson 2

Name _____

Activity

Directions Say: *Alex sees 2 stars in the sky. He draws 2 stars in a cloud. Place counters in the large cloud on the workmat to show how many stars. How can you show how many stars Alex sees in other ways? Draw or use objects to show other ways in the small, empty cloud.*

I can ...
read and write the numbers 1, 2, and 3.

© **Content Standards** K.CC.A.3
Also K.CC.B.5
Mathematical Practices MP.3, MP.5, and MP.6

3

3

three

☆ Guided Practice

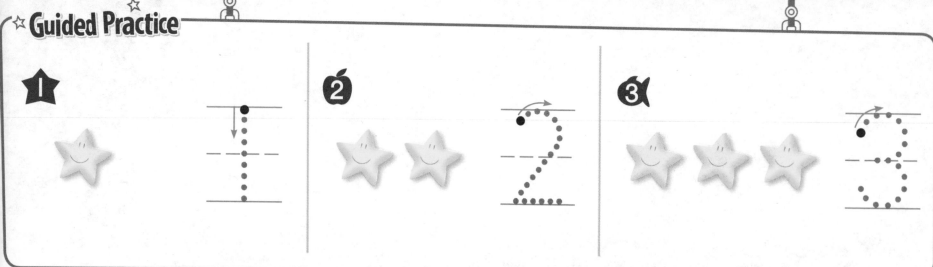

1

2

3

Directions ⭐–❸ Have students count the stars, and then write the number to tell how many.

Name _____

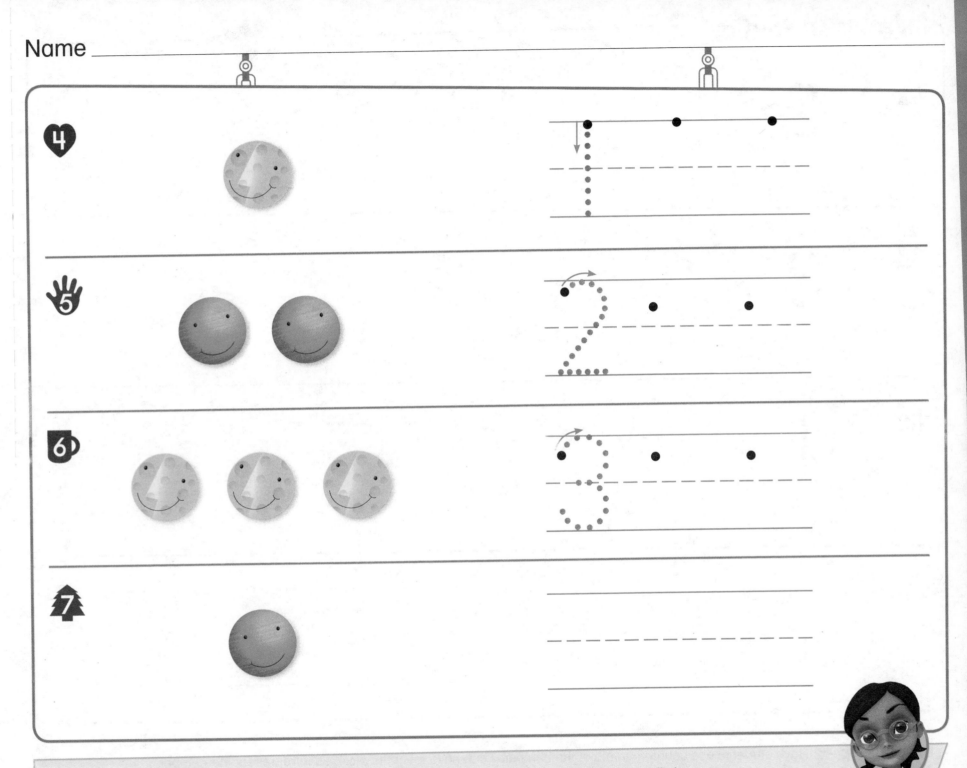

Directions ❤️–🌲 Have students count the objects, and then practice writing the number that tells how many.

fifteen **15**

Topic 1 | Lesson 3

Independent Practice

Tools Assessment

8 2

9 3

10 1

11

Directions 8–10 Have students use counters to make the number. Then have them draw circles to represent the number. 11 **Higher Order Thinking** Have students draw 1, 2, or 3 stars, and then practice writing the number that tells how many.

Solve & Share

Name _____

Activity

Directions Have students place 5 counters in the tree on the workmat. Then say: *Chips the chipmunk found these nuts. Draw a circle around the colored box that shows how many nuts Chips found. Tell how you know you are correct.*

I can ...
count 4 and 5 objects.

© **Content Standards** K.CC.B.4a
Also K.CC.B.5
Mathematical Practices MP.3, MP.4, and MP.5

Go Online | SavvasRealize.com

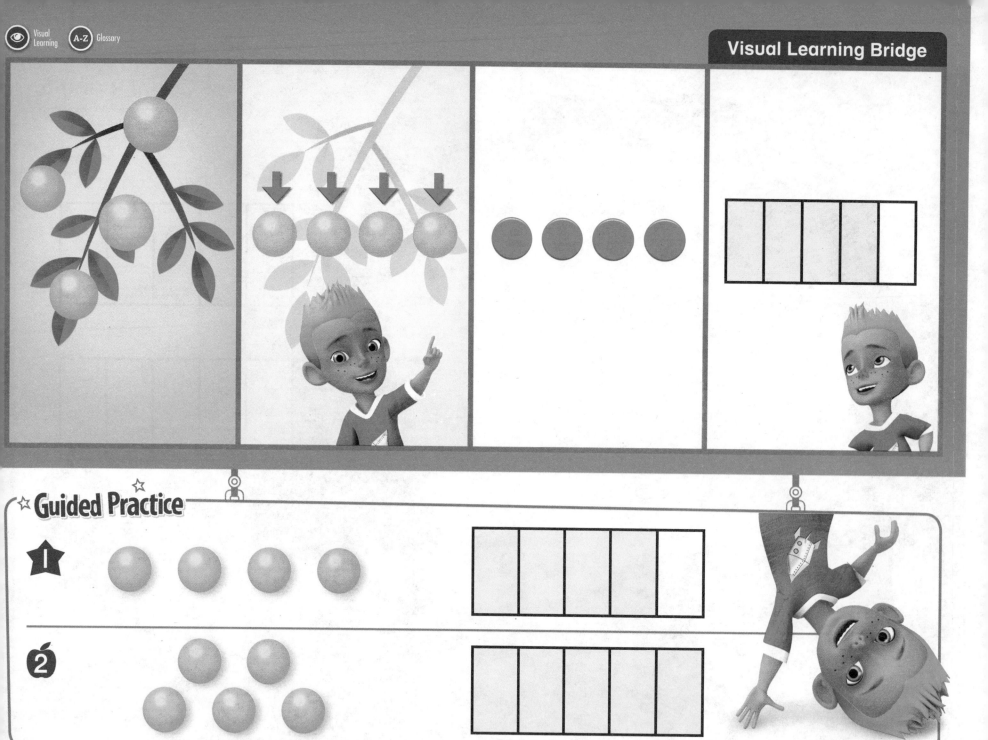

☆ Guided Practice

1

2

Directions ⭐ and ② Have students color a box as they count each orange to show how many.

Name

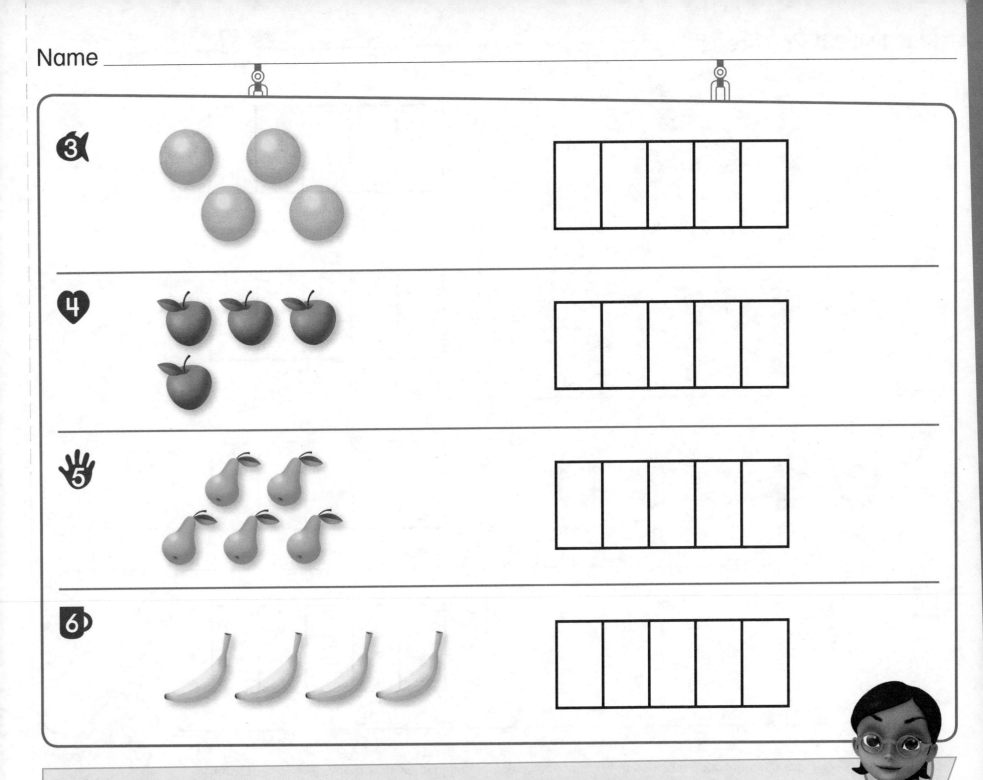

Directions ❸–❻ Have students color a box as they count each piece of fruit to show how many.

Independent Practice

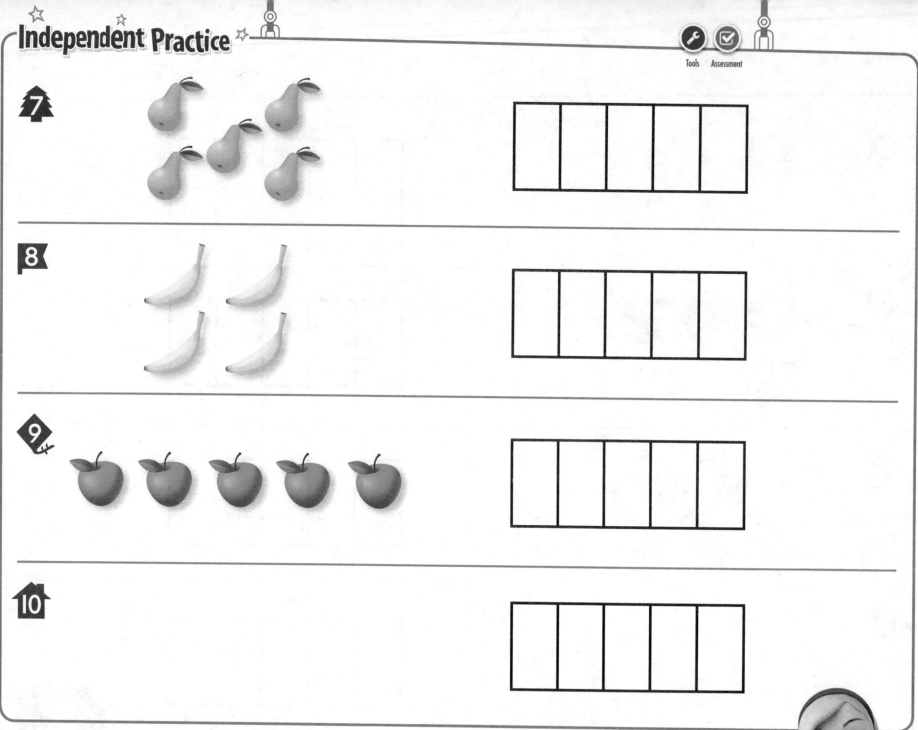

7

8

9

10

Directions **7**–**9** Have students color a box as they count each piece of fruit to show how many. **10** **Higher Order Thinking** Have students draw 4 or 5 oranges, and then color a box as they draw each orange to show how many.

Topic I | Lesson 4

Solve & Share

Name _____

Activity

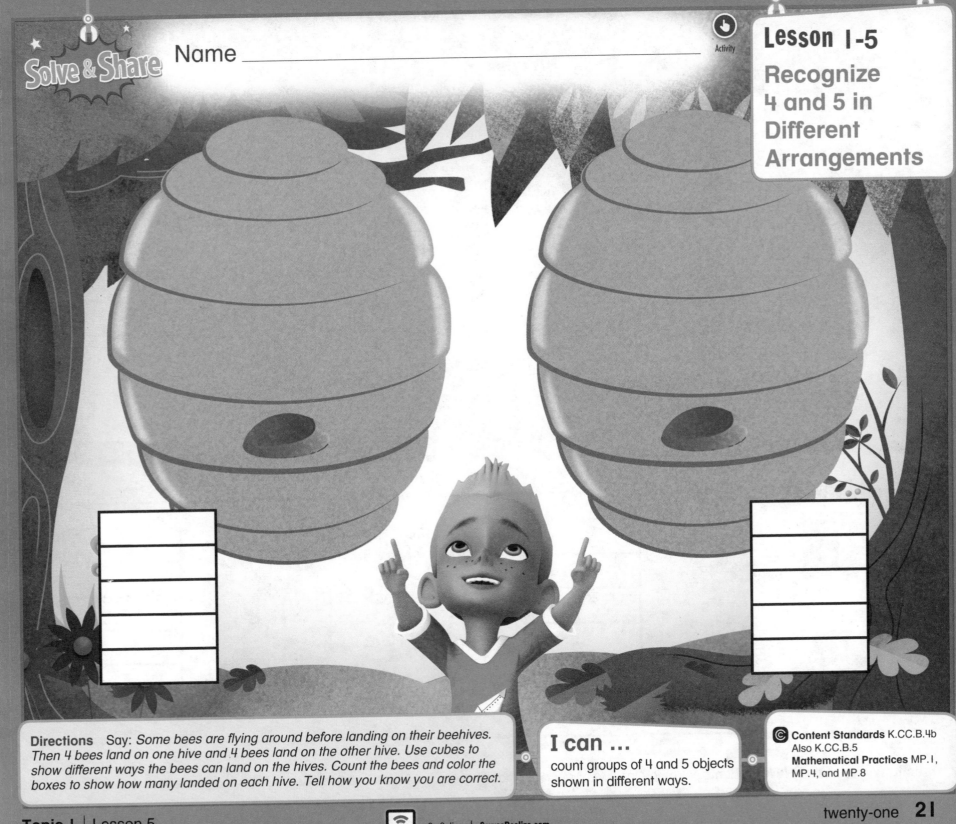

Directions Say: *Some bees are flying around before landing on their beehives. Then 4 bees land on one hive and 4 bees land on the other hive. Use cubes to show different ways the bees can land on the hives. Count the bees and color the boxes to show how many landed on each hive. Tell how you know you are correct.*

I can ...
count groups of 4 and 5 objects shown in different ways.

© **Content Standards** K.CC.B.4b
Also K.CC.B.5
Mathematical Practices MP.1, MP.4, and MP.8

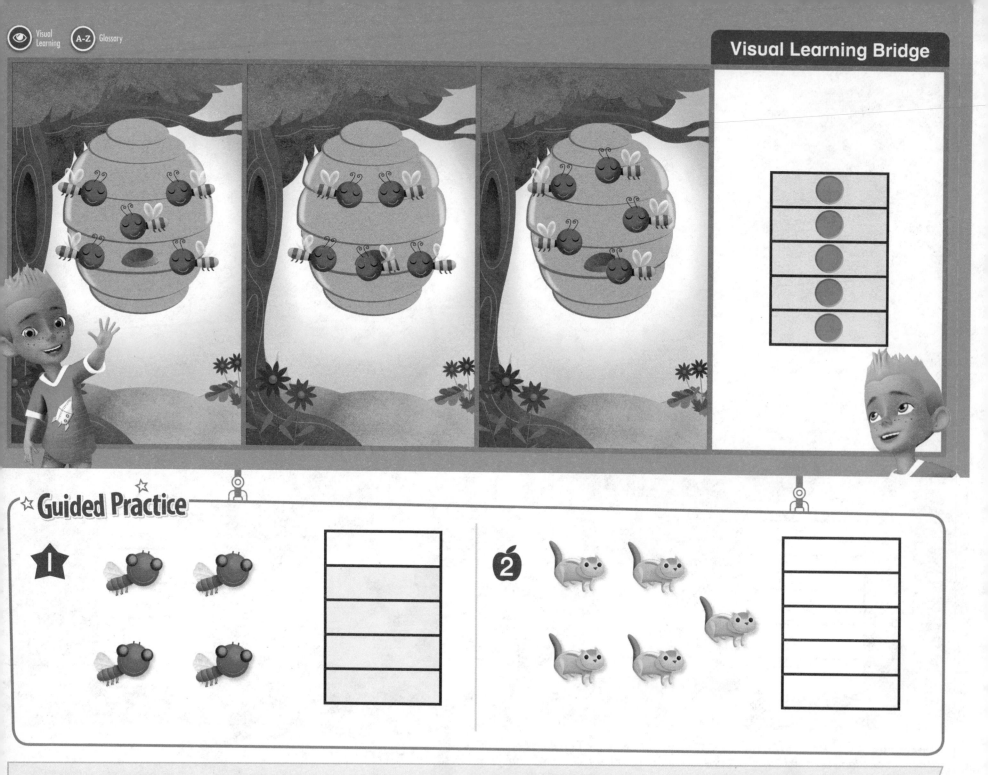

☆ Guided Practice

1

2

Directions ⭐ and 🍎 Have students count the insects or animals in each group, and then color the boxes to show how many.

Name _____

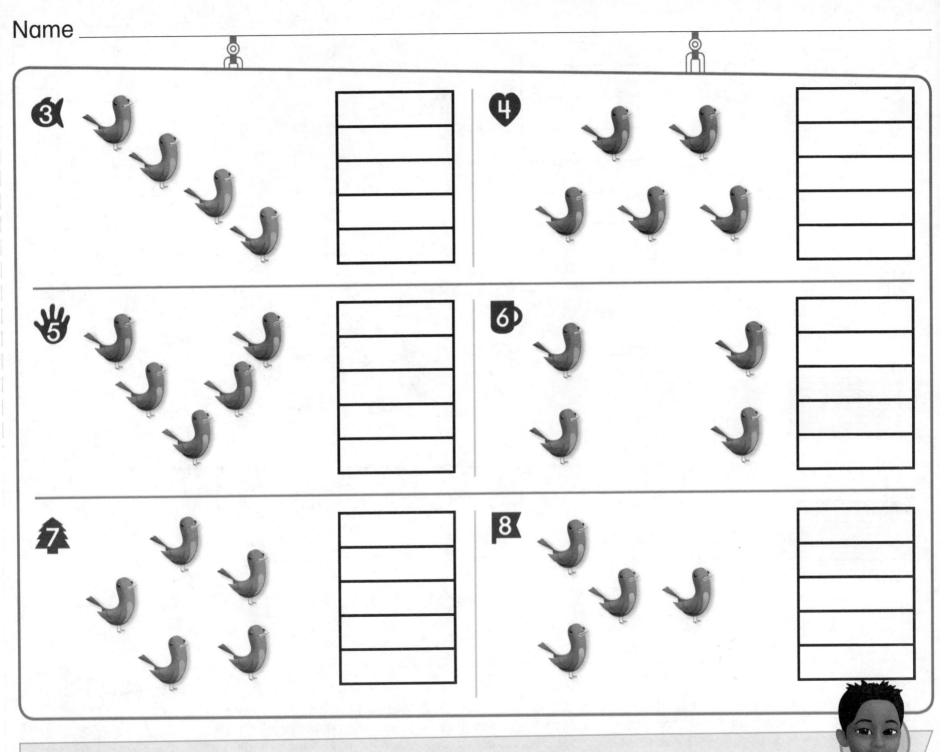

Directions ❸–❽ Have students count the birds, and then color the boxes to show how many.

Topic I | Lesson 5

twenty-three 23

Independent Practice

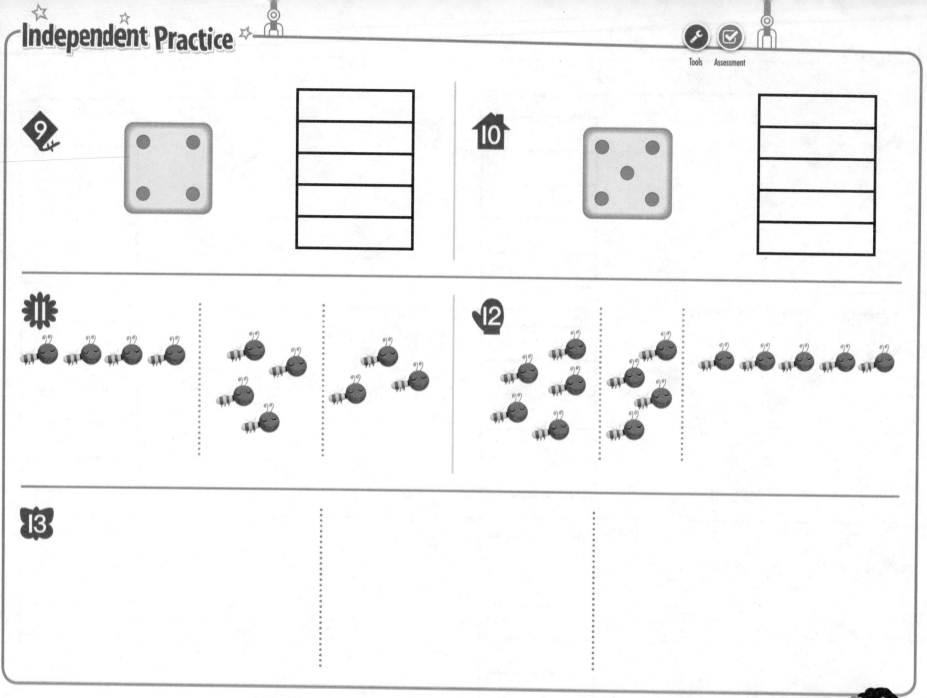

Solve & Share

Name _____

Activity

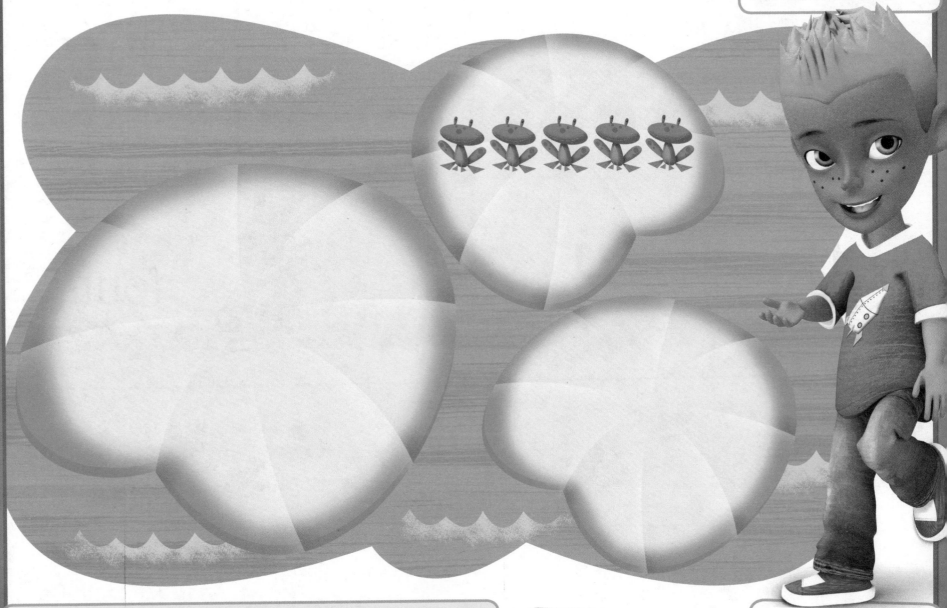

Directions Say: *Alex sees some frogs sitting on a lily pad. Show how many frogs he sees by placing counters on the large lily pad. Count and tell how many. Then draw or use objects to show how many frogs in other ways on the small, empty lily pad on the workmat.*

I can ...
read and write the numbers 4 and 5.

© **Content Standards** K.CC.A.3 Also K.CC.B.5
Mathematical Practices MP.2, MP.4, and MP.6

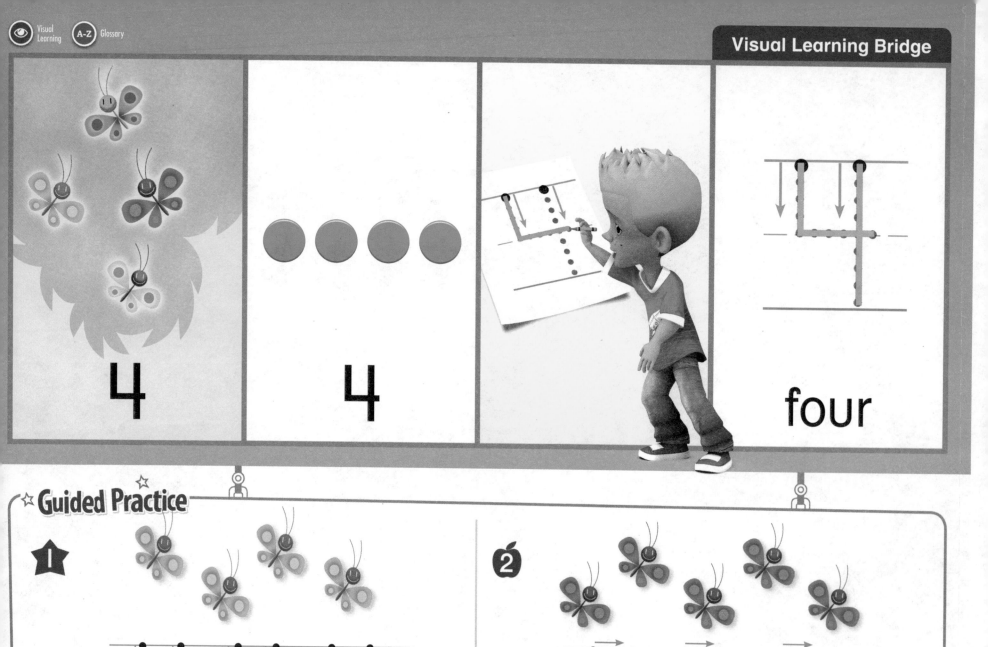

4

4

four

☆ **Guided Practice**

1

2

Directions ⭐ and ② Have students count the butterflies, and then practice writing the number that tells how many.

Topic I | Lesson 6

Name _____

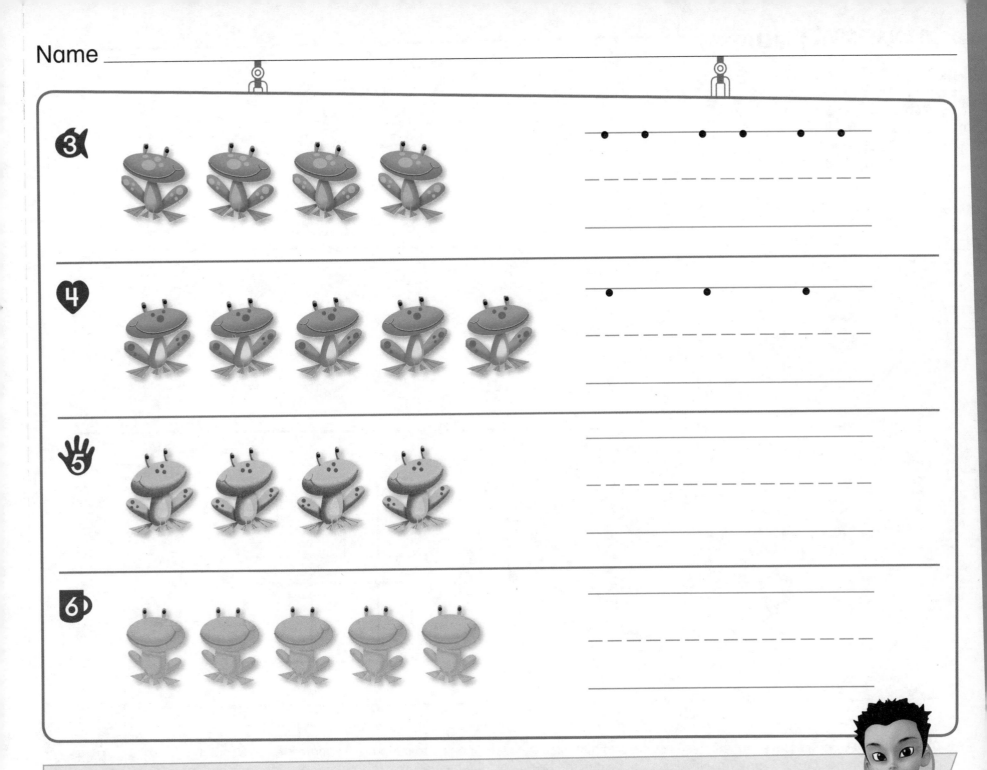

3

4

5

6

Directions 3–6 Have students count the frogs, and then practice writing the number that tells how many.

Topic 1 | Lesson 6

twenty-seven **27**

Independent Practice

 4

 5

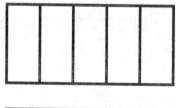

Directions ⓐ and ⓑ Have students use counters to make the number. Then have them draw squares to represent the number. ⓒ **Higher Order Thinking** Have students count the blue birds and the yellow birds, color a box for each bird, and then write the numbers to tell how many.

Topic I | Lesson 6

Solve & Share

Name _____

Directions Say: *Alex has a vegetable garden. Toss a number cube to see how many potatoes he has in his basket. Place counters on the basket to show how many. What does it mean if the cube face you roll has no dots? How can Alex use the boxes to show that there are no potatoes in the basket?*

I can ...
use zero to tell when there are no objects.

© **Content Standards** K.CC.B.4a Also K.CC.B.5
Mathematical Practices MP.1, MP.4, and MP.6

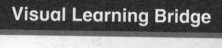
Visual Learning Bridge

☆ Guided Practice

1

2

Directions ★ and ❷ Have students color a box as they count each apple to show how many.

30 thirty

Topic I | Lesson 7

Name

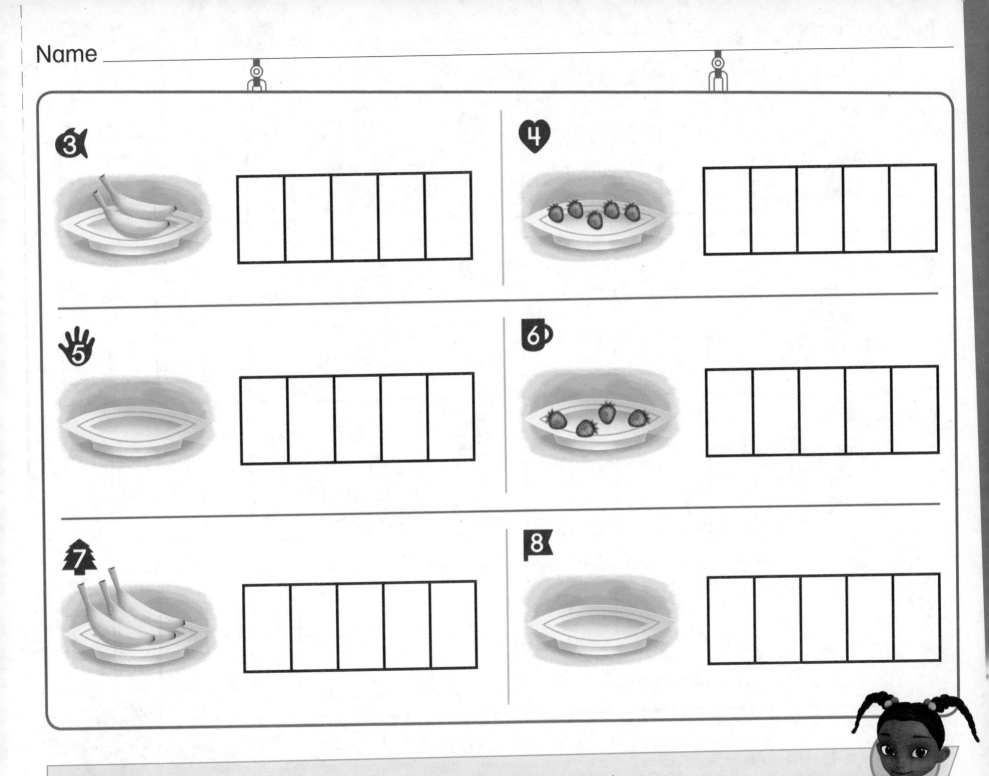

Directions 3–8 Have students color a box as they count each piece of fruit to show how many.

thirty-one 31

Topic 1 | Lesson 7

Independent Practice

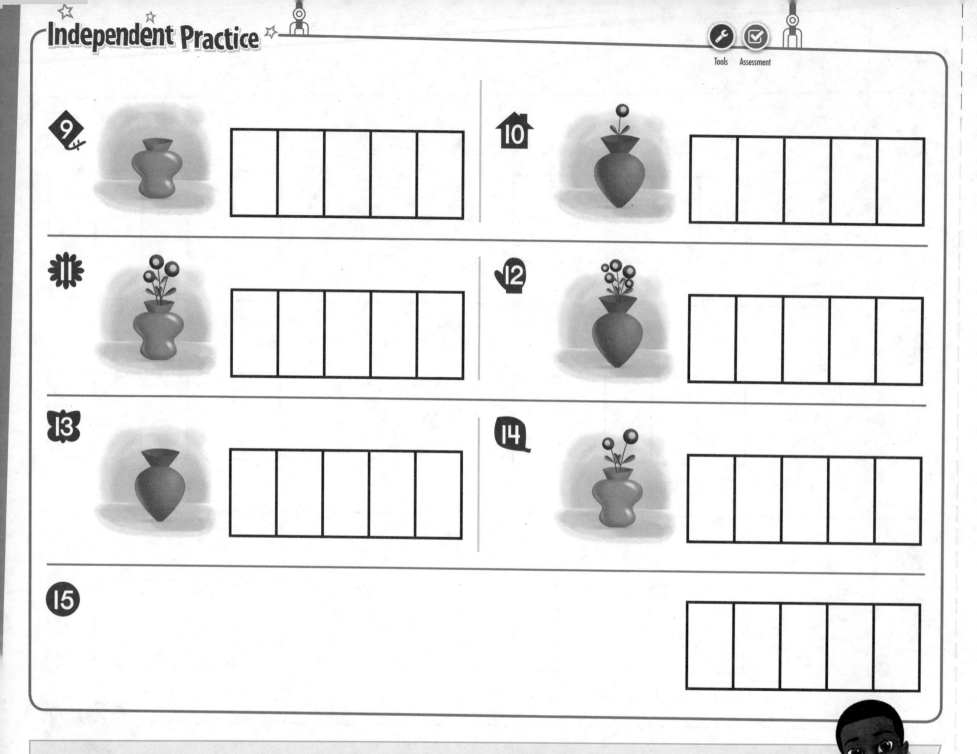

9

10

11

12

13

14

15

Directions **9–14** Have students color a box as they count each flower in the vase to show how many. **15 Higher Order Thinking** Have students pick a number between 0 and 5, draw that many flowers, and then color the boxes to show how many.

Topic 1 | Lesson 7

☆ ☆ Solve & Share

Name _____

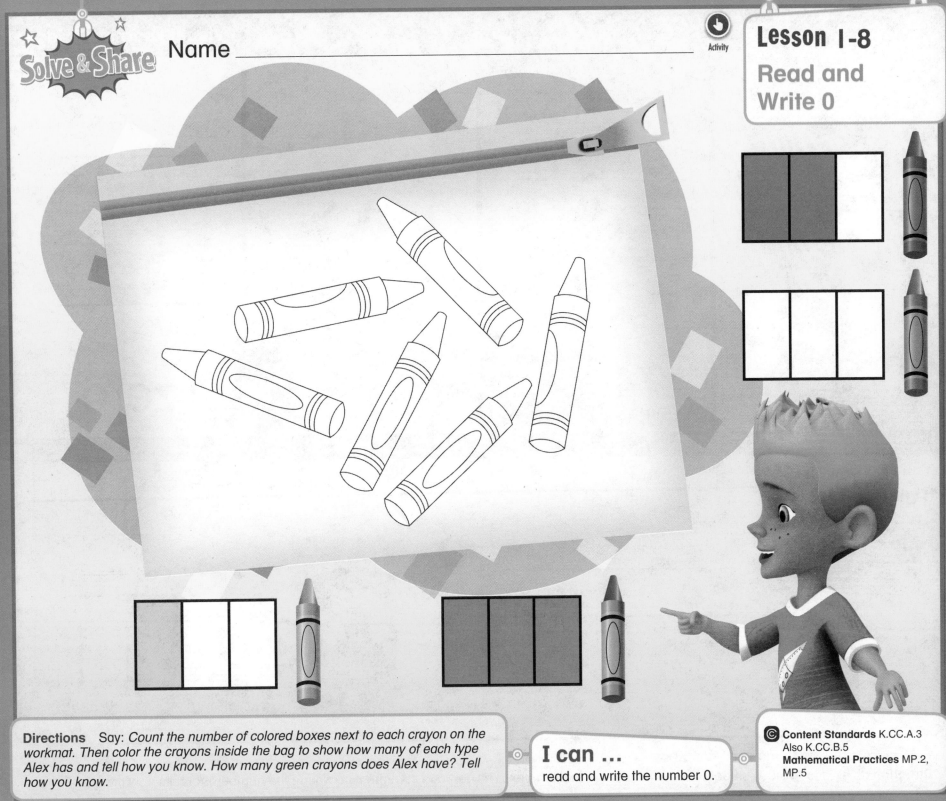

Directions Say: *Count the number of colored boxes next to each crayon on the workmat. Then color the crayons inside the bag to show how many of each type Alex has and tell how you know. How many green crayons does Alex have? Tell how you know.*

I can ...
read and write the number 0.

© **Content Standards** K.CC.A.3
Also K.CC.B.5
Mathematical Practices MP.2, MP.5

zero

☆ Guided Practice

1

2

Directions ⬆ and ❷ Have students count the pencils in each pencil holder, and then practice writing the number that tells how many.

Name _____

3 ● ● ●
- - - - - - - - - - - - - - - - - - -

4 ● ● ●
- - - - - - - - - - - - - - - - - - -

5 ●———●———●
- - - - - - - - - - - - - - - - - - -

6 ●———●———●
- - - - - - - - - - - - - - - - - - -

7
- - - - - - - - - - - - - - - - - - -

8
- - - - - - - - - - - - - - - - - - -

Directions **3–8** Have students count the pencils in each pencil holder, and then practice writing the number that tells how many.

thirty-five **35**

Independent Practice

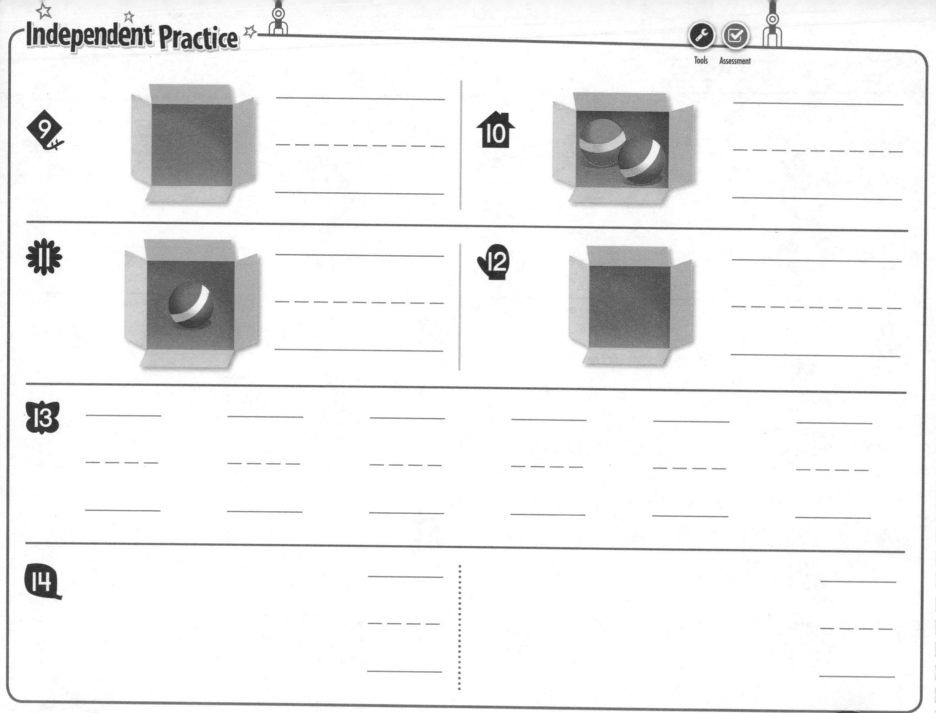

9 _____

_____

10 _____

_____

11 _____

_____

12 _____

_____

13 _____   _____   _____   _____   _____

_____   _____   _____   _____   _____

14 _____

_____

_____

_____

Directions Have students: **9–12** count the balls in each box, and then practice writing the number that tells how many; **13** practice writing the numbers 0 to 5. **14 Higher Order Thinking** Have students draw zero counters and write the number to tell how many, and then draw 1 to 5 counters and write the number to tell how many.

36 thirty-six

Topic 1 | Lesson 8

Solve & Share

Name _____

Activity

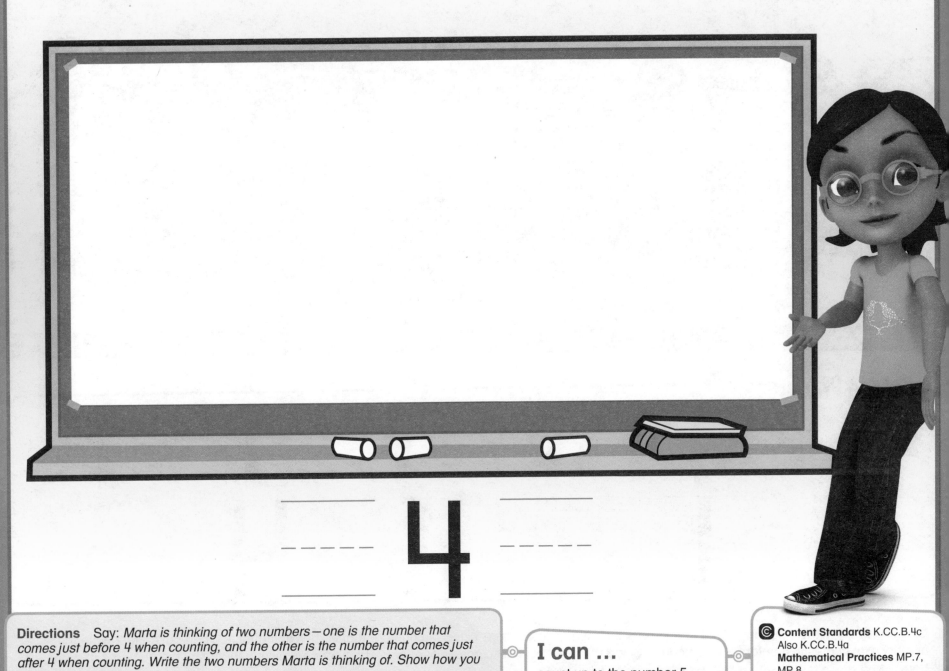

4

Directions Say: *Marta is thinking of two numbers—one is the number that comes just before 4 when counting, and the other is the number that comes just after 4 when counting. Write the two numbers Marta is thinking of. Show how you know you are correct.*

I can ...
count up to the number 5.

© **Content Standards** K.CC.B.4c Also K.CC.B.4a
Mathematical Practices MP.7, MP.8

☆ Guided Practice

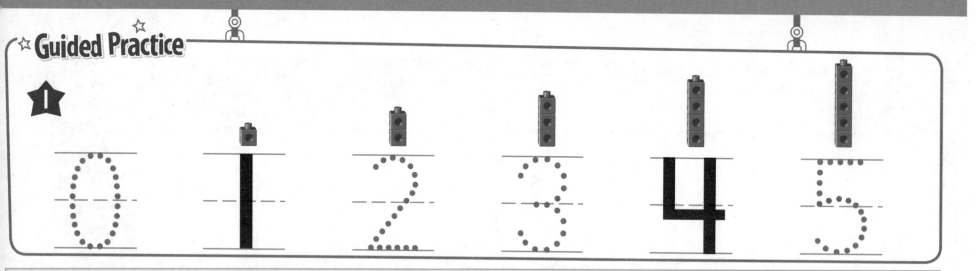

Directions ⭐ Have students write the number that comes just before 1 and the number that comes just after 1. Then have them write the number that comes just before 4 when counting, and the number that comes just after 4 when counting. Have them say the numbers in order from 0 to 5.

Topic 1 | Lesson 9

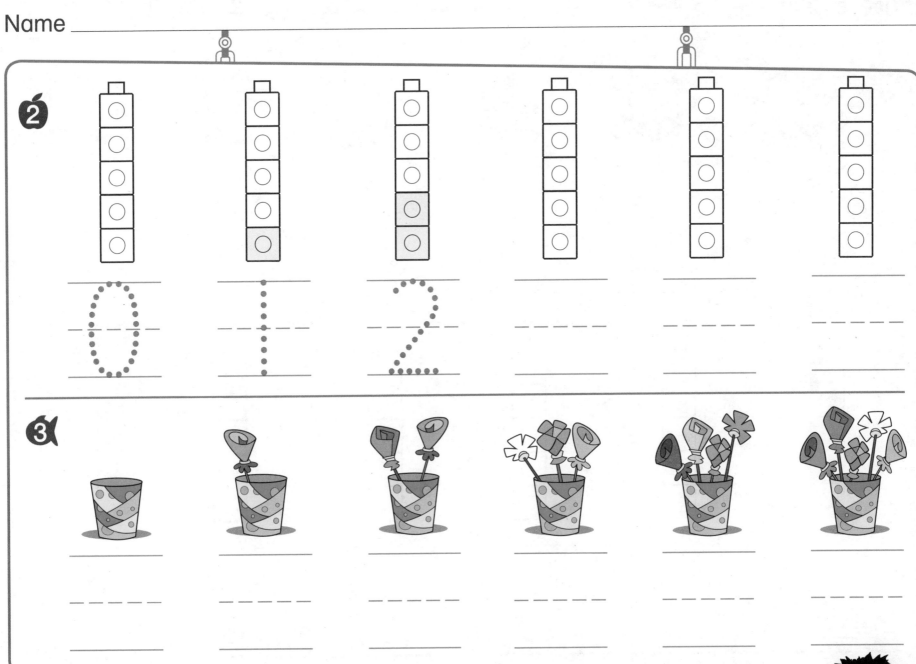

2

0   1   2

3

Directions Have students: **2** color the cubes to show each number, write the numbers in order, and then draw a circle around the number that comes just after 1 when counting; **3** count the flowers in each vase, write the numbers, and then say the numbers in order from 0 to 5.

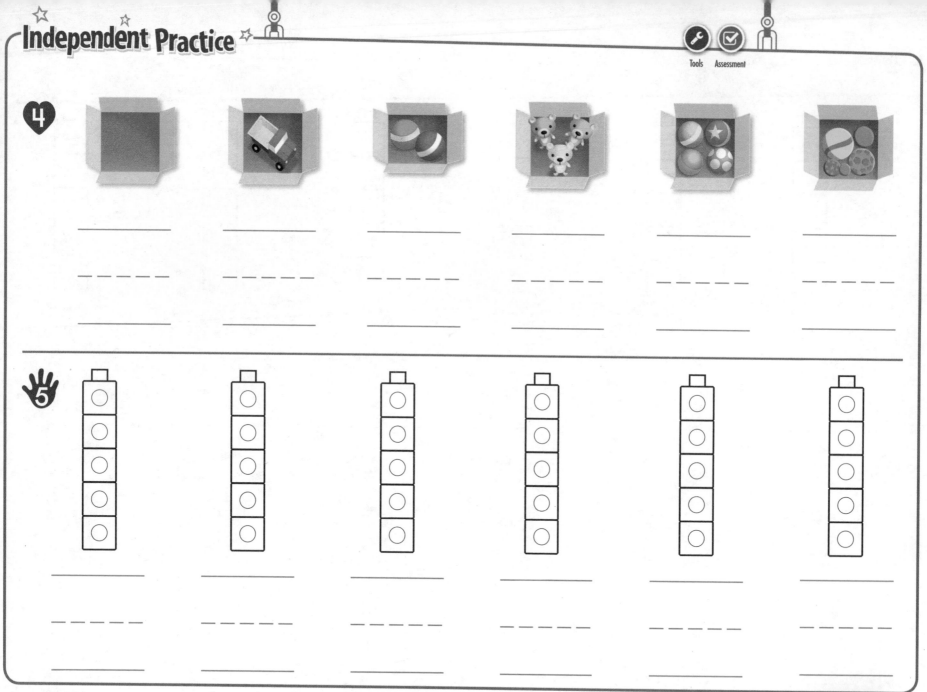

4

5

Directions ❤ Have students count the toys in each box, write the numbers, and then draw a circle around the number that comes just after 4 when counting how many. ✋ **Higher Order Thinking** Have students color 5 cubes, and then write the number. Have them color cubes to show the number that comes next when counting backwards from 5, and then write the number of cubes they colored in the tower. Repeat for the remaining towers.

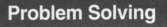

Think.

_____

_ _ _ _ _

_____

Directions Say: *Alex needs to count the group of shapes. How can you count these shapes? Use objects or words to help. Write the number to tell how many shapes. Tell why your number is correct.*

I can ...
use math to explain what I know about counting.

Ⓒ **Mathematical Practices** MP.3
Also MP.2, MP.5
Content Standards K.CC.B.4a
Also K.CC.B.4b, K.CC.B.5

How can I explain?

Numbers

1 2 3

3

☆ Guided Practice

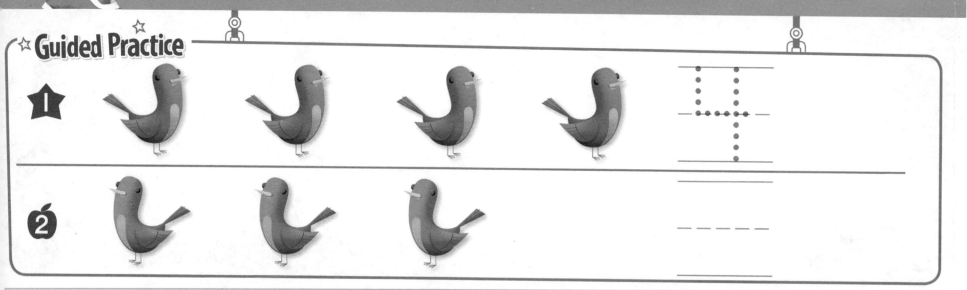

1

2

Directions 🌟 and 🍎 Have students make a math argument about how many birds are in each row, and then write the number. Have them use objects, words, or a method of their choice to explain their arguments and tell why they are correct.

Tools   Assessment

Independent Practice

3

_ _ _ _ _

_____

4

_____

_ _ _ _

_____

5

_____

_ _ _ _ _

_____

6

_____

_ _ _ _ _

_____

Directions **3–5** Have students make a math argument about how many leaves are in each row, and then write the number. Have them use objects, words, or a method of their choice to explain their arguments and tell why they are correct. **6 enVision® STEM** Say: *Chlorophyll makes leaves green. There is less sunlight in the winter, so trees save their chlorophyll. This turns leaves brown, orange, red, and yellow.* Have students make a math argument about how many orange leaves are in the row, and then write the number. Have them use objects, words, or a method of their choice to explain their arguments and tell why they are correct.

Problem Solving

Performance Task

_____

– – – – – –

_____

Name _____

⭐**1**

A   **2**

🍎**2**

_____

‑ ‑ ‑ ‑ ‑ ‑ ‑ ‑ ‑ ‑ ‑ ‑ ‑

_____

🐟**3**

2   **4**

❤**4**

Directions **Understand Vocabulary** Have students: ⭐ draw a circle around the **number**; 🍎 write the number that means **none**; 🐟 draw a circle around the number **four**; ❤ mark an X on the **one** red cube, and draw a circle around all **five** cubes in the group.

5

1

6

3

_____

- - - - - - - - - -

_____

7

_____

- - - - - - - - - -

_____

8

- -

Directions Understand Vocabulary Have students: ✋ draw a circle around the number **one**; ☕ write the number **three**; 🌲 **count** the number of cubes, and then write the number to tell how many; 🚩 write the numbers 0 to 5 in **order,** and then draw counters to show that many of each number.

46 forty-six

Topic 1 | Vocabulary Review

Name ______________________

TOPIC 1

Set A

Reteaching

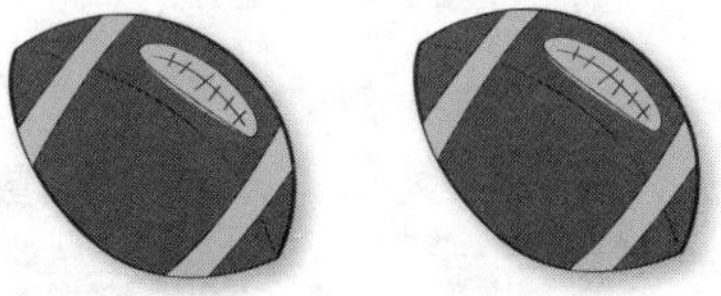

1 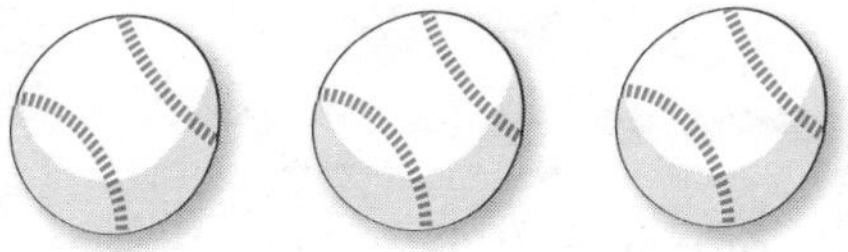

2 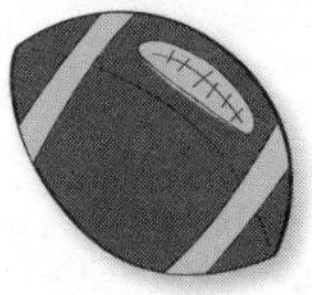

Set B

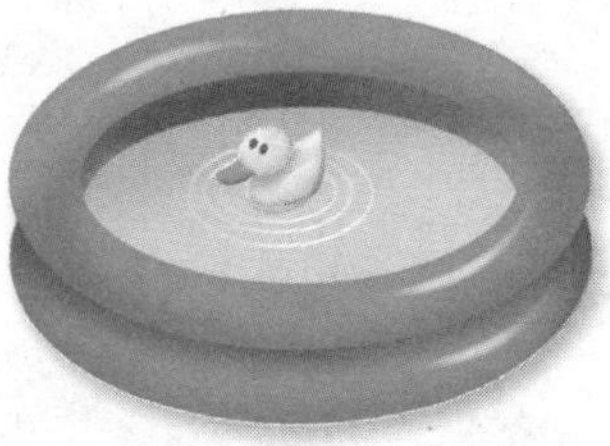

1

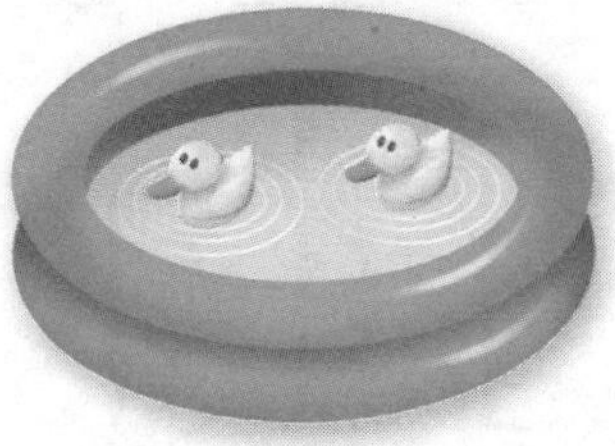

2

3 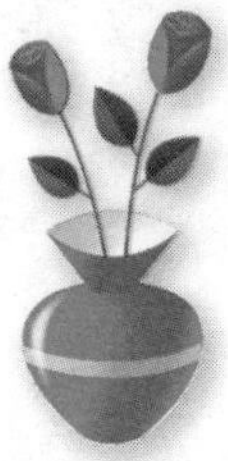

4 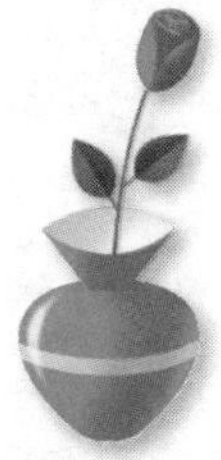

Directions Have students: 1 and 2 color a box as they count each ball to show how many; 3 and 4 count the flowers in the vase, and then practice writing the number that tells how many.

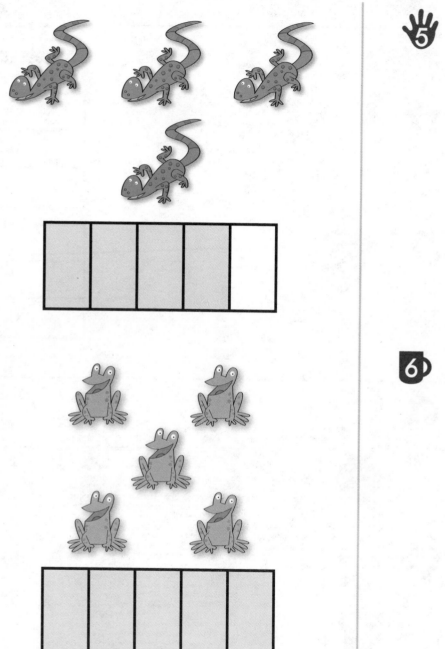

Directions 👋 and 🄍 Have students color a box as they count each animal to show how many.

48 forty-eight

Topic 1 | Reteaching

Name _____

_____

7

3 4 5

3

_____

0

8

9

Directions Have students: 7 write the numbers that are 1 less than 3 and 1 more than 3 when counting; 8 and 9 count the flowers in the vase, and then practice writing the number that tells how many.

Topic 1 | Reteaching

forty-nine **49**

4

3

5

50 fifty

Topic 1 | Reteaching

Name _____

1 Ⓐ

Ⓑ

Ⓒ

Ⓓ

2

Ⓐ I

Ⓑ 2

Ⓒ 3

Ⓓ 4

3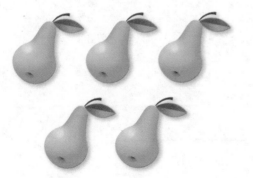

2   3   4   5
Ⓐ   Ⓑ   Ⓒ   Ⓓ

4

Ⓐ   Ⓑ   Ⓒ   Ⓓ

Directions Have students mark the best answer. **1** Which shows 3 flowers? **2** How many counters are there? **3** How many pears are there? **4** Which box has 0 toys in it?

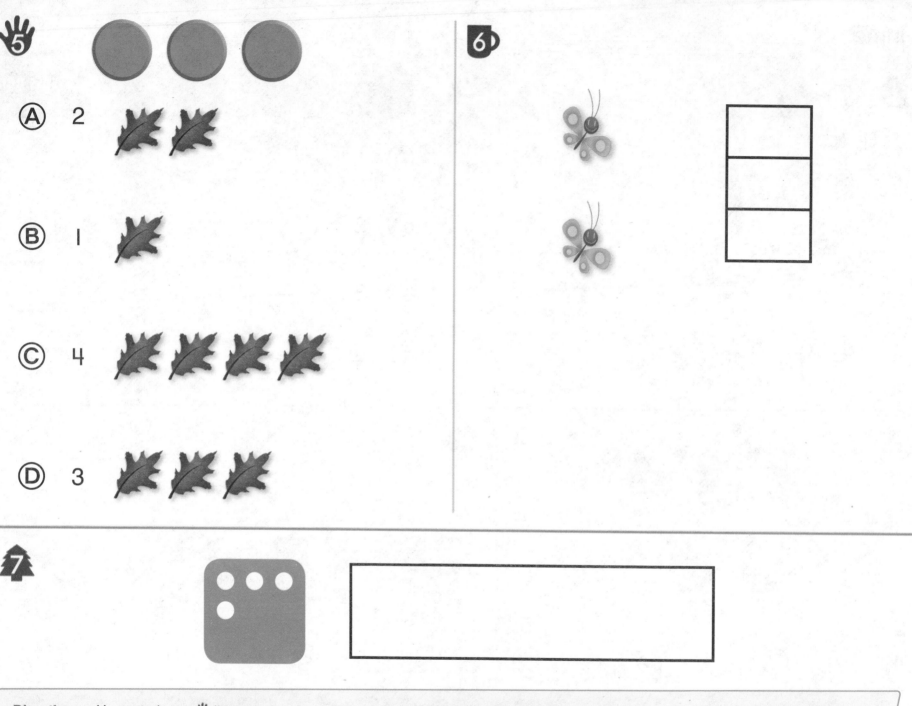

5

A) 2

B) 1

C) 4

D) 3

6

7

Directions Have students: ✋ listen to the story: *Tina is counting leaves. She uses these counters to show how many leaves she has counted so far. Which of these shows the next number of leaves she will count?* 🍵 count the butterflies, and then color the boxes to show how many; 🌲 count the number of dots and then draw counters in the box to show the same number of dots.

Topic 1 | Assessment Practice

Name _____

8   ❄   ❄❄   ❄❄❄   ❄❄❄❄

_____   _____   _____   _____   _____

- - - - -   - - - - -   - - - - -   - - - -

_____   _____   _____   _____   _____

9

_____   _____

- - - - -   - - - - -

_____   _____

Directions Have students: **8** count the snowflakes, and then write the number to tell how many; **9** listen to the story: *Jack has some red and some yellow counters. He uses the counters to show one way to make 4. Write numbers to tell how many of each color he used.*

_____

- - - - - - -

_____

- - - - - - -

_____

Directions Have students: ⓾ count the plates, and then write the number to tell how many; ⓫ count the number of apples on the plate, and then color the apples to show how many; ⓬ draw 5 marbles, and then write the number to tell how many.

Topic 1 │ Assessment Practice

Name _____

⭐ 1

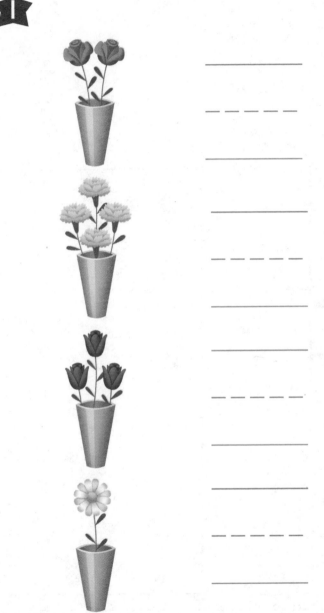

_____

_____

_____

_____

Directions Flower Cart Say: *Michael's family sells flowers from a flower cart.* 🟊 Have students count how many of each kind of flower, and then write the number to tell how many.

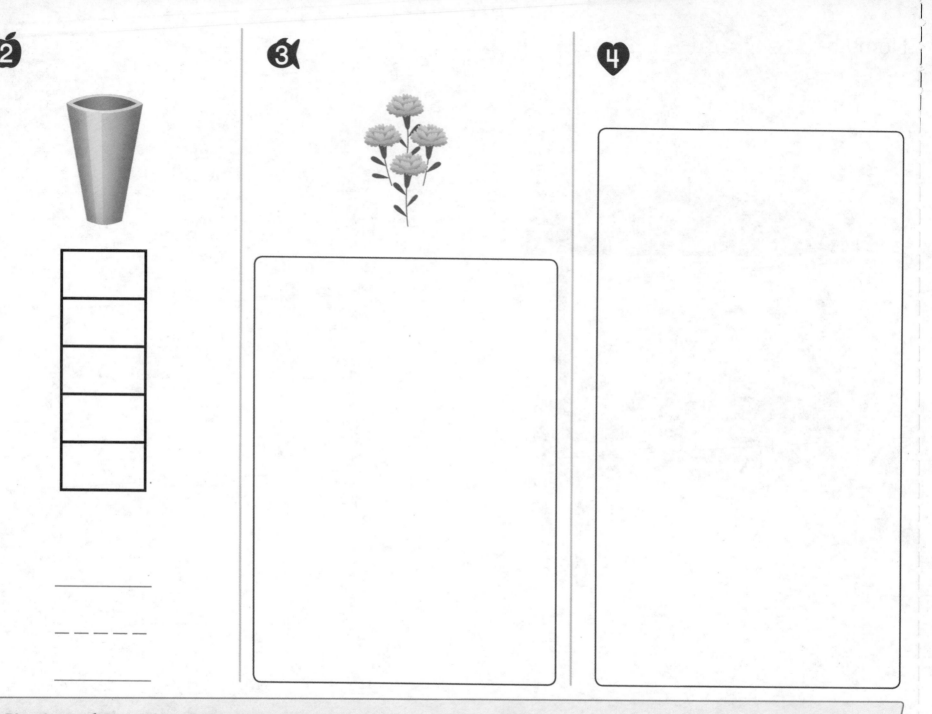

2

3

4

56 fifty-six

Topic 1 | Performance Task

Compare Numbers 0 to 5

Essential Question: How can numbers from 0 to 5 be compared and ordered?

Snow

Be careful.

ēnVision STEM Project: Severe Weather

Directions Read the character speech bubbles to students. **Find Out!** Have students name different types of severe weather that occur around the world. Say: *Not all places have the same types of severe weather. Talk to your friends and relatives about severe weather that has happened in the world in the past month. Ask them if they have ever seen that type of severe weather.* **Journal: Make a Poster** Have students make a poster. Ask them to draw up to 5 items people might need to be safe in a snowstorm. Have them draw up to 5 items people might need to be safe during a drought. Ask them to write the number of objects in each group, compare them, and then draw a circle around the number that is greater than the other number.

Name _____

 1

0	2

2

3	1

3

4	5

4

_____

– – – – – – –

_____

5

_____

– – – – – – –

_____

6

_____

– – – – – – –

_____

Name _____

A

B

Directions Say: *You will choose one of these projects. Look at picture* **A**. *Think about this question: What do you know about spiders? If you choose Project A, you will make a spider poster. Look at picture* **B**. *Think about this question: Are all flowers the same? If you choose Project B, you will make a flower model.*

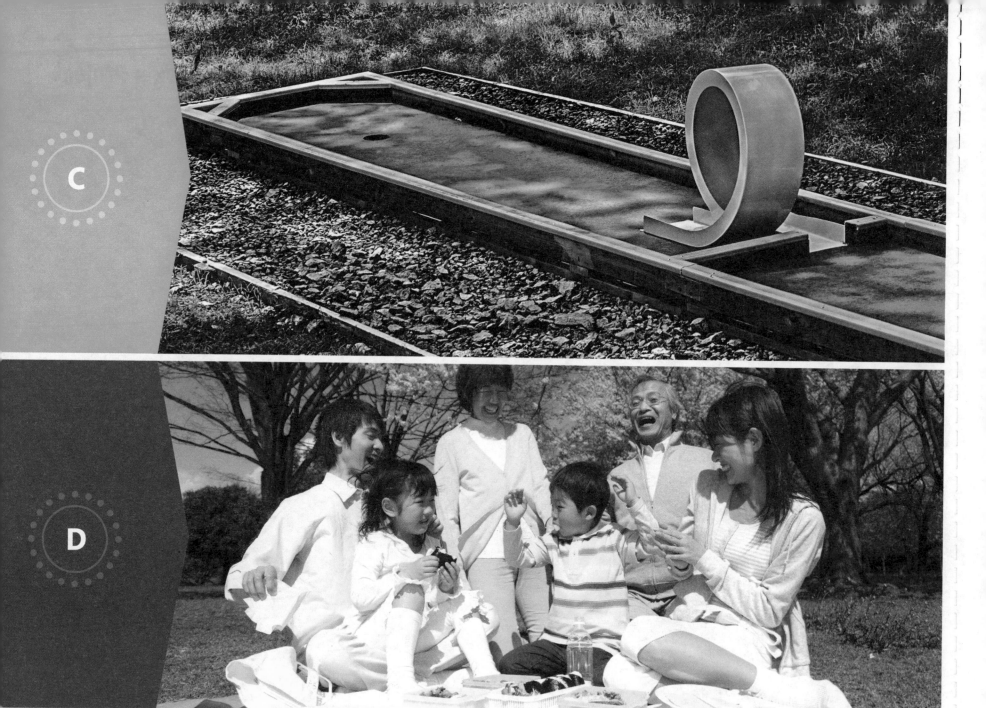

Directions   Say: *You will choose one of these projects. Look at picture* **C.** *Think about this question: How many shots does it take to get the golf ball into the hole? If you choose Project C, you will design a mini-golf hole. Look at picture* **D.** *Think about this question: What do you need when you go on a picnic? If you choose Project D, you will make a list of picnic items.*

60   sixty

Name _____

Activity

Directions Say: *Marta has some toy cars. Are there the same number of red cars as there are yellow cars on the rug? How do you know? Use counters to show your work.*

I can ...
compare groups to see whether they are equal by matching.

© Content Standards K.CC.C.6
Also K.CC.B.5
Mathematical Practices MP.2,
MP.6, and MP.7

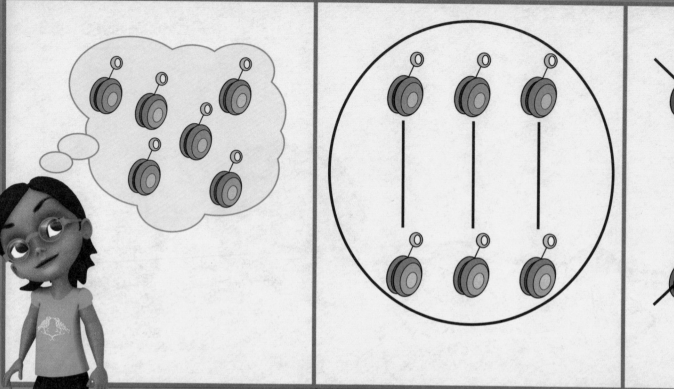

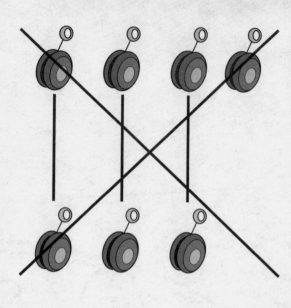

☆ Guided Practice

1

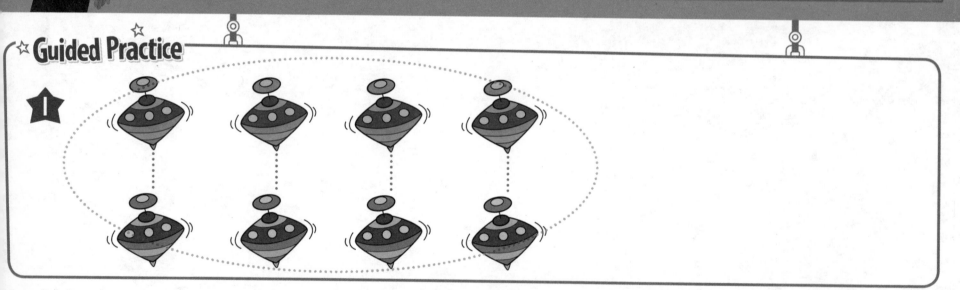

Directions ⭐ Have students draw lines between the toys in the top group to the toys in the bottom group. Then have them draw a circle around the groups if they are equal in number, or mark an X on the groups if they are NOT equal in number.

Topic 2 | Lesson 1

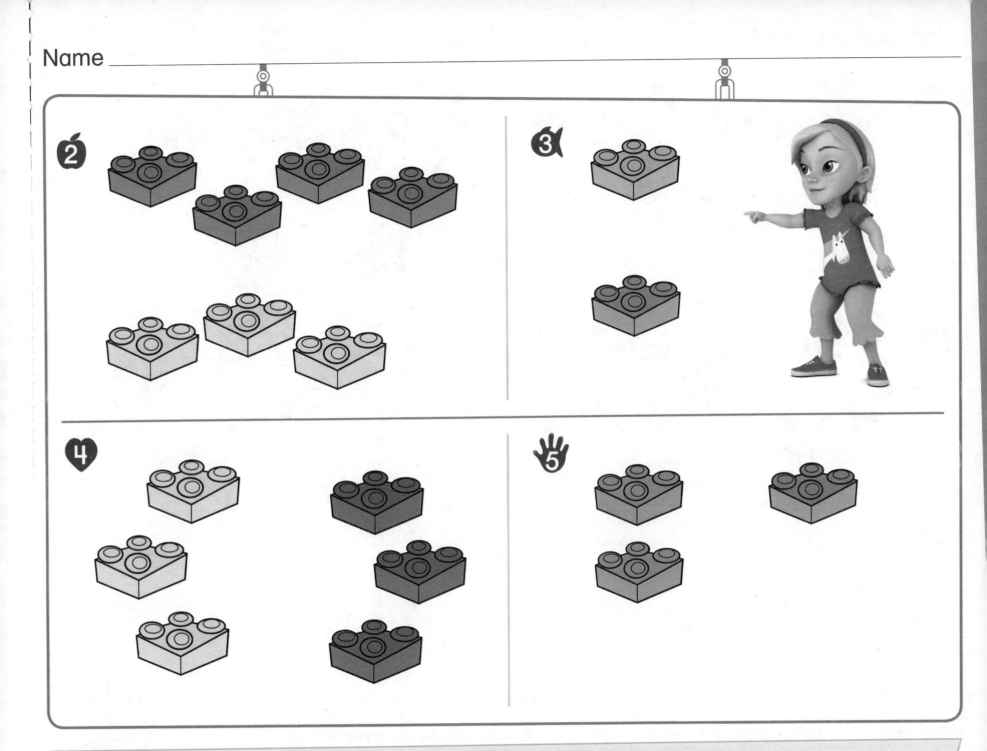

2

3

4

5

Directions 2–5 Have students draw lines from the blocks in one group to the blocks in the other group. Then have them draw a circle around the groups if they are equal in number, or mark an X on the groups if they are NOT equal in number.

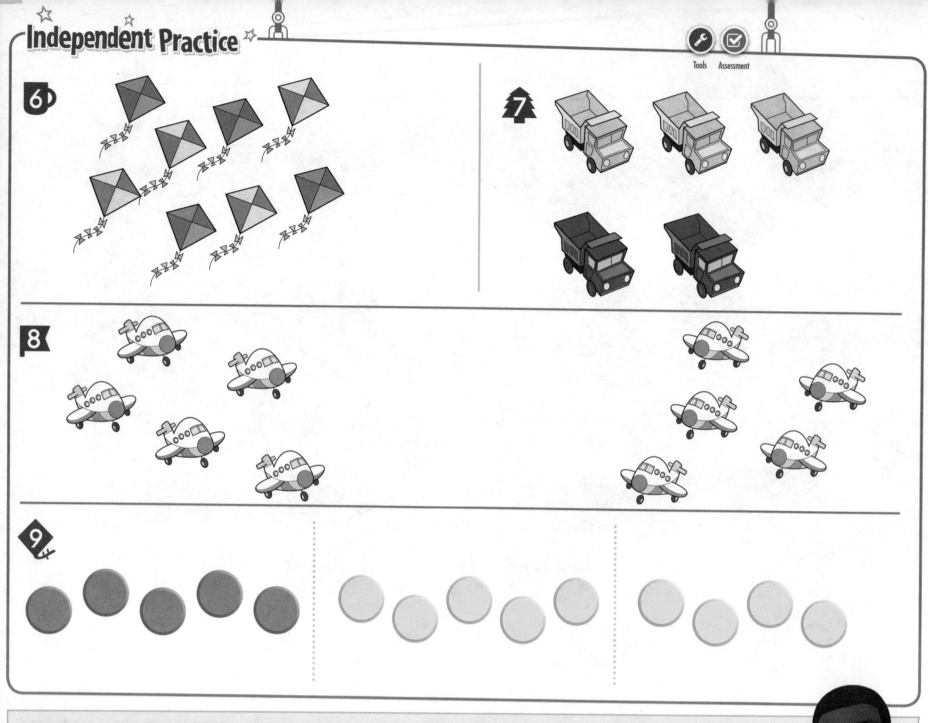

6

7

8

9

Directions **6**–**8** Have students draw lines from the toys in one group to the toys in the other group. Then have them draw a circle around the groups if they are equal in number, or mark an X on the groups if they are NOT equal in number. **♦ Higher Order Thinking** Have students draw a circle around the group of yellow counters that is NOT equal in number to the group of red counters.

64 sixty-four   Copyright © SAVVAS Learning Company LLC. All Rights Reserved.   **Topic 2** | Lesson 1

Solve & Share

Name _____

Directions Say: *Marta's class goes to the park. Mr. Leeman brings 4 soccer balls and 3 basketballs. Which group of balls has more? How do you know? Use counters to show your work.*

I can ...
tell whether one group is greater in number than another group.

© **Content Standards** K.CC.C.6 Also K.CC.B.5 **Mathematical Practices** MP.2, MP.3, and MP.6

Topic 2 | Lesson 2

Go Online | SavvasRealize.com

sixty-five **65**

☆ Guided Practice

1

2

Name _____

🖐 5

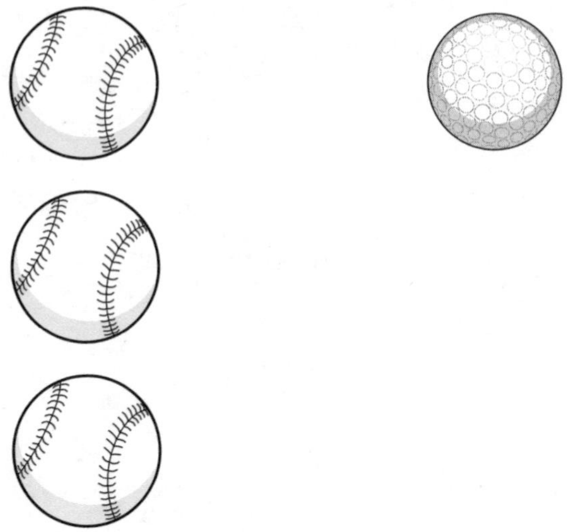

Directions ⭐–🖐 Have students draw lines to match objects from one group to the other group. Have them draw a circle around the group that is greater in number than the other group, and then explain why they are correct.

Independent Practice

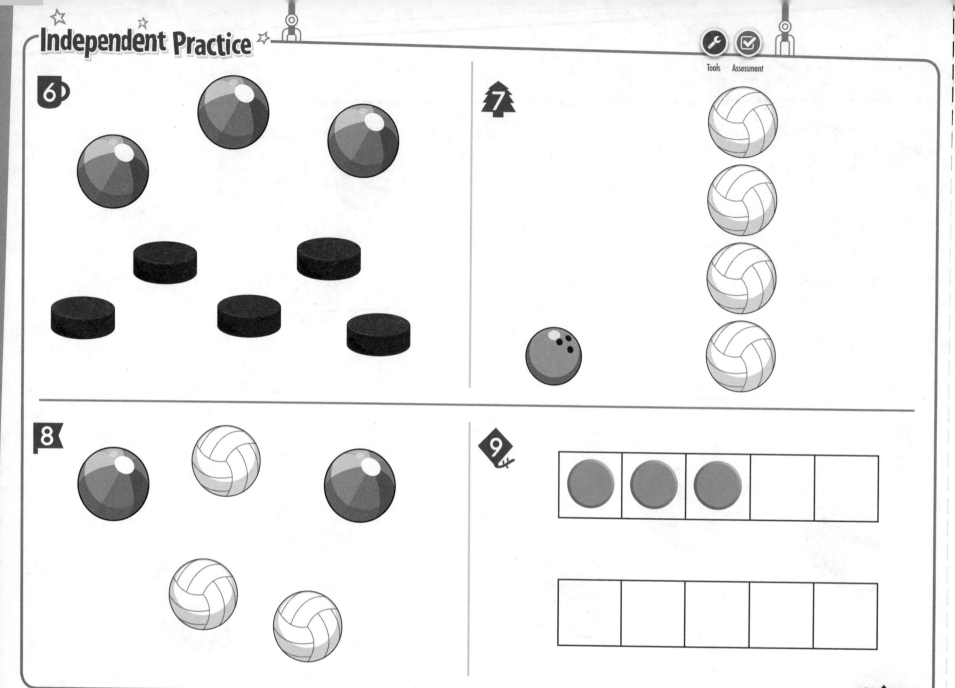

6

7

8

9

68 sixty-eight

Topic 2 | Lesson 2

Directions Say: *Marta puts 5 stuffed animals on a shelf. She puts 3 teddy bears on a different shelf. Which group has fewer stuffed toys? How do you know? Use counters to show your work.*

I can ...
tell whether one group is less in number than another group.

© **Content Standards** K.CC.C.6
Also K.CC.B.5
Mathematical Practices MP.3, MP.4

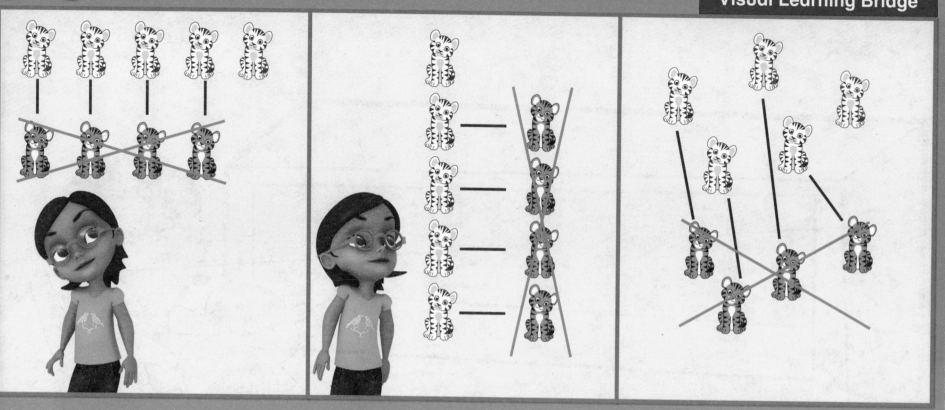

Guided Practice

1

2

Directions ★ and ② Have students draw lines to match the toys from one group to the other group. Have them mark an X on the group that is less in number than the other group, and then explain why they are correct.

Topic 2 | Lesson 3

Name _____

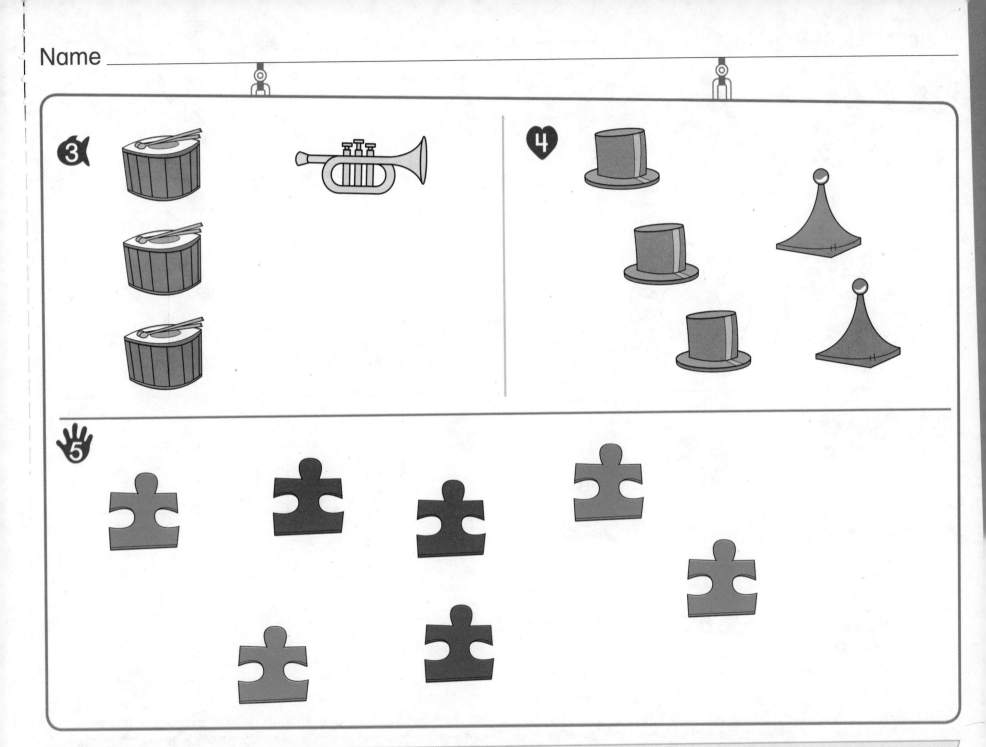

Directions ❸–✋ Have students draw lines to match the toys from one group to the other group. Have them mark an X on the group that is less in number than the other group, and then explain why they are correct.

Topic 2 | Lesson 3

seventy-one **71**

Tools Assessment

6

7

8

9

Directions **6** **enVision® STEM** Ask students what a raindrop means in a weather forecast. Have students draw lines between groups to match the raindrop stickers to the sun stickers. Have them mark an X on the group that is less in number than the other group, and then explain why they are correct. **7** and **8** Have students draw lines to match the objects from one group to the other group. Have them mark an X on the group that is less in number than the other group, and then explain why they are correct. **9** **Higher Order Thinking** Have students draw a group of yellow counters that is less in number than the group of red counters.

Topic 2 | Lesson 3

Solve & Share

Name _____

Activity

_____   _____

- - - - - -   - - - - -

_____ red   _____ blue

Directions Say: *Marta builds a tower with red and blue blocks. Count how many red blocks and how many blue blocks she uses. Write the numbers to tell how many. Then draw a circle around the number that is less than the other number.*

I can ... compare numbers.

Content Standards K.CC.C.6 Also K.CC.A.3, K.CC.B.5 **Mathematical Practices** MP.3, MP.6, and MP.8

Visual Learning Bridge

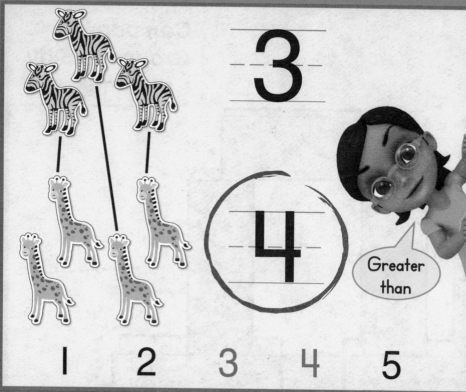

☆ Guided Practice

Directions ⋆ Have students count the monkey and banana stickers, and then write the numbers to tell how many. Then have them draw a circle around the number that is greater than the other number and mark an X on the number that is less than the other number.

Topic 2 | Lesson 4

Name _____

Directions ❷–✋ Have students count the stickers, write the numbers to tell how many, and then draw a circle around the number that is greater than the other number and mark an X on the number that is less than the other number, or draw a circle around both numbers if they are equal.

Topic 2 | Lesson 4

Independent Practice

6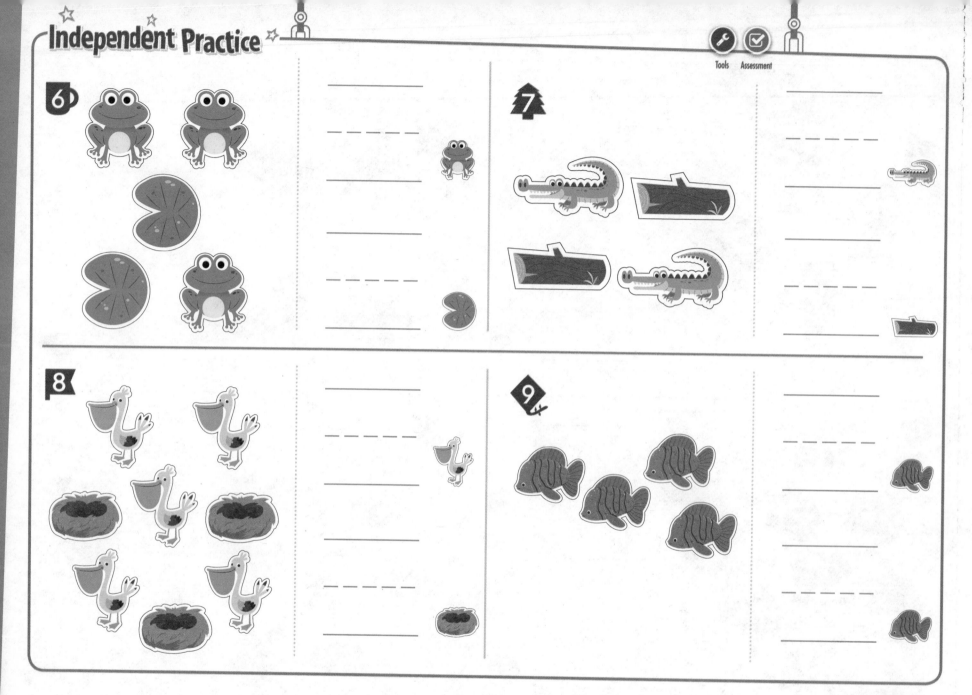

7

8

9

Directions **6–8** Have students count the stickers, write the numbers to tell how many, and then draw a circle around the number that is greater than the other number and mark an X on the number that is less than the other number, or draw a circle around both numbers if they are equal. **❖ Higher Order Thinking** Have students count the fish stickers, draw a group of fish stickers that is less in number than the group shown, and then write the numbers to tell how many.

Topic 2 | Lesson 4

Name _____

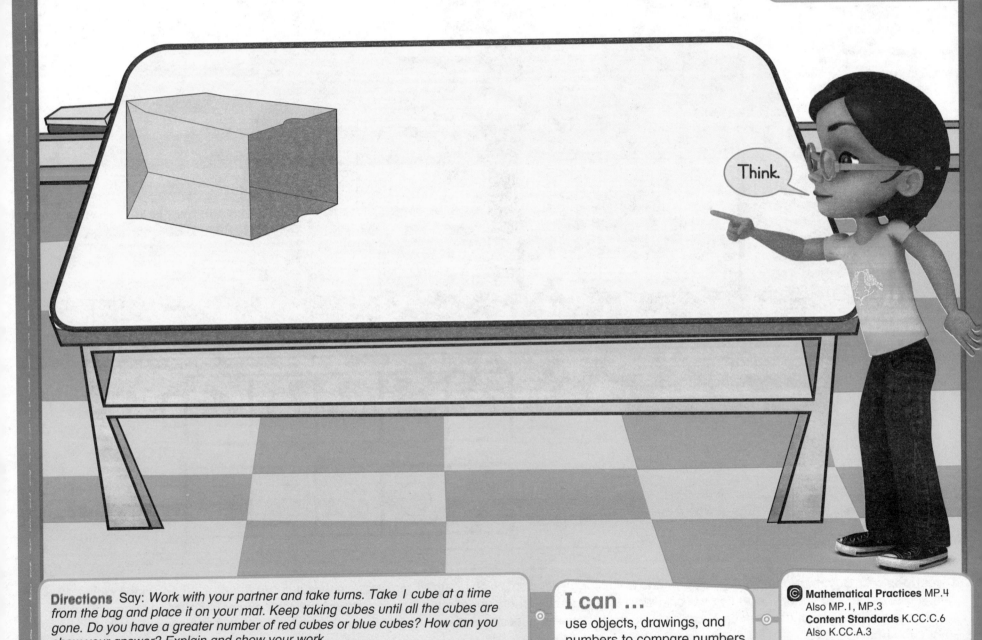

Think.

Directions Say: *Work with your partner and take turns. Take 1 cube at a time from the bag and place it on your mat. Keep taking cubes until all the cubes are gone. Do you have a greater number of red cubes or blue cubes? How can you show your answer? Explain and show your work.*

I can ...
use objects, drawings, and numbers to compare numbers.

Ⓒ **Mathematical Practices** MP.4
Also MP.1, MP.3
Content Standards K.CC.C.6
Also K.CC.A.3

Speech bubbles: How can I show it? · Cubes · Drawings · Numbers

☆ Guided Practice

1

Directions 🏠 Say: *Marta has 5 fish stickers and 2 flamingo stickers. Which group of stickers is less in number than the other group? How can you use cubes to show how to find the answer?* Have students create cube trains for each group, color the number of cubes to show the number of stickers, and then mark an X on the cube train that shows less stickers in number than the other cube train. Have them explain their cube trains.

Topic 2 | Lesson 5

Independent Practice

2

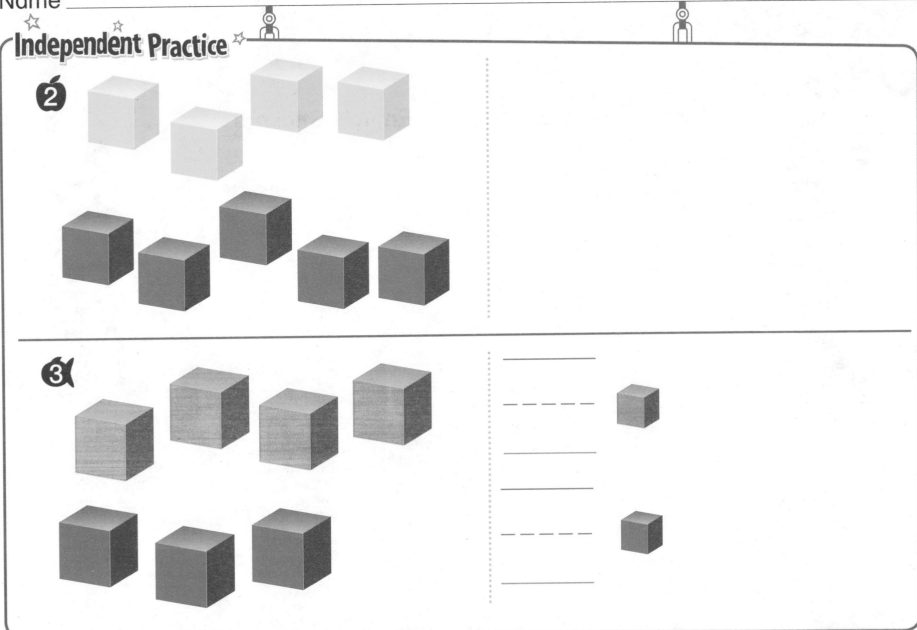

3

Directions **2** Say: *Carlos has 4 yellow blocks and 5 blue blocks. Which group of blocks is greater in number than the other group? How can you use a drawing to show your answer?* Have students create a drawing to show and explain their answer. **3** Say: *Carlos has 4 red blocks and 3 blue blocks. Which group of blocks is less in number than the other group? How can you use numbers to show your answer?* Have students use numbers to show and explain their answer.

Problem Solving

Marta's Stickers

Emily's Stickers

Directions Read the problem aloud. Then have students use multiple problem-solving methods to solve the problem. Say: *Marta has 2 stickers. Emily has a greater number of stickers than Marta. How many stickers could Emily have?* 🕹 **Make Sense** *What do you know about the problem? Can Emily have 1 sticker? Tell a partner why or why not.* ✋ **Model** *Use cubes, draw a picture, or use numbers to show how many stickers Marta has and Emily could have.* ☕ **Explain** *Tell a partner why your work for Emily's stickers is correct.*

Name _____

1

2

I

- - - - - - - -

3

4

Directions **Understand Vocabulary** Have students: **1** draw 5 counters in a **group**; **2** write the number that is **less than** the number shown; **3** draw a group of counters that is **equal** in number to the group of counters shown; **4** **compare** red and yellow counters using matching to find which group is less in number than the other, and then mark an X on that group.

5

 4 _____ - - - - - - _____

3 2

8

Topic 2 | Vocabulary Review

Set A

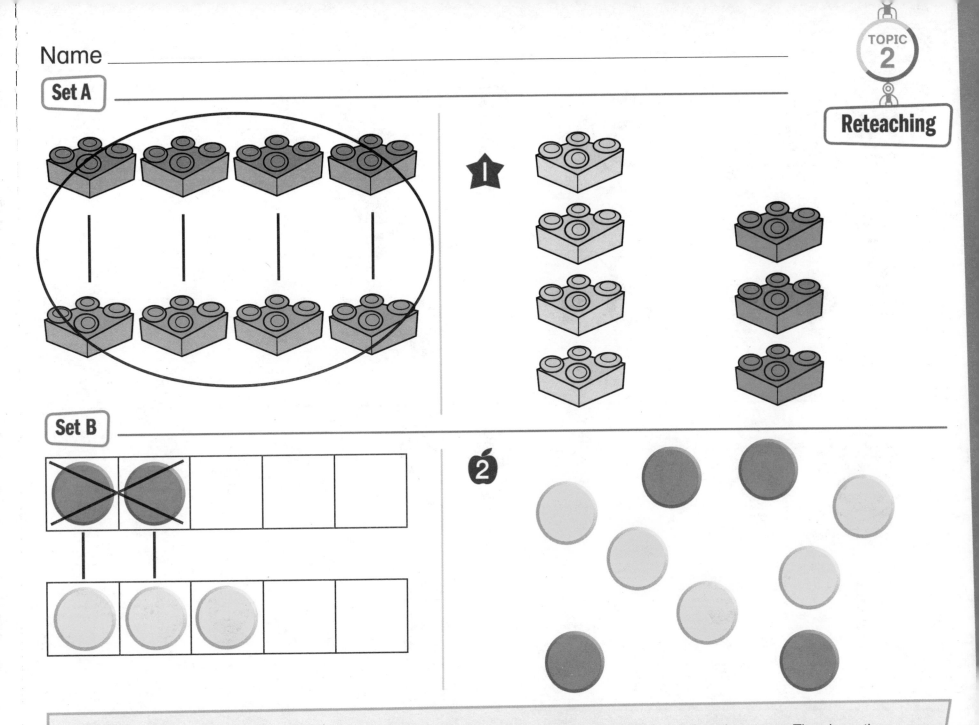

Set B

Directions Have students: ⭐ draw lines between the rows to match the blocks from one group to the other group. Then have them draw a circle around the groups if they are equal, or mark an X on the groups if they are NOT equal; ② draw lines to match the groups of red and yellow counters. Have them draw a circle around the group that is greater in number than the other group, and then explain why they are correct.

Directions Have students: ❸ count the stickers, write numbers to tell how many of each type, and then draw a circle around the number that is greater than the other number and mark an X on the number that is less than the other number; ❹ count the balloons, and then draw a circle around the number that is greater than the other number, or draw a circle around both numbers if the groups of balloons are equal in number.

Name _____

 1

Ⓐ

Ⓑ

Ⓒ

Ⓓ

 2

☐

☐

☐

☐

3

4   4

Directions 1 *Look at the group of baseballs. Which group of tennis balls is greater in number than the group of baseballs?* 2 *Mark all the groups of red counters that are NOT equal in number to the group of yellow counters.* 3 *Have students draw counters to represent each number. Then have students draw a circle around the number that is greater than the other number, or draw a circle around both numbers if they are equal.*

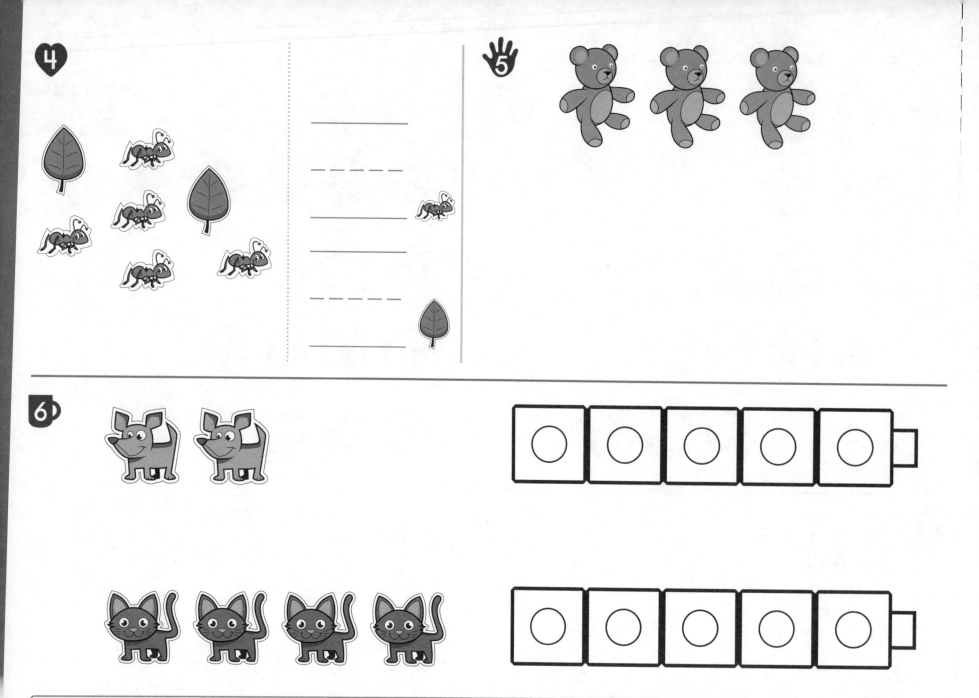

Topic 2 | Assessment Practice

Name _____

⭐ 1

_____

_ _ _ _ _ _ _ _ _ _ _

_____

_____

_ _ _ _ _ _ _ _ _ _ _

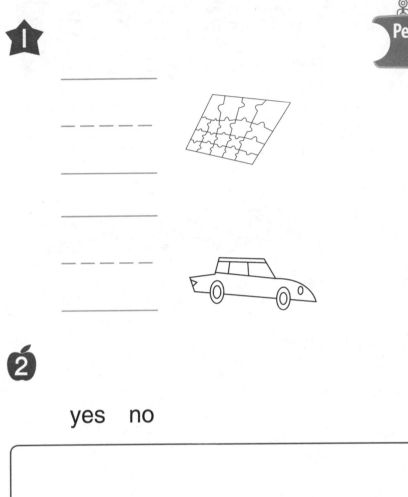

🍎 2

yes   no

Directions   **Toy Chest** Say: *David keeps his toys in a toy chest.* ⭐ Have students count the large puzzles and cars that David can see in the toy chest, and then write the numbers to tell how many of each toy. Then have them draw a circle around the number that is greater than the other number and mark an X on the number that is less than the other number. 🍎 Say: *David says that his group of toy cars is greater than his group of alphabet blocks. Do you agree with him?* Have students draw a circle around **yes** or **no**, and then have them draw a picture to explain their answer.

3

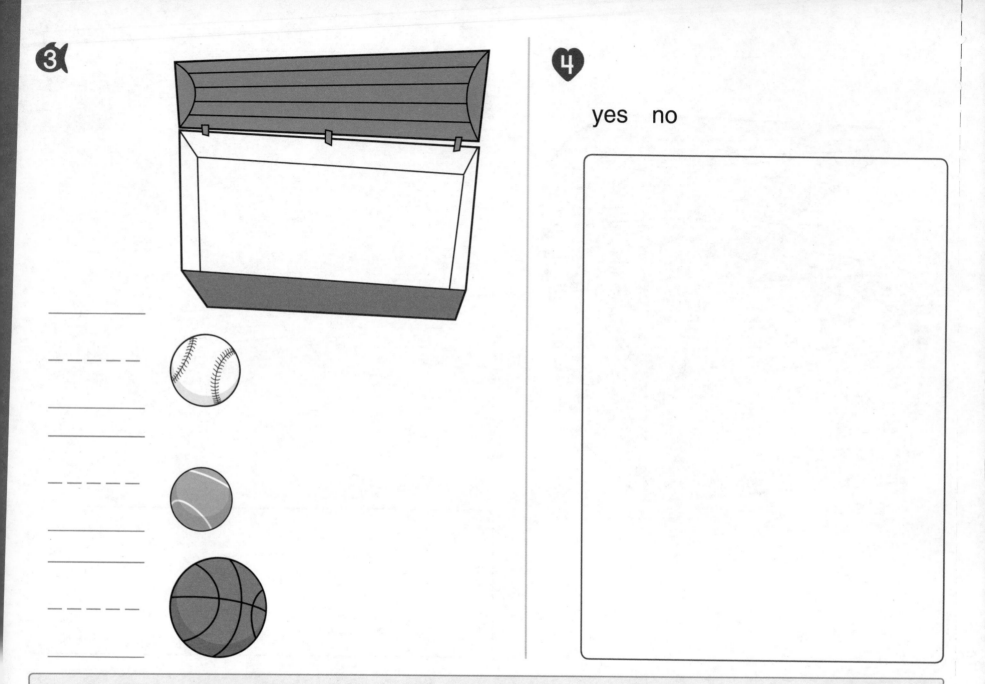

_____

- - - - - -

_____

- - - - - -

_____

- - - - - -

4

yes no

Directions ❸ Say: _David's sister Sara likes sports. She keeps balls for different sports in her toy chest._ Then have students use the following clues to draw how many of each ball she could have in her toy chest, and then write the numbers to tell how many. _Sara has 3 baseballs. She has a group of tennis balls that is equal in number to the group of baseballs. Her group of basketballs is less in number than her group of tennis balls._ ❹ Say: _David said that Sara could have zero basketballs in her toy chest. Do you agree with him?_ Draw a circle around **yes** or **no**. Then have students draw a picture to explain their answer.

Topic 2 | Performance Task

Numbers 6 to 10

Essential Question: How can numbers from 6 to 10 be counted, read, and written?

Digital Resources

Interactive Student Edition · Activity · Visual Learning · Video · Practice

Assessment · Games · Tools · Glossary

enVision STEM Project: Types of Weather

Directions Read the character speech bubbles to students. **Find Out!** Have students discuss different types of weather they have experienced. Say: *Talk to friends and relatives about weather. Ask which types of weather they have seen.* **Journal: Make a Poster** Have students make a poster. Have them draw 10 pictures to represent good and bad weather they have experienced. Ask them to sort their pictures into two groups that show types of weather they enjoy and types they do not enjoy. Have students count how many are in each group and write the numbers.

Name _____

 1

 2

 **3**

 **4**

_____

- - - - - - -

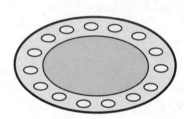

- - - - - - -

 5

Directions Have students: ★ draw a circle around the group that is greater in number than the other group; 🍎 mark an X on the number that is less than the other number; ↩ mark an X on the group that is less in number than the other group; ♥ count the objects, write the number to tell how many of each, and then draw a circle around the number that is greater than the other number; ✋ draw a group of counters that is equal in number to the group of counters shown.

Name _____

A

B

C

Directions Say: *You will choose one of these projects. Look at picture* **A.** *Think about this question: What fruits and vegetables are grown locally? If you choose Project A, you will write a song. Look at picture* **B.** *Think about this question: Where would you go if you had a private plane? If you choose Project B, you will design a model plane. Look at picture* **C.** *Think about this question: How many animals live in a coral reef? If you choose Project C, you will make a poster of a coral reef.*

What did the green grape say to the purple grape? Breathe!

Directions Read the robot's speech bubble to students. **Generate Interest** Ask students what foods they like to eat by the handful. Say: *Can you hold more apples or strawberries in your hand? How many tennis balls can you hold in one hand?* Provide time to practice picking up objects and then counting them.

I can ...
model with math to count groups and compare to solve a problem.

Ⓒ **Mathematical Practices** MP.4
Also MP.7, MP.8
Content Standards K.CC.C.6
Also K.CC.A.2, K.CC.A.3,
K.CC.B.4a, K.CC.B.5

Solve & Share

Name _____

Activity

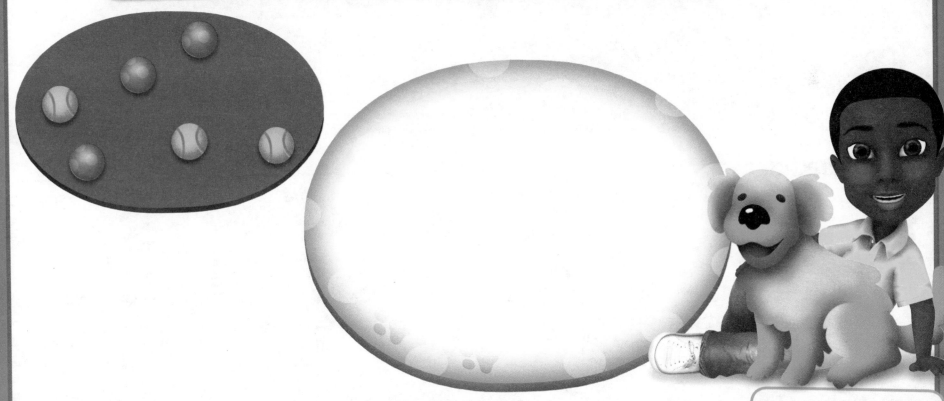

Directions Say: *Jackson's dog, Rex, has some balls on the red rug. Use counters and draw a picture on the empty dog bed to show how many balls Rex has. Tell how you know you are correct.*

I can ...
count the numbers 6 and 7.

© **Content Standards** K.CC.B.4a
Also K.CC.B.5
Mathematical Practices MP.2, MP.3, and MP.4

☆ Guided Practice

1

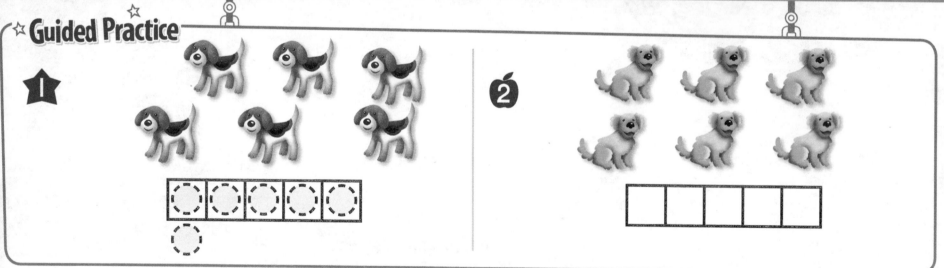

2

94 ninety-four

Name _____

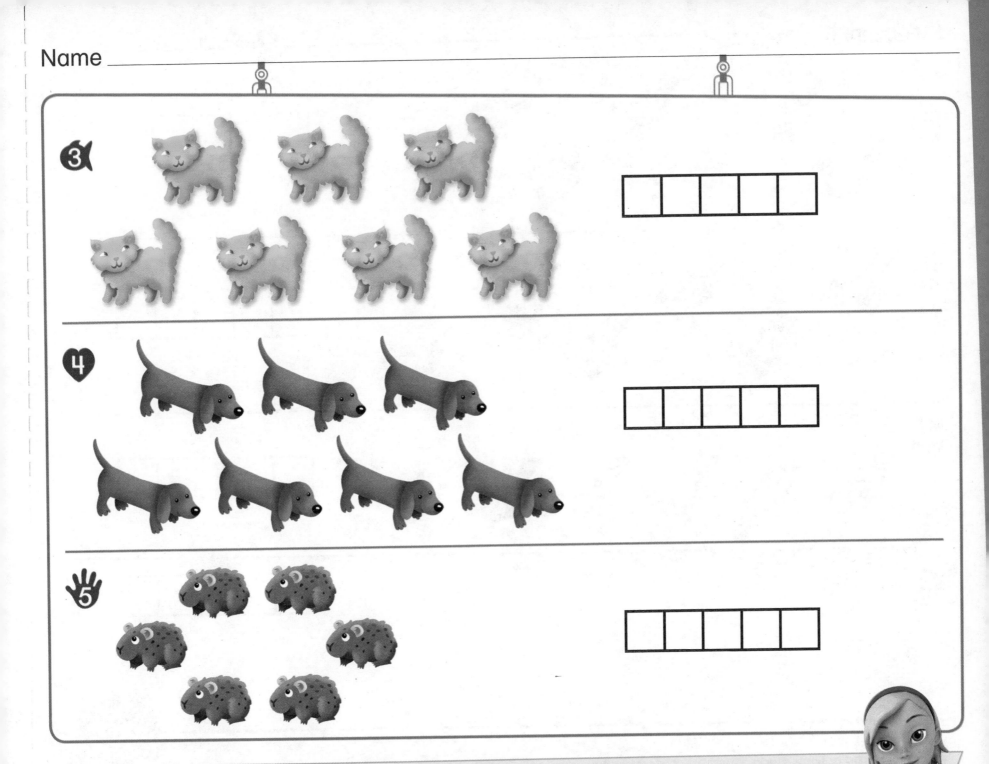

③

④

🖐5

Directions ③–🖐 Have students draw a counter as they count each animal to show how many.

Topic 3 | Lesson 1

ninety-five **95**

Independent Practice

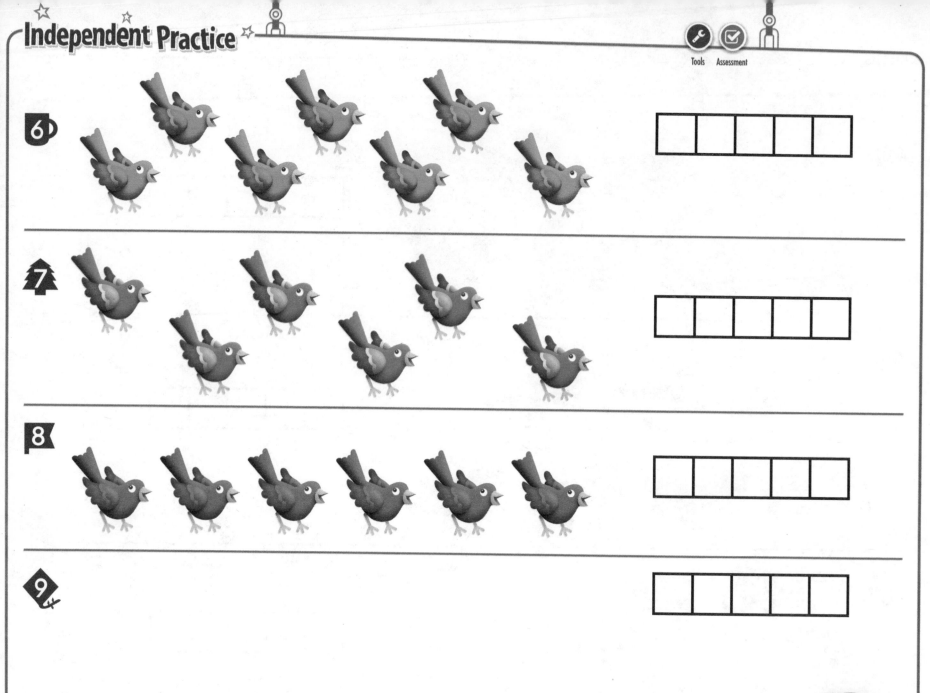

6

7

8

9

Directions **6–8** Have students draw a counter as they count each bird to show how many. **9 Higher Order Thinking** Have students draw 6 or 7 eggs, and then draw a counter as they draw each egg to show how many.

Topic 3 | Lesson 1

Solve & Share

Name _____

Directions Say: *Jackson sees some beach balls. Choose a number card to tell how many. Use connecting cubes to show the number on the beach blanket. Count the cubes and show your partner. Then use the cubes to show another way to make the number. Now look at the other number card and repeat the activity.*

I can ...
read and write the numbers 6 and 7.

Content Standards K.CC.A.3
Also K.CC.B.5
Mathematical Practices MP.2,
MP.5, and MP.6

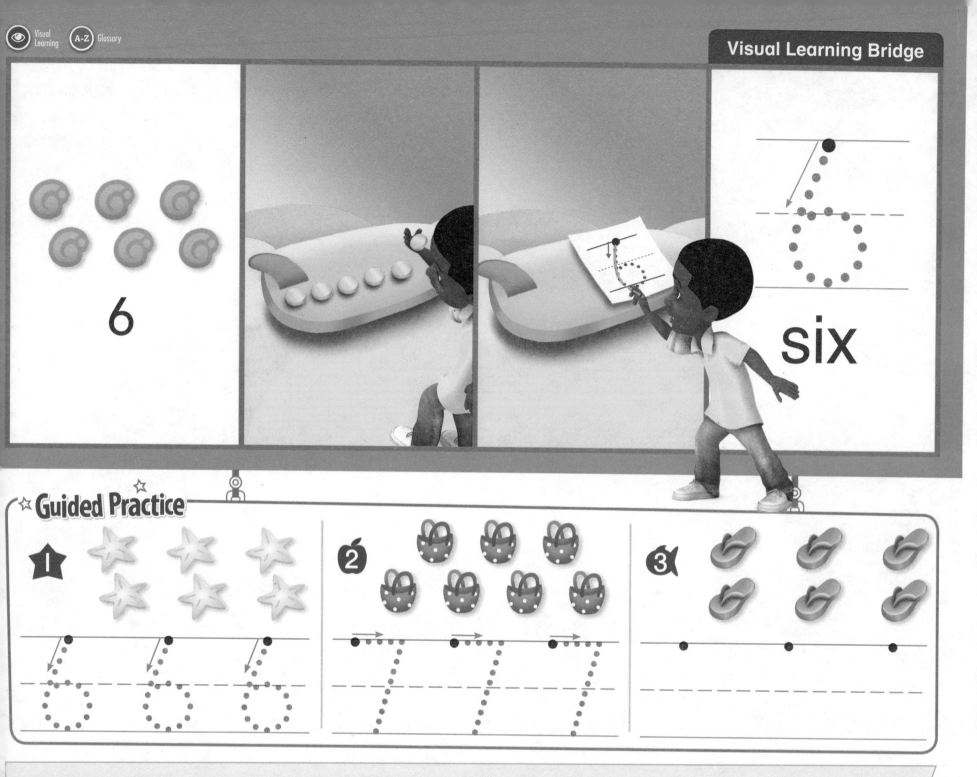

6

six

☆ Guided Practice

1

2

3

Directions 🌟–③ Have students count the objects, and then practice writing the number that tells how many.

Name _____

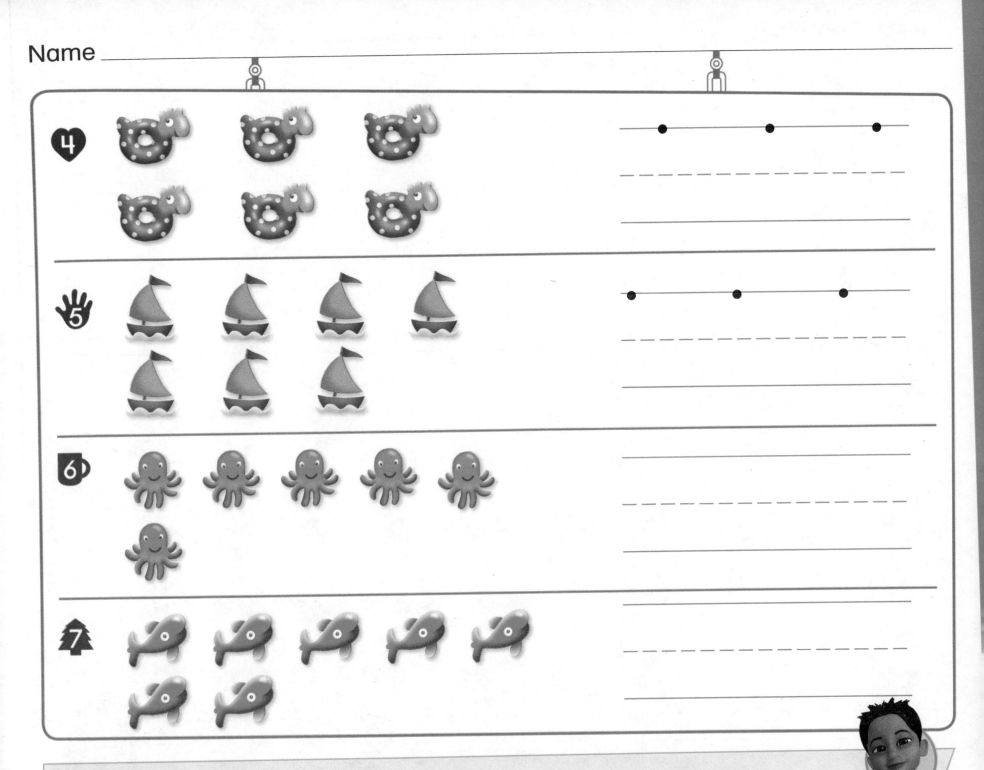

Directions ♥–🌲 Have students count the objects, and then practice writing the number that tells how many.

Topic 3 | Lesson 2

ninety-nine **99**

Independent Practice

8 6

9 7

10

_____   _____    _____   _____

Directions 🔟 and ✏️ Have students use counters to make the number. Then have them draw circles to represent the number. 🔟 **Higher Order Thinking** Have students count each group of objects, and then write the numbers to tell how many.

Topic 3 | Lesson 2

Name _____

Activity

Directions Say: *Jackson makes some sandwiches for lunch at the beach. Use counters and draw a picture on the blank sign to show how many sandwiches Jackson makes. Tell how you know you are correct.*

I can ...
count the numbers 8 and 9.

© **Content Standards** K.CC.B.4a
Also K.CC.B.5
Mathematical Practices MP.2, MP.3

Topic 3 | Lesson 3

Go Online | SavvasRealize.com

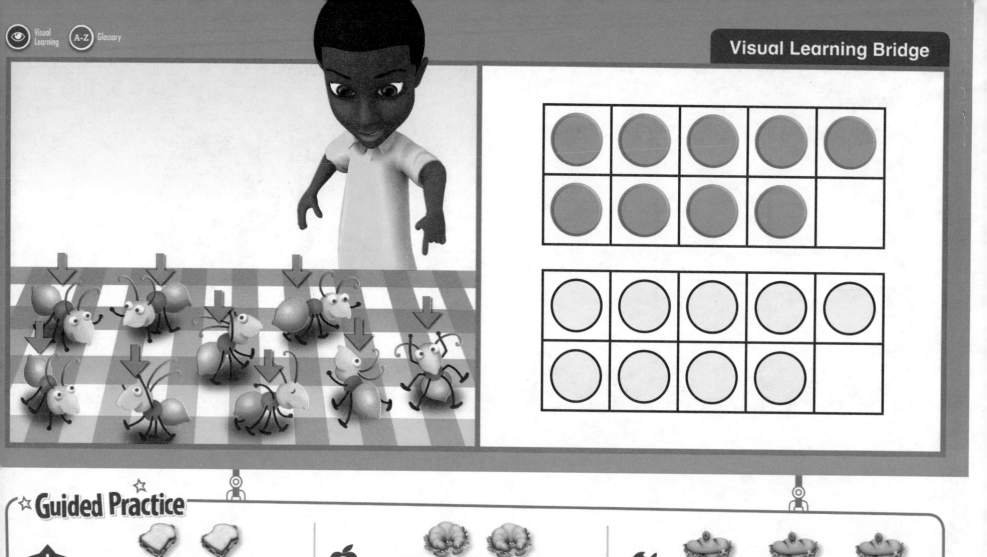

☆ Guided Practice

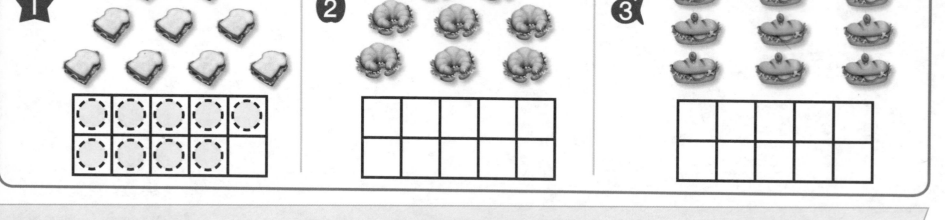

1

2

3

Directions **1**—**3** Have students count the sandwiches, and then draw counters to show how many.

Name _____

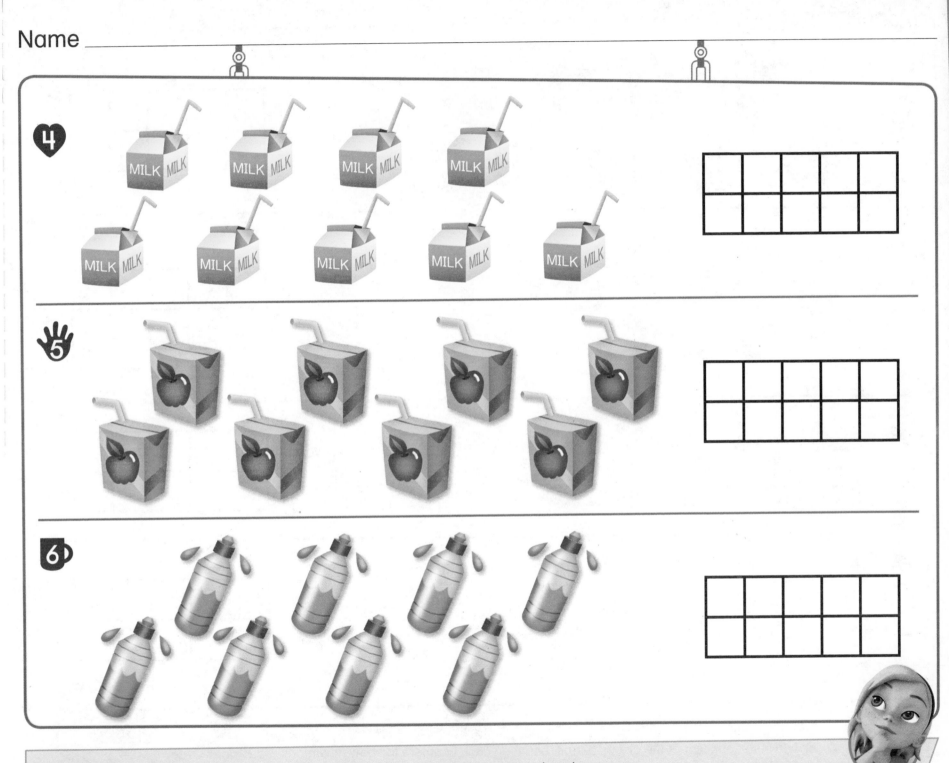

Directions ♥—🍵 Have students count the drinks, and then draw counters to show how many.

Topic 3 | Lesson 3

one hundred three **103**

Independent Practice

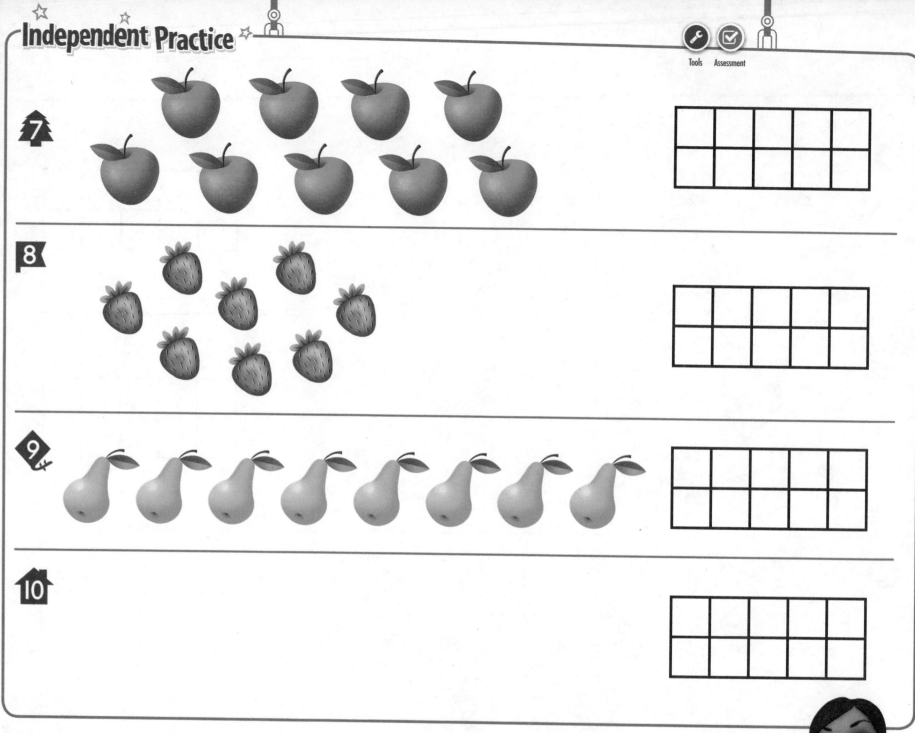

7

8

9

10

Directions 7–9 Have students count the pieces of fruit, and then draw counters to show how many. 10 **Higher Order Thinking** Have students draw 8 or 9 oranges, and then draw counters to show how many.

Topic 3 | Lesson 3

Name _____

Directions Say: *Jackson sees some turtle eggs. Draw a number card to tell how many. Count out that many counters and place them across the top of the workmat. What are some different ways to make the number? Draw two ways on the turtle shells. Are there different ways to count the number? Tell how you know.*

I can ...
read and write the numbers 8 and 9.

© **Content Standards** K.CC.A.3 Also K.CC.B.5
Mathematical Practices MP.3, MP.5, and MP.6

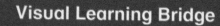

8

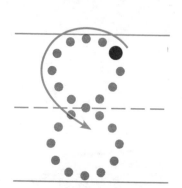

eight

☆ Guided Practice

1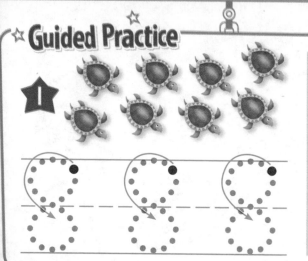

2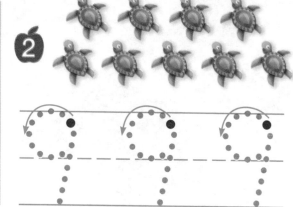

3

Directions ⭐–🐟 Have students count the turtles, and then practice writing the number that tells how many.

106 one hundred six

Topic 3 | Lesson 4

Name _____

4 ♥

5 ✋

6 ☕

7 🌲

Directions **4**–**7** Have students count the animals, and then practice writing the number that tells how many.

Topic 3 | Lesson 4

one hundred seven **107**

Tools Assessment

8 8

9 9

10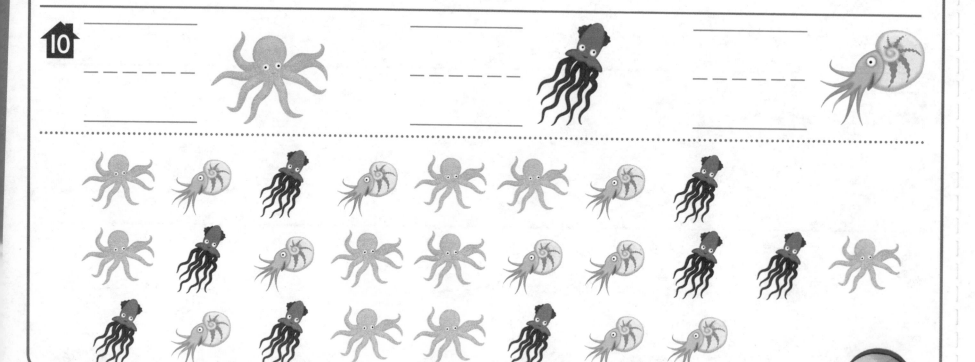

Topic 3 | Lesson 4

☆ ☆ ☆
Solve & Share

Name _____

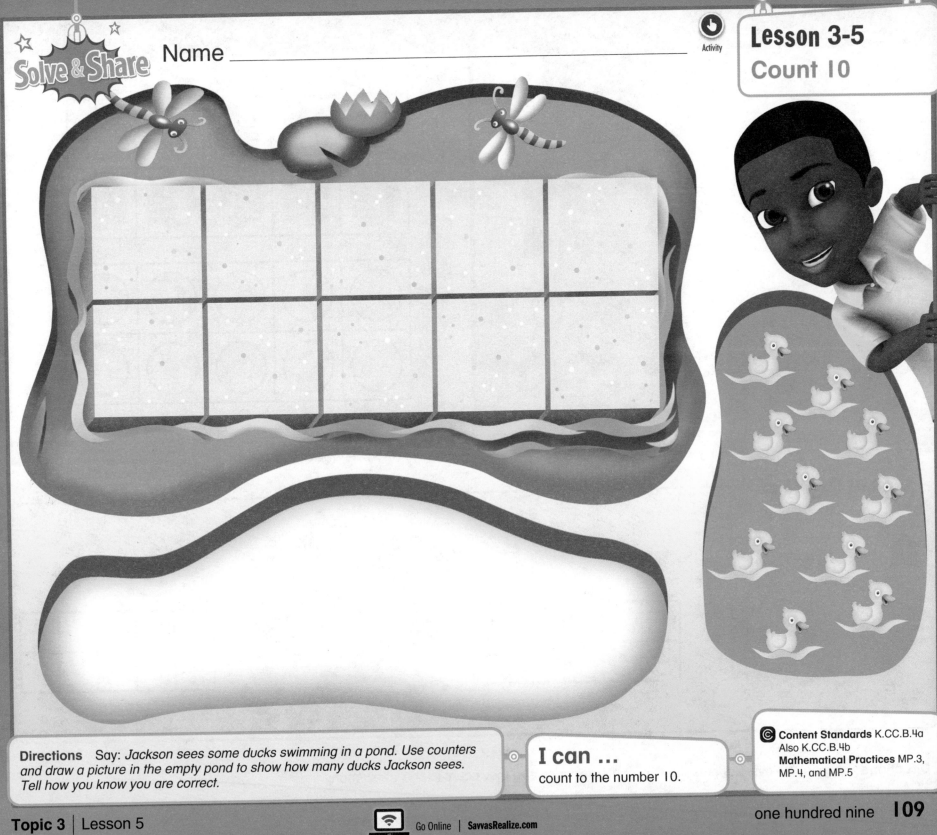

Content Standards K.CC.B.4a
Also K.CC.B.4b
Mathematical Practices MP.3,
MP.4, and MP.5

Directions Say: *Jackson sees some ducks swimming in a pond. Use counters and draw a picture in the empty pond to show how many ducks Jackson sees. Tell how you know you are correct.*

I can ...
count to the number 10.

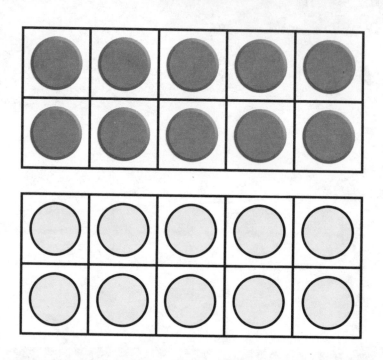

☆ Guided Practice

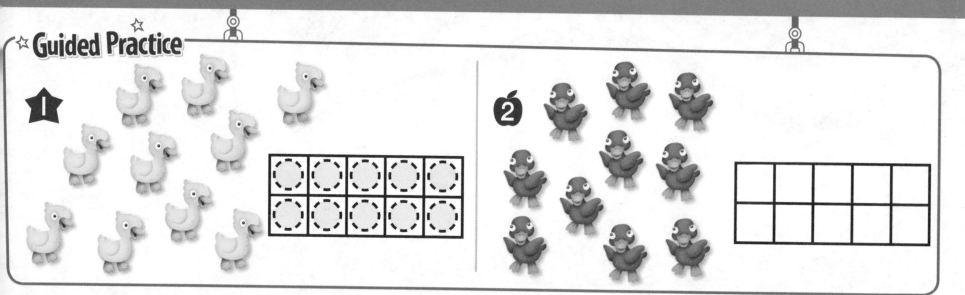

1

2

Directions 1 and 2 Have students draw a counter for each bird they count to show how many.

Topic 3 | Lesson 5

Name _____

3

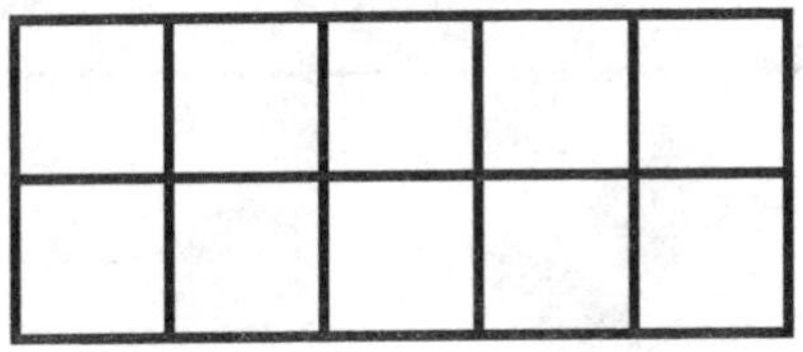

4

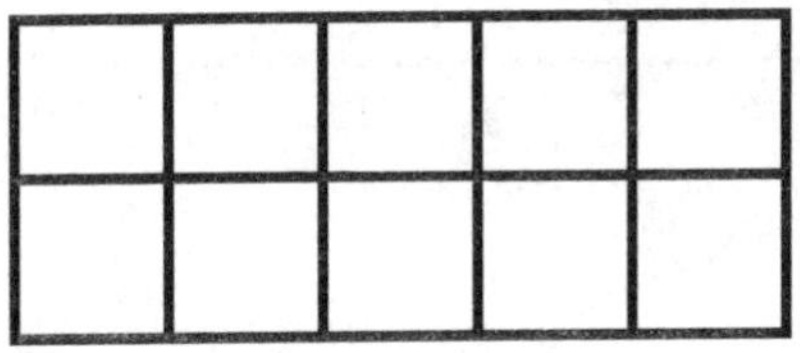

Directions **3** and **4** Have students draw a counter for each bird they count to show how many.

Topic 3 | Lesson 5

one hundred eleven **111**

Independent Practice

Solve & Share

Name _____

Activity

Lesson 3-6
Read, Make, and
Write 10

Directions Say: *Jackson sees some fish in the water. Count how many and use cubes to show the number on the side of the boat. Remove the cubes and use your crayons to draw 10 squares on the boat. Are there different ways to show the number? Tell how you know.*

I can ...
read and write the number 10.

© **Content Standards** K.CC.A.3
Also K.CC.B.5
Mathematical Practices MP.2, MP.5, and MP.8

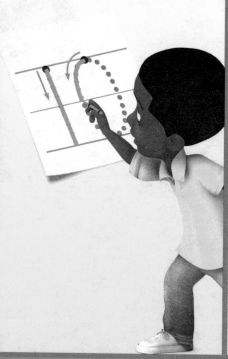

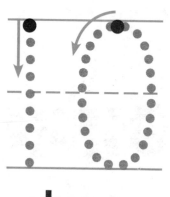

10   10   ten

☆ Guided Practice

1

2

3

Directions ★—3 Have students count the boats, and then write the number to tell how many.

114   one hundred fourteen

Topic 3 | Lesson 6

Name _____

♥ 4

_____

- - - - - - -

_____

✋ 5

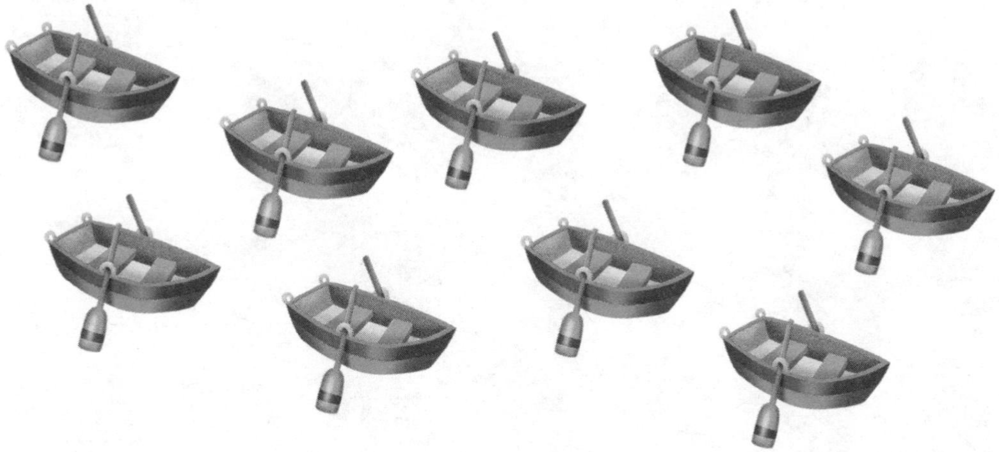

_____

- - - - - - -

_____

Directions ♥–✋ Have students count the boats, and then write the number to tell how many.

Topic 3 | Lesson 6

one hundred fifteen **115**

Independent Practice

6

_____

- - - - - - - -

7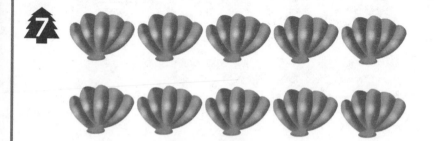

_____

- - - - - - - -

_____

8

_____

- - - - - - - -   _____   _____

- - - -    - - - - -

_____

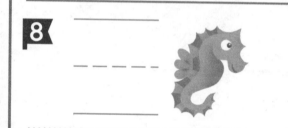

Directions Number Sense 6 and 7 Have students count the shells, and then write the number to tell how many.
8 Higher Order Thinking Have students count each group of sea horses, and then write the numbers to tell how many.

116 one hundred sixteen

Topic 3 | Lesson 6

Solve & Share

Name _____

_____   8   _____

Directions Say: *Emily thinks of two numbers, one that is 1 less than 8 and another that is 1 more than 8. Write the two numbers Emily is thinking of. Show how you know you are correct.*

I can ...
count groups of numbers to 10.

Content Standards K.CC.A.2 Also K.CC.B.4c, K.CC.C.6 **Mathematical Practices** MP.2, MP.3, and MP.7

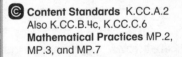

☆ Guided Practice

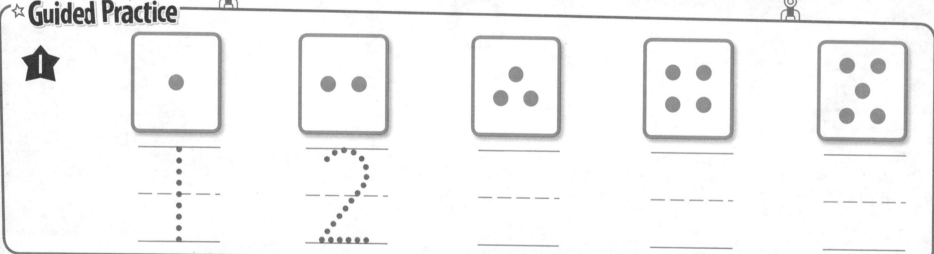

1

Directions ★ Have students count, and then write the number that is 1 greater than the number before.

2

[dot card showing 6 dots]   - - - -   [dot card showing 5 dots]   **7**   [dot card showing 8 dots]   - - - -

3

6	9
8	7

_____ _____ _____ _____

- - - - - - - - - - - - - - - -

4

3	6
5	4

_____ _____ _____ _____

- - - - - - - - - - - - - - - -

Directions 🍎 **Vocabulary** Have students count to find the number that is 1 **less than** and 1 **greater than** the given number, and then write the numbers. 🟣 and ❤ Have students write the smallest number, and then count forward and write the number that is 1 greater than the number before.

Independent Practice

5 ⬜ _ _ _ _   • | _ _ _   •• _ _ _ _

6 [six dots] _ _ _ _   [nine dots] **9**   [nine dots] _ _ _ _

7 8 9 7 10 _ _ _   _ _ _   _ _ _

8 9 6 7 _ _ _   _ _ _   _ _ _

Topic 3 | Lesson 7

Name _____

Think.

Directions Say: *Jackson decorates his sand castle with 3 shells. He has two different colors of shells. How can he use a number pattern to show ways to make groups of 3 shells? Use two-colored counters to show the shell pattern and write the number pattern on the sand castle.*

I can ...
use counting patterns to solve a problem.

Ⓒ **Mathematical Practices** MP.7
Also MP.5, MP.8
Content Standards K.CC.B.4b
Also K.CC.A.3

Visual Learning Bridge

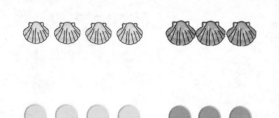

How can I show all the ways?

Make a pattern.

☆ Guided Practice

1

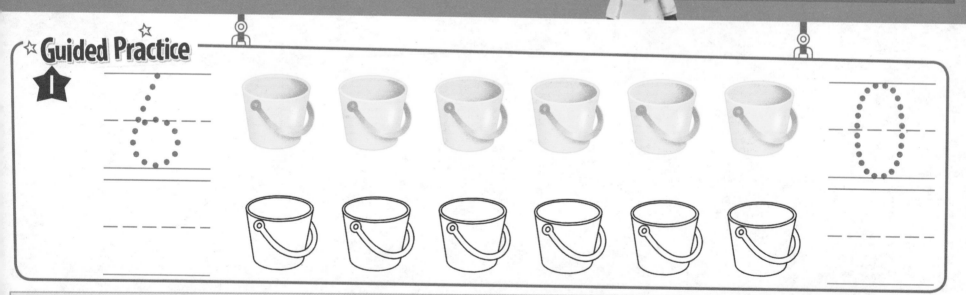

Directions Say: *How can you color the pails to show different ways to make groups of 6?* ⭐ Have students use red and yellow crayons to make a pattern showing two ways to make groups of 6, and then write the number of red pails and yellow pails in each row. Have them describe the pattern.

Topic 3 | Lesson 8

Independent Practice

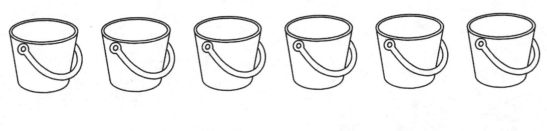

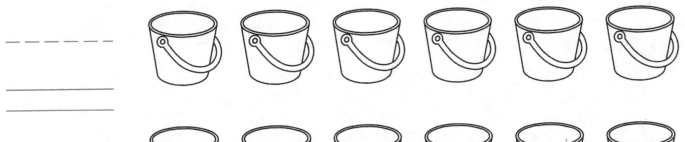

Directions Say: *How can you color the pails to show different ways to make groups of 6?* ❷ Have students look at Items 1 and 2, and then use red and yellow crayons to complete the pattern showing ways to make groups of 6. Then have them write the number of red pails and yellow pails in each row, and describe the pattern.

3 4 5

Directions Read the problem to students. Then have them use multiple problem-solving methods to solve the problem. Say: *Mr. Sand runs a game at the beach. The prizes are red and blue beach balls. He displays them in a pattern. What is the next row in the pattern?* 3 **Use Tools** *What tool can you use to help solve the problem?* 4 **Generalize** *How can the ways that are shown help you find the next way to make a group of 9 beach balls?* 5 **Look for Patterns** *What is the next way in the pattern? Write the number of red and blue beach balls for that way.*

⭐ 1

_____

- - - - - -

_____

🍎 2

8   9

🐦 3

_____

5 - - - - - 7

_____

❤️ 4

_____

- - - - -

_____

_____

- - - - -

_____

Directions Understand Vocabulary Have students: ⭐ write the number **eight**; 🍎 draw a circle around the number **nine**; 🐦 write the missing number and then say it aloud; ❤️ write the number of red cubes and the number of blue cubes used to make the group of 10.

5

10   9

 6

_____

- - - - - - - - -

_____

 7

_____

- - - - - - - - -

_____

8

_____ _____ _____ _____ _____

- - - - - - - - - - - - - - - - - - - - - - - - - - - - - - - - - - -

_____ _____ _____ _____ _____

- - - - - - - - - - - - - - - - - - - - - - - - - - - - - - - - - - -

_____ _____ _____ _____ _____

Directions **Understand Vocabulary** Have students:  draw a circle around the number **ten**; write the number **seven**; count the number of cubes, and then write the number to tell how many; write numbers 1 to10 in order.

Topic 3 | Vocabulary Review

Name _____

Set A

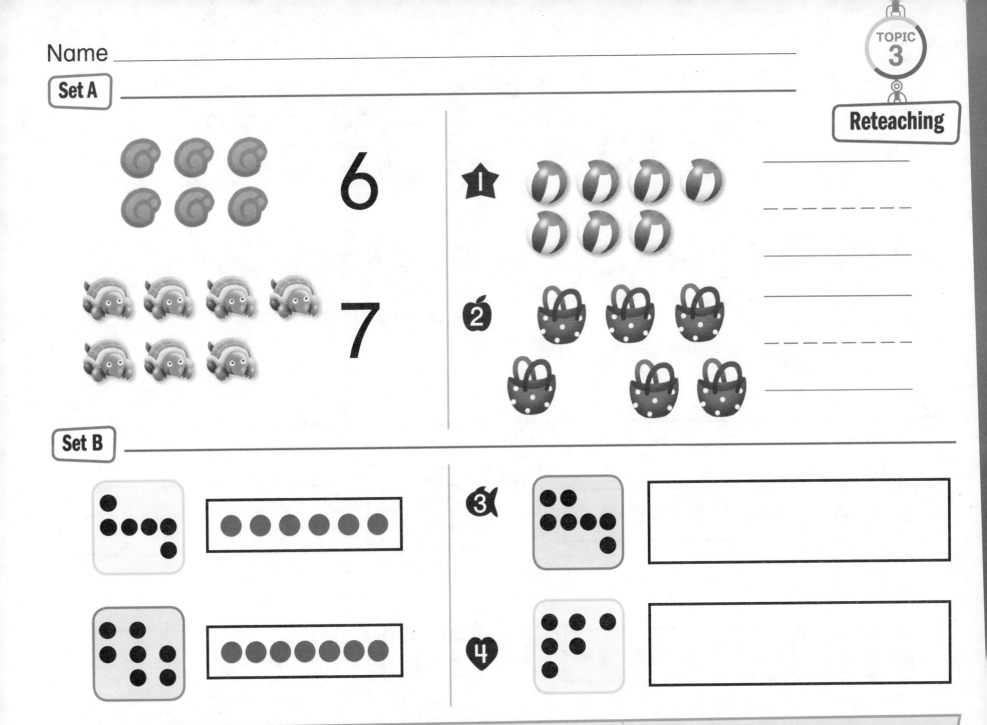

6

7

⭐1 _____

🍎2 _____

Set B

✴3

♥4

Directions Have students: ⭐ and 🍎 count the objects, and then write the numbers to tell how many; ✴ and ♥ count the number of dots, place a counter for each dot they count, and then draw counters in the box to show the same number of counters as dots in a different way.

Topic 3 | Reteaching

one hundred twenty-seven **127**

 8

 9

Directions Have students: 🖐5 and 🍵6 count the objects, and then write the number to tell how many; 🌲7 and ⬛8 count the number of dots, place a counter as they count each dot, and then draw counters in the box to show the same number of counters as dots in a different way.

128 one hundred twenty-eight

Topic 3 | Reteaching

Name _____

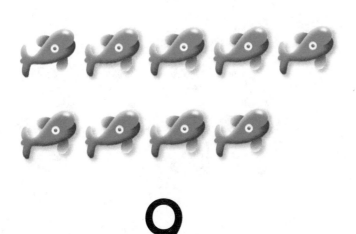

9

_____

– – – – – – – – – – – – – – – –

_____

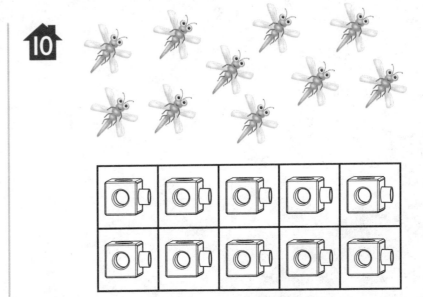

Directions Have students: 🐾 count the objects, and then practice writing the number that tells how many; 🏠 count the insects, use connecting cubes to show that number, and then color a connecting cube for each insect they count.

3   ● ● ●   0

2   ● ● ○   1

1   ● ○ ○   2

0   ○ ○ ○   3

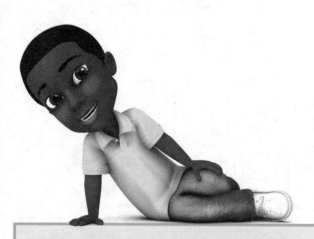

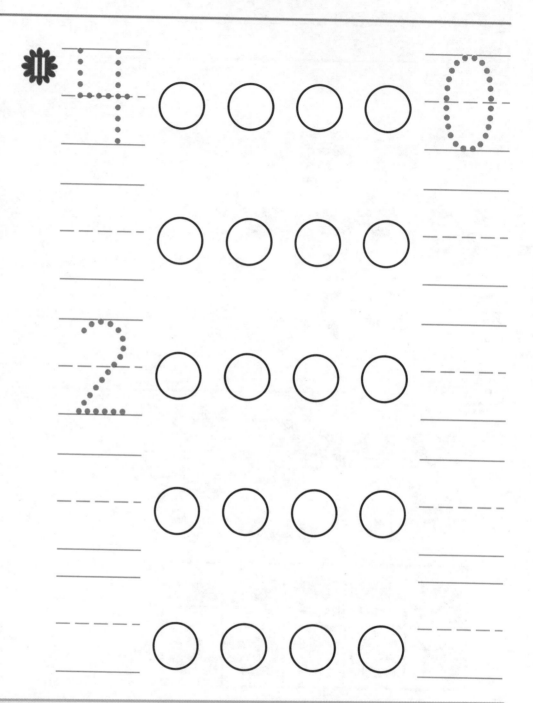

Directions ✽ Have students use two different colored crayons to make an ordered pattern showing rows of 4 counters, and then write the numbers to describe the pattern.

130   one hundred thirty

Name _____

4   5   6   7

Ⓐ   Ⓑ   Ⓒ   Ⓓ

2

7   8   9   10

Ⓐ   Ⓑ   Ⓒ   Ⓓ

3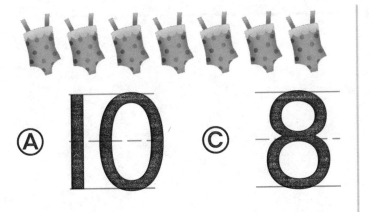

Ⓐ 10   Ⓒ 8

Ⓑ 9   Ⓓ 7

4

Directions Have students mark the best answer. ⭐ How many fish are there? ② How many turtles are there? ③ Which number tells how many swimsuits? ④ Mark all the answers that do NOT show 9.

5

8

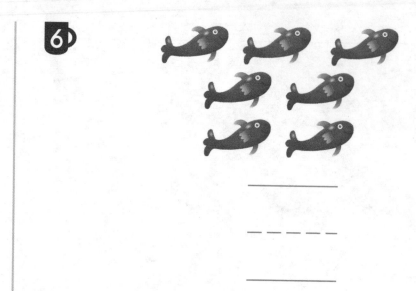

6

———————

- - - - -

———————

7

———————

- - - - -

———————

8

_____ _____

- - - - -   - - - - -

_____ and _____

_____

- - - - -

_____

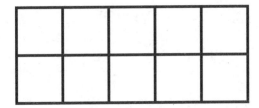

Directions Have students: **8** color the apples red and yellow to show one way to make a group of 10; write numbers to tell how many apples of each color there are; and write the number that tells how many apples in all; **9** draw more turtles to show 10, and then draw counters to show how many turtles in all.

Topic 3 | Assessment Practice

one hundred thirty-three **133**

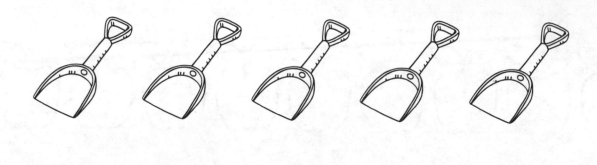

_____

- - - - - - -

red   _____

_____

- - - - - - -

yellow   _____

_____

- - - - - - -

total   _____

Directions 🏠 Have students color the shovels using red and yellow crayons to show one way to make a group of 5. Write the number of red shovels and the number of yellow shovels that they colored. Then write the number that tells how many shovels in all.

     Topic 3 | Assessment Practice

Name _____

 1

_ _ _ _ _ _ _

_ _ _ _ _ _ _

_ _ _ _ _ _ _

_ _ _ _ _ _ _

2

_ _ _ _   _ _ _ _

_ _ _ _   _ _ _ _

Directions **The Beach** Say: *Lexi sees many interesting things at the beach.* ⭐ Have students count how many there are of each object, and then write the number to tell how many. ② The fish that Lexi sees show one way to make 10. Color the fish red and yellow to show two different ways to make a row of 10 fish. Then write the numbers.

Directions ③ Say: *The beach towels that Lexi sees show one way to make 7.* Have students color the beach towels (e.g., some blue and some red) to make an ordered pattern showing rows of 7 towels, and then write numbers to describe the pattern.

Topic 3 | Performance Task

Compare Numbers 0 to 10

Essential Question: How can numbers from 0 to 10 be compared and ordered?

Lightning

Weather can be dangerous.

enVision STEM Project: Weather Changes

Directions Read the character speech bubbles to students. **Find Out!** Have students find out about weather changes. Say: *The weather changes from day to day. Talk to friends and relatives about the weather. Ask them to help you record the number of sunny days and rainy days during the week.*
Journal: Make a Poster Have students make a poster. Have them draw up to 10 lightning bolts above one house and up to 10 lightning bolts above another house. Ask them to write the number of lightning bolts above each house, and then draw a circle around the number that is greater than the other, or draw a circle around both numbers if they are the same.

Name _____

Review What You Know

1

2

3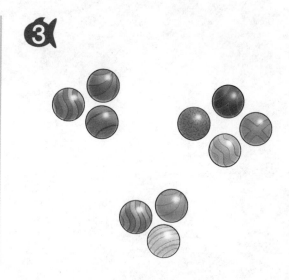

4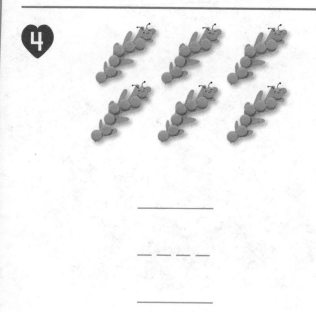

_____

- - - - -

_____

5

_____

- - - - -

6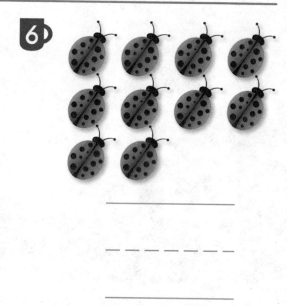

_____

- - - - -

_____

Directions Have students: ⭐ draw a circle around the group of birds that is less than the other group; 🍎 draw a circle around the group of dogs that is greater than the other group; 🔵 draw a circle around the two groups that have an equal number of marbles; ❹–❻ count the number of objects, and then write the number to tell how many.

138 one hundred thirty-eight

Topic 4

A

B

Directions Say: *You will choose one of these projects. Look at picture **A**. Think about this question: How can you train to go into space? If you choose Project A, you will act out an exercise skit. Look at picture **B**. Think about this question: What kinds of fruit would you put into a fruit salad? If you choose Project B, you will create a fruit salad recipe.*

C

D

Directions Say: *You will choose one of these projects. Look at picture **C**. Think about this question: What is the most exciting ride at a theme park? If you choose Project C, you will design a ride. Look at picture **D**. Think about this question: What do you like to do on a vacation? If you choose Project D, you will make a list.*

Name _____

Directions Say: *Work with a partner. Take turns drawing one cube from the bag and placing it on your page in the rectangle of the same color. When the bag is empty, do you have more red or blue cubes? How do you know? Draw a picture of your cubes in the rectangles showing which color is more.*

I can ...
compare groups of up to 10 objects.

© **Content Standards** K.CC.C.6 Also K.CC.B.5
Mathematical Practices MP.3, MP.4, and MP.8

Visual Learning · A-Z Glossary

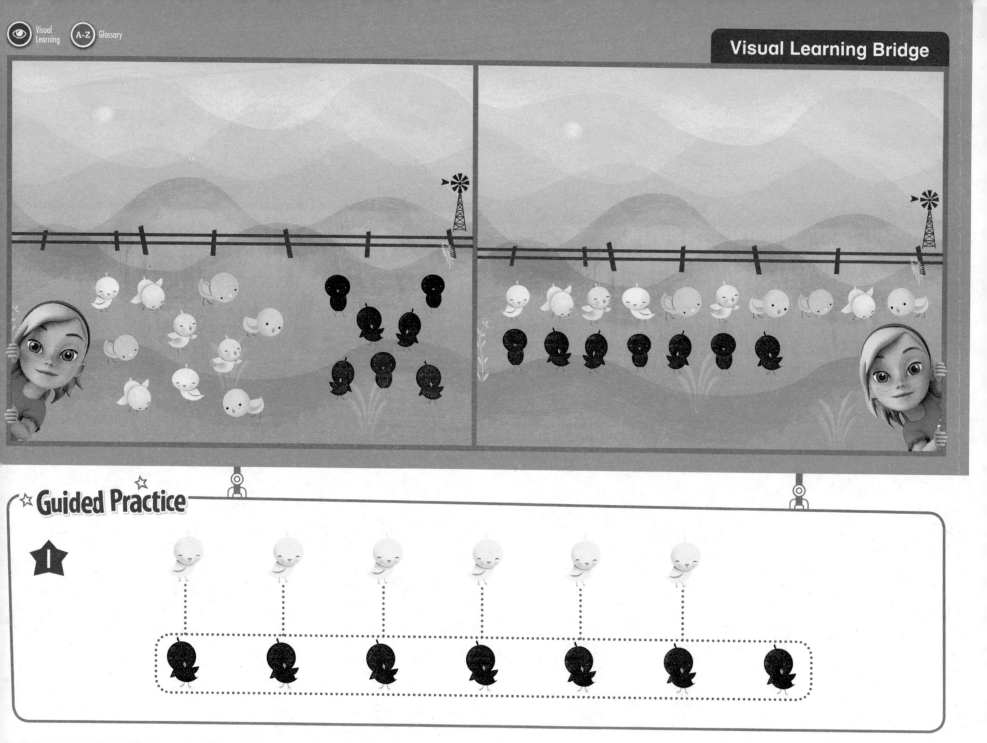

☆ Guided Practice

1

Directions ☆ Have students compare the groups, draw a line from each chick in the top group to a chick in the bottom group, and then draw a circle around the group that is greater in number than the other group.

Topic 4 | Lesson 1

Name _____

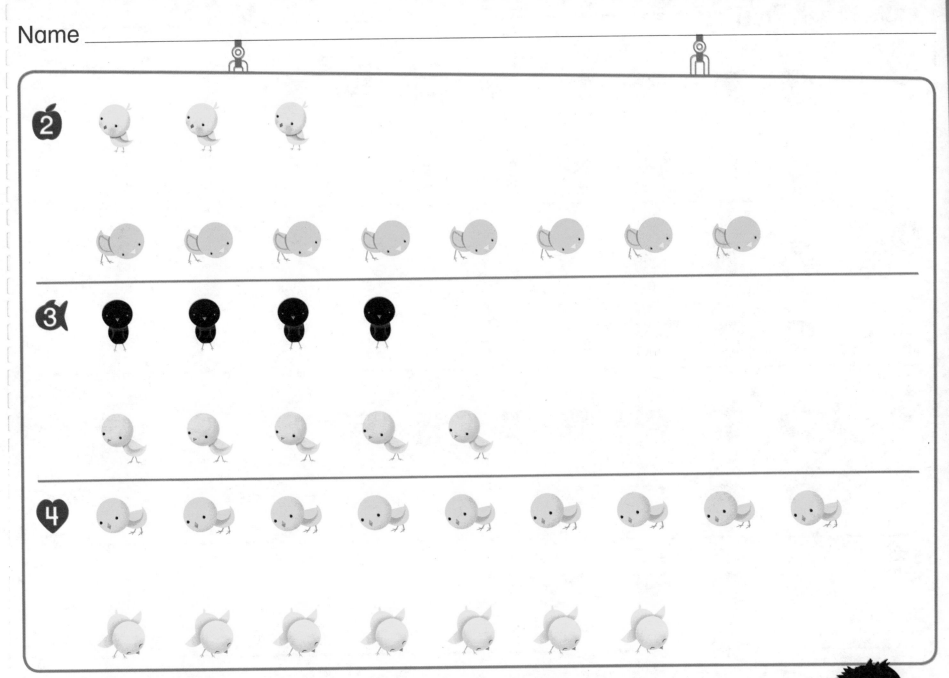

Directions 🍎 **enVision**® STEM Say: *Chicks live in coops. Coops protect chicks in different types of weather.* Have students compare the groups, draw a line from each chick in the top group to a chick in the bottom group, and then draw a circle around the group that is greater in number than the other group. 🍎 and ♥ Have students compare the groups, draw a line from each chick in the top group to a chick in the bottom group, and then draw a circle around the group that is less in number than the other group.

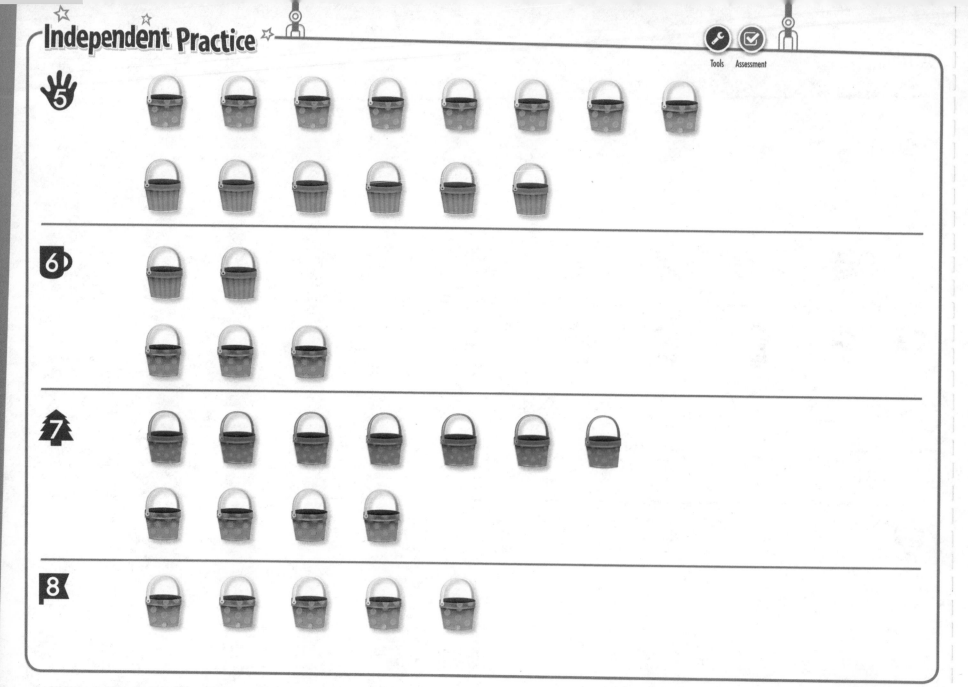

Directions Have students: ✋ compare the groups, draw a line from each bucket in the top group to a bucket in the bottom group, and then draw a circle around the group that is greater in number than the other group; 6 and 7 compare the groups, draw a line from each bucket in the top group to a bucket in the bottom group, and then draw a circle around the group that is less in number than the other group. 8 **Higher Order Thinking** Have students draw a group of buckets that is greater in number than the group shown.

Topic 4 | Lesson 1

Name _____

– – – – –

– – – – –

Directions Say: *Emily is planting seedlings, or little plants. She plants 5 red pepper seedlings and 7 yellow pepper seedlings. Use counters to show the groups of seedlings. Write the numbers, and then circle the number that tells which group has more.*

I can ...
compare groups of numbers using numerals to 10.

© **Content Standards** K.CC.C.7
Also K.CC.B.6
Mathematical Practices MP.1,
MP.2

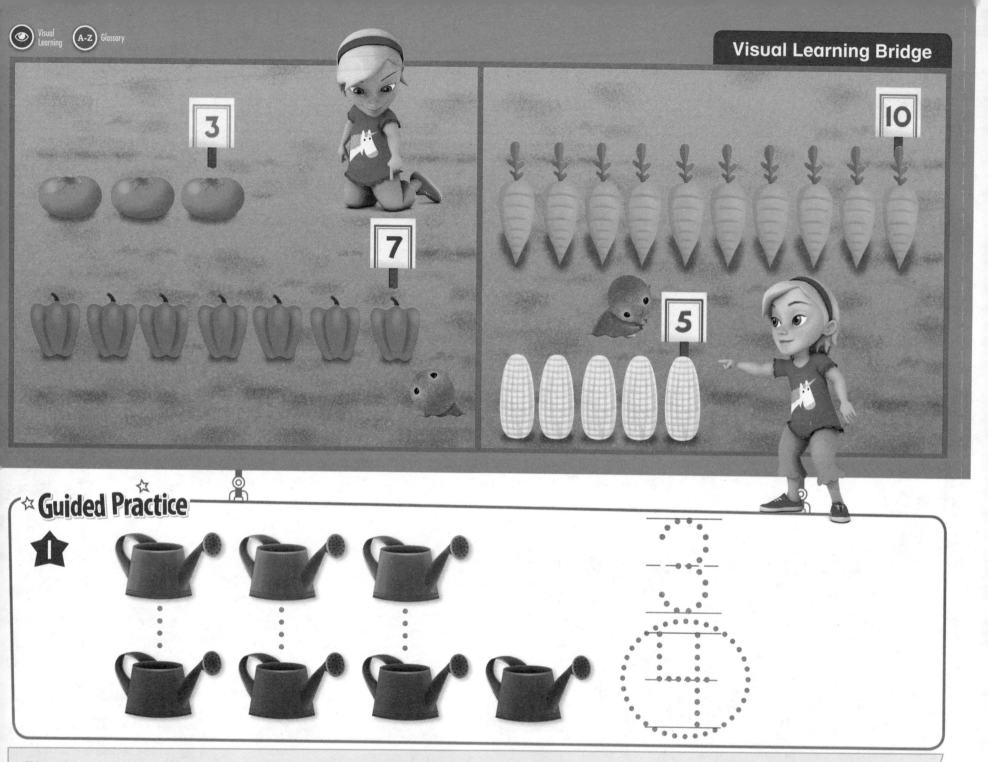

☆ Guided Practice

Directions ★ Have students count the watering cans in each group, write the number to tell how many, draw a line from each watering can in the top group to a watering can in the bottom group, and then draw a circle around the number that is greater than the other number.

Topic 4 | Lesson 2

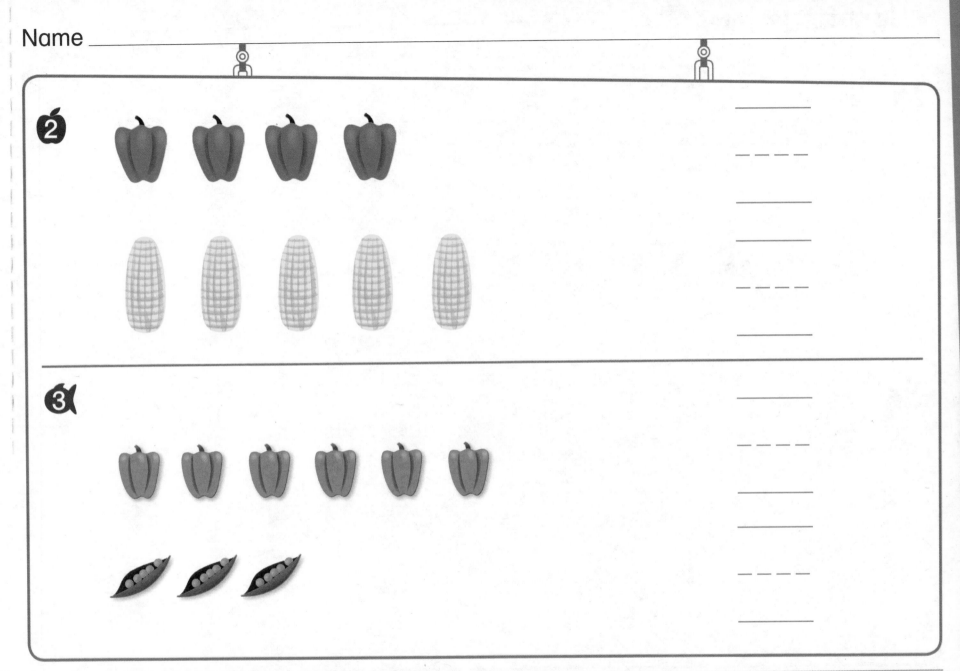

2

3

Directions **2** Have students count the vegetables in each group, write the number to tell how many, draw a line from each vegetable in the top group to a vegetable in the bottom group, and then mark an X on the number that is less than the other number. **3 Number Sense** Have students count the vegetables in each group, draw more pea pods to make the groups equal, write the numbers to tell how many in each group, and then draw a line from each vegetable in the top group to a vegetable in the bottom group to compare.

Tools Assessment

4

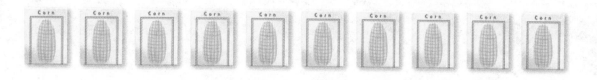

5

Directions ❹ Have students count the seed packets in each group, write the number to tell how many, draw a line from each seed packet in the top group to a seed packet in the bottom group, and then mark an X on the number that is less than the other number. ✋ **Higher Order Thinking** Have students count the flowers in the group, draw a group of flowers that is less than the group shown, and then write the numbers to tell how many.

Name _____

Activity

Lesson 4-3
Compare Groups to 10 by Counting

I can ...
compare groups of numbers by counting.

Ⓒ **Content Standards** K.CC.C.6
Also K.CC.A.2, K.CC.C.7
Mathematical Practices MP.2, MP.5, and MP.6

8

6

1 2 3 4 5 ⑥ 7 ⑧ 9 10

☆ Guided Practice

1 2 3 4 5 6 7 8 9 10

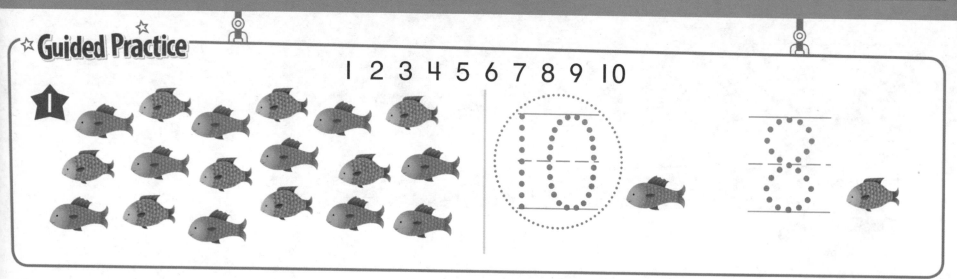

1

Directions 🐟 Have students count the number of each color fish, write the numbers to tell how many, and then draw a circle around the number that is greater than the other number. Use the number sequence to help find the answer.

Name _____

1 2 3 4 5 6 7 8 9 10

🍎❷ _____ _____

❸ _____ _____

💜❹ _____ _____

✋❺ _____ _____

Directions Have students count the number of each color fish, write the numbers to tell how many, and then: ❷ draw a circle around the number that is greater than the other number; ❸ draw a circle around both numbers if they are equal, or mark an X on both numbers if they are NOT equal; ❹ and ✋ mark an X on the number that is less than the other number. Use the number sequence to help find the answer for each problem.

Independent Practice

1 2 3 4 5 6 7 8 9 10

Directions Have students count the number of each critter, write the numbers to tell how many, and then: **6** draw a circle around both numbers if they are equal, or mark an X on both numbers if they are NOT equal; **7** mark an X on the number that is less than the other number; **8** draw a group of spiders that is two greater in number than the number of tarantulas shown, and then write the number to tell how many. **9 Higher Order Thinking** Have students count the butterflies, and then write all the numbers up to 10 that are greater than the number of butterflies shown. Use the number sequence to help find the answer for each problem.

Topic 4 | Lesson 3

Name _____

1 2 3 4 5 6 7 8 9 10

Directions Say: *Emily's mother asked her to bring the towels in off the line. Her basket can hold less than 7 towels. How many towels might Emily bring in? You can give more than one answer. Show how you know your answers are right.*

I can ...
compare two numbers.

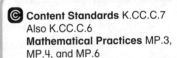
Content Standards K.CC.C.7 Also K.CC.C.6
Mathematical Practices MP.3, MP.4, and MP.6

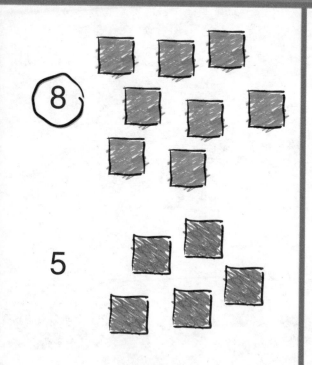

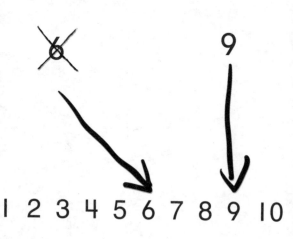

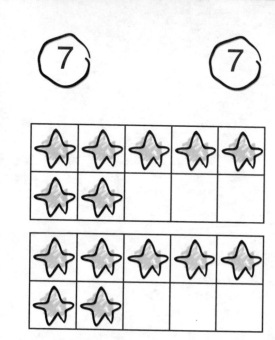

Guided Practice

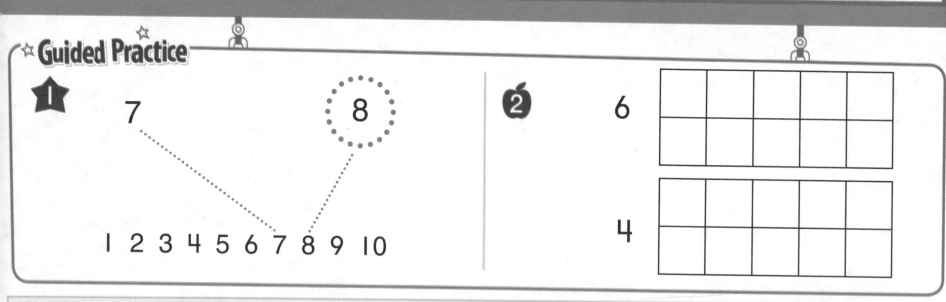

1 7   8

1 2 3 4 5 6 7 8 9 10

2 6

4

Directions Have students: **1** count the numbers 1 to 10 and use the number sequence to show how they know which number is greater than the other, and then draw a circle around the number that is greater; **2** draw counters in the ten-frames to show how they know which number is greater than the other, and then draw a circle around the number that is greater.

Topic 4 | Lesson 4

Name _____

3

6

9

4

8

8

5

9   10

1 2 3 4 5 6 7 8 9 10

6

9

8

Directions Have students: **3** draw pictures to show how they know which number is greater than the other, and then draw a circle around the number that is greater; **4** draw counters in the ten-frames to show how they know if the numbers are equal, and then draw a circle around both numbers if they are equal, or mark an X on both numbers if they are NOT equal; **5** use the number sequence to show how they know which number is less than the other number, and then mark an X on the number that is less; **6** draw pictures to show how they know which number is less than the other number, and then mark an X on the number that is less.

Independent Practice

7

6

8

8

9   7

1 2 3 4 5 6 7 8 9 10

9

8   _____   _____
    - - - - -
    _____   _____

10

5   _____
    - - - - -   9
    _____

Directions Have students: **7** draw pictures to show how they know which number is less than the other number, and then mark an X on the number that is less; **8** use the number sequence to show how they know which number is less than the other number, and then mark an X on the number that is less. **9 Higher Order Thinking** Have students write the next two numbers that are greater than the number shown, and then tell how they know. **10 Higher Order Thinking** Have students write a number that is greater than the number on the left, but less than the number on the right.

Topic 4 | Lesson 4

Name _____

Activity

Think.

Directions Say: *There are 7 fish in a bowl. Emily puts 1 more fish in the bowl. How many fish are in the bowl now? How can you solve this problem?*

I can ...
repeat something from one problem to help me solve another problem.

© **Mathematical Practices** MP.8
Also MP.1, MP.5
Content Standards K.CC.A.2
Also K.CC.B.4c

Topic 4 | Lesson 5

Go Online | SavvasRealize.com

one hundred fifty-seven **157**

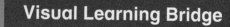

Is there a shortcut?

Repeat 3, and then 1 more.

4

☆ Guided Practice

1

     5

Directions 🔼 Say: *Carlos sees 4 frogs at the pond. Then he sees 1 more. How many frogs are there now?* Have students use reasoning to find the number that is 1 greater than the number of frogs shown. Draw counters to show the answer, and then write the number. Have students explain their reasoning.

Topic 4 | Lesson 5

Tools Assessment

Independent Practice

2

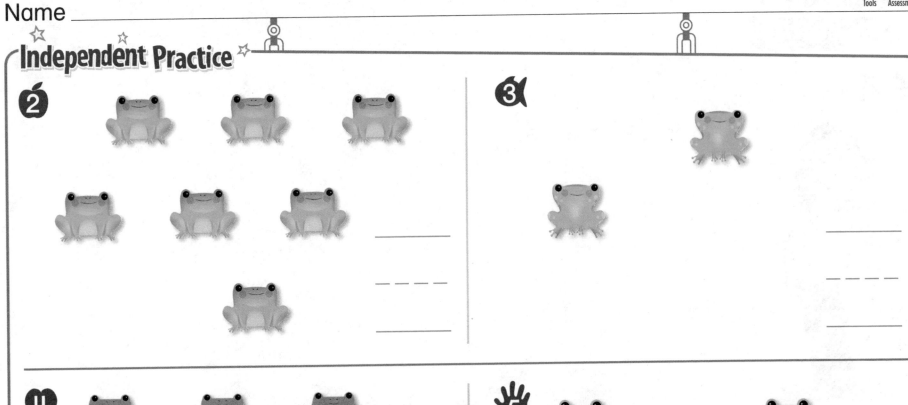

3

_____

- - - - -

4

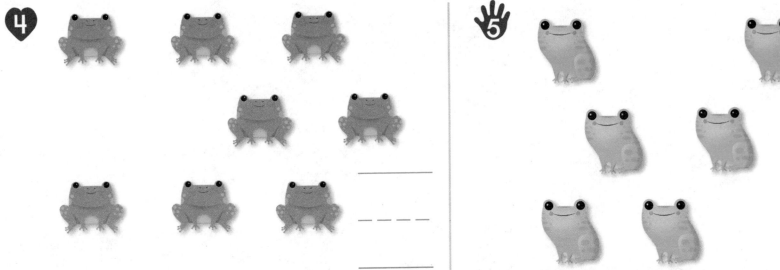

_____

- - - - -

5

_____

- - - - -

Directions Say: *Alex sees frogs at the pond. Then he sees 1 more. How many frogs are there now?* **2**–**5** Have students use reasoning to find the number that is 1 greater than the number of frogs shown. Draw counters to show the answer, and then write the number. Have students explain their reasoning.

Problem Solving

Marta's Family Pets

· ·

_____ _____

_ _ _ _

_____

Directions Read the problem aloud. Then have students use multiple problem-solving methods to solve the problem. Say: *Marta's family has 5 pets. Then her family gets 1 more. How many pets do they have now?* ⑥ **Generalize** *Does something repeat in the problem? How does that help?* ⑦ **Use Tools** *What tool can you use to help solve the problem? Use the tool to find the number of pets in Marta's family now.* ⑧ **Make Sense** *Should the answer be greater than or less than 5?*

160 one hundred sixty

Topic 4 | Lesson 5

⭐1

6   9

🍎2

_____
- - - - - - - - - -
_____

🐟3

_____
- - - - - - - - - -
_____

❤4

_____
- - - - - - - - - -
_____

Directions **Understand Vocabulary** Have students: ⭐ draw a circle around the number that is **greater than** 7; 🍎 **count** the counters, and then write the number to tell how many; 🐟 write the number that means **none**; ❤ count how many of each color cube there is, draw a circle around the group that has a number of cubes that is **less than** the other group, and then write the number to tell how many there are in that group.

5 3   **6** 8

_____

_ _ _ _ _ _ _

_____

7

_____

_ _ _ _ _ _ _

_____

8

_ _ _ _ _   5   _ _ _ _ _   9

Topic 4 | Vocabulary Review

Name _____

Set A

⭐

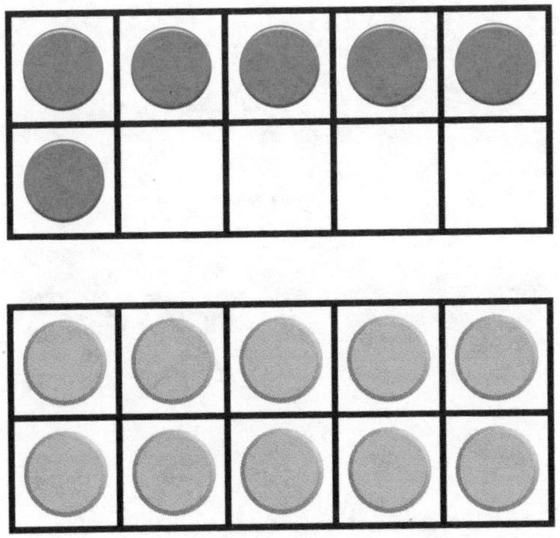

Set B

⑥

④

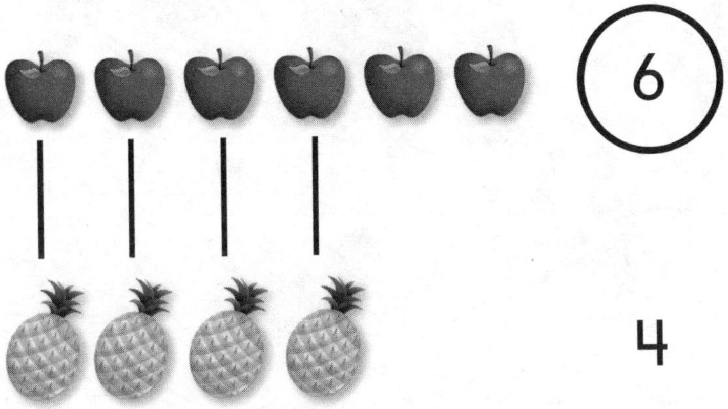

②

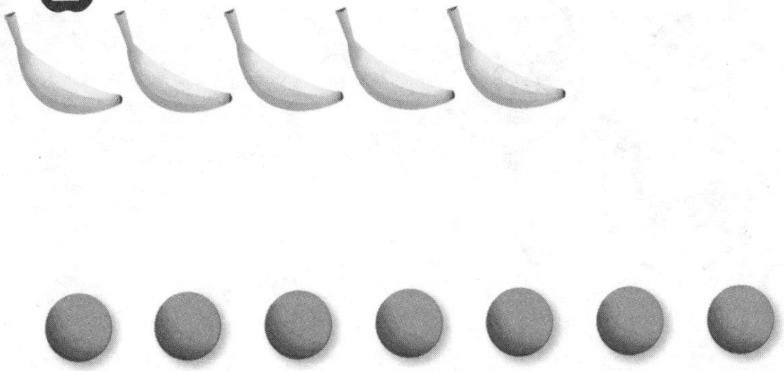

Directions Have students: ⭐ compare the groups, and draw a circle around the group that is less in number than the other group; ② count the fruit in each group, write the numbers that tell how many, draw a line from each piece of fruit in the top group to a piece of fruit in the bottom group, and then draw a circle around the number that is greater than the other number.

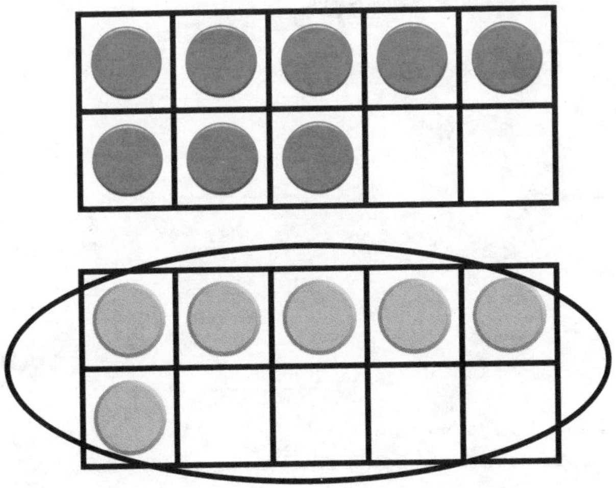

5

✗

_____   _____

- - - - - - -   - - - - - - -

_____   _____

8

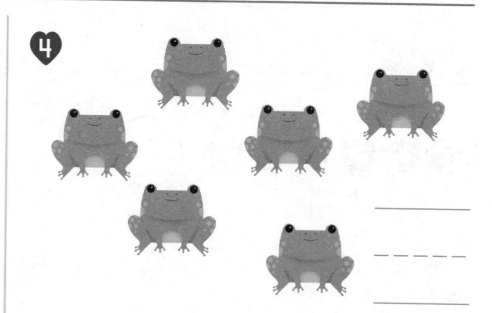

_____

- - - - - - -

_____

Directions Have students: ③ count the number of each critter, write the numbers, and then mark an X on the number that is less than the other number; ④ Say: *April sees frogs at the pond. Then she sees 1 more. How many frogs does she see now?* Have students use reasoning to find the number that is 1 greater than the number of frogs shown. Draw counters to show the answer, and then write the number.

Name _____

⭐

Ⓐ

Ⓑ

Ⓒ

Ⓓ

②

| 7 |

1 2 3 4 5 6 7 8 9 10

☐ 9

☐ 6

☐ 5

☐ 3

③

_____   _____

- - - - - - -   - - - - - - -

Directions Have students mark the best answer. ⭐ Which group of blue birds is greater in number than the group of yellow birds? ② Look at the number line. Then mark all the numbers that are less than the number on the card. ③ Have students count the number of lemons and limes, write the number that tells how many of each, and then draw a circle around the number that is greater.

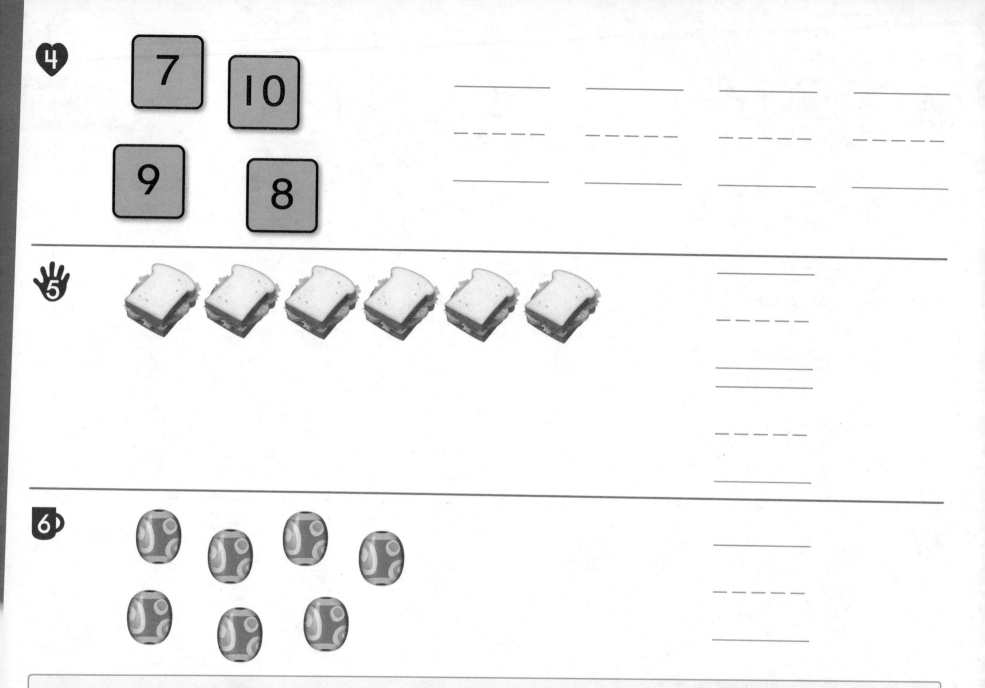

4

7   10

9   8

_ _ _ _ _   _ _ _ _ _   _ _ _ _ _   _ _ _ _ _

_ _ _ _ _

5

_ _ _ _ _

_ _ _ _ _

6

_ _ _ _ _

_ _ _ _ _

_ _ _ _ _

Directions Have students: **4** write the number that is counted first among the 4 number cards, and then count forward and write the number that is 1 greater than the number before; **5** count the sandwiches in the group, draw a group of juice boxes that is less than the group of sandwiches shown, and then write the numbers to tell how many. **6** Say: *Kayla has 7 beads to make a bracelet. Then she buys 1 more. How many beads does she have now?* Have students use reasoning to find the number that is 1 greater than the number of beads shown. Draw counters to show the answer, and then write the number to tell how many.

Topic 4 | Assessment Practice

Name _____

 1 2 3 4 5 6 7 8 9 10

_____   _____

- - - - -    - - - - -

Directions **Forest Animals** Say: *The forest is home to woodland animals. One part of the forest has many different animal homes in it.* ★ Have students study the picture. Say: *How many skunks live in this part of the forest? How many raccoons live in this part of the forest? Count the number of each type of animal and write the numbers.* Then have students draw a circle around the number that is greater than the other number and mark an X on the number that is less than the other number. Have them use the number sequence to help find the answers.

2

_____ ⬛(fox) _____   _____   _____   _____   _____

3

5

5

4

- - - - 🐦   - - - 🐦

Directions Have students look at the picture on the page before. **2** Say: _How many foxes live in this part of the forest? Count how many and write the number._ Then have students write all the numbers through 10 that are greater than the number of foxes. **3** Say: _5 chipmunks and 5 frogs move out of this part of the forest. Draw a circle around both numbers if they are equal, or mark an X on both numbers if they are NOT equal. Show how you know you are correct._ **4** Say: _How many birds live in this part of the forest? Count how many and write the number. 1 more bird flies into the forest. How many birds are in this part of the forest now?_ Have students use tools to solve the problem and write the number. Then have them show how they found the answer.

Classify and Count Data

Essential Question: How can classifying data help answer questions?

Some cows are brown and some are black.

Cows can be different colors.

ënVision STEM Project: Sorting Animals

Directions Read the character speech bubbles to students. **Find Out!** Have students find out about animals that can be organized by color. Say: *Talk to friends and relatives about animals. Talk about how an animal can be one color, but another of the same animal can be a different color.* **Journal: Make a Poster** Have students make a poster. Have them choose one animal they learned about, and then draw a group of 6–10 animals. Ask them to color the animals using two different colors, and then write the numbers to tell how many of each color.

Review What You Know

1

2

3

4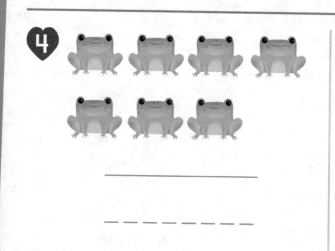

5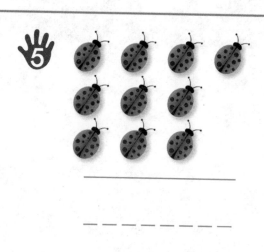

6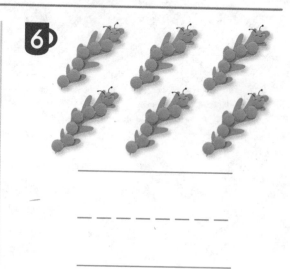

Directions Have students: **1** draw a circle around the group with 10 bugs; **2** draw a circle around the group that has a number of birds that is less than 5; **3** draw a circle around the group that has a number of birds that is greater than 5; **4**–**6** count the frogs or bugs in each group, and then write the number to tell how many.

Topic 5

Directions Say: *You will choose one of these projects. Look at picture* **A.** *Think about this question: What would our class flag look like? If you choose Project A, you will design a flag. Look at picture* **B.** *Think about this question: How do you go? If you choose Project B, you will make a model. Look at picture* **C.** *Think about this question: How does an instrument make music? If you choose Project C, you will act out playing instruments and making music.*

I always thought those were elephants!

Directions Read the robot's speech bubble to students. **Generate Interest** Ask students what they use to color pictures at home. Say: *What colors would you use to color a dog? What colors would you never use?* Have them draw their own dogs and color them in creative or unusual ways.

I can ...

model with math to make equal groups to solve a problem.

ⓒ **Mathematical Practices** MP.4 Also MP.2, MP.8
Content Standards K.MD.B.3 Also K.CC.A.2, K.CC.B.5, K.OA.A.1

4 legs

NOT 4 legs

Pet Fair

Directions Say: *Carlos' kindergarten class is having a pet fair. The pets need to be put into two tents. One tent is for pets with 4 legs. The other tent is for pets that do NOT have 4 legs. Draw pictures of 5 pets. How many animals are in the 4 legs tent? How many animals are in the NOT 4 legs tent? Count the legs and talk about your pictures.*

I can ...
classify objects into categories and tell why they are in each category.

© **Content Standards** K.MD.B.3 Also K.CC.B.5
Mathematical Practices MP.1, MP.3, and MP.6

Hair

NO Hair

Classify.

☆ Guided Practice

1

Directions ☆ Have students draw a circle around the animals that have feathers, and then mark an X on the animals that do NOT have feathers.

Topic 5 | Lesson 1

Name _____

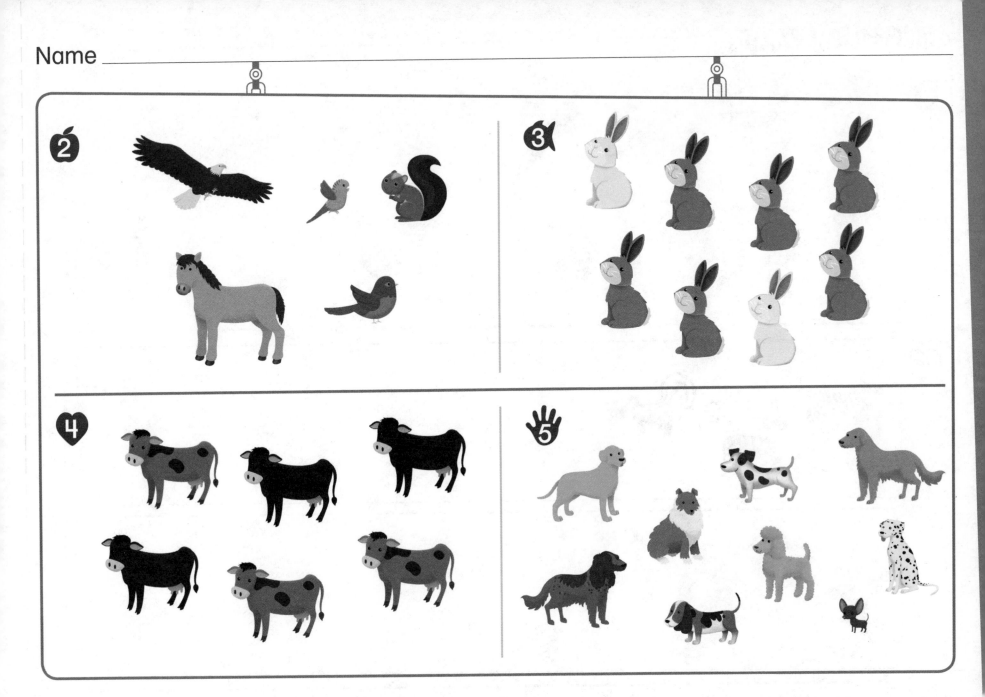

Directions ✷ **enVision®** STEM Say: *What can most animals with wings do?* Have students draw a circle around the animals that have wings, and then mark an X on the animals that do NOT have wings. Have students: ✷ draw a circle around the rabbits that are white, and then mark an X on the rabbits that are NOT white; ✷ draw a circle around the cows that are brown, and then mark an X on the cows that are NOT brown; ✷ draw a circle around the dogs that have spots, and then mark an X on the dogs that do NOT have spots.

Independent Practice

Directions Have students: ⑥ draw a circle around the birds that are green, and then mark an X on the birds that are NOT green; ⑦ draw a circle around the animals that have tails, and then mark an X on the animals that do NOT have tails. ⑧ **Higher Order Thinking** Say: *The animals have been classified into two categories. How were the animals classified?* Have students draw a picture of an animal that belongs in each category.

Topic 5 | Lesson I

Activity

Lesson 5-2
Count the
Number of
Objects in
Each Category

Solve & Share

Name _____

_____

- - - - - -

_____

On the ground

_____

- - - - - -

NOT on the ground

Directions Say: *Carlos goes outside and sees some creatures. How many creatures does he see on the ground? How many does he see that are NOT on the ground? Tell how you know you counted all of the creatures.*

I can ...
count how many objects are in different categories.

© **Content Standards** K.MD.B.3
Also K.CC.B.5
Mathematical Practices MP.2,
MP.6, and MP.8

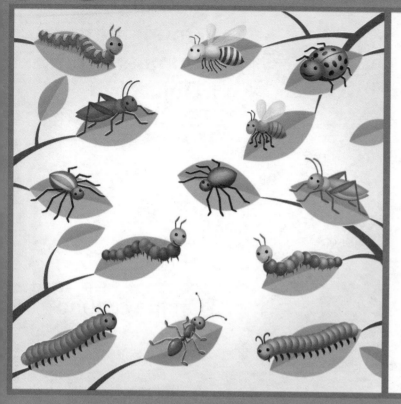

Count.

6 | 7

☆ Guided Practice

1

6 | 5

Directions ⭐ Have students draw lines in the chart as they count the animals that are in the pond and the animals that are NOT in the pond, and then write the numbers to tell how many in another chart.

Name _____

2

3

Directions **2** **Vocabulary** Have students draw lines in the chart as they count the animals that have 8 legs and the animals that do NOT have 8 legs, and then write the numbers to tell how many are in each **category** in another chart. **3** Have students draw lines in the chart as they count the birds that are in the trees and the birds that are NOT in the trees, and then write the numbers to tell how many are in each category in another chart.

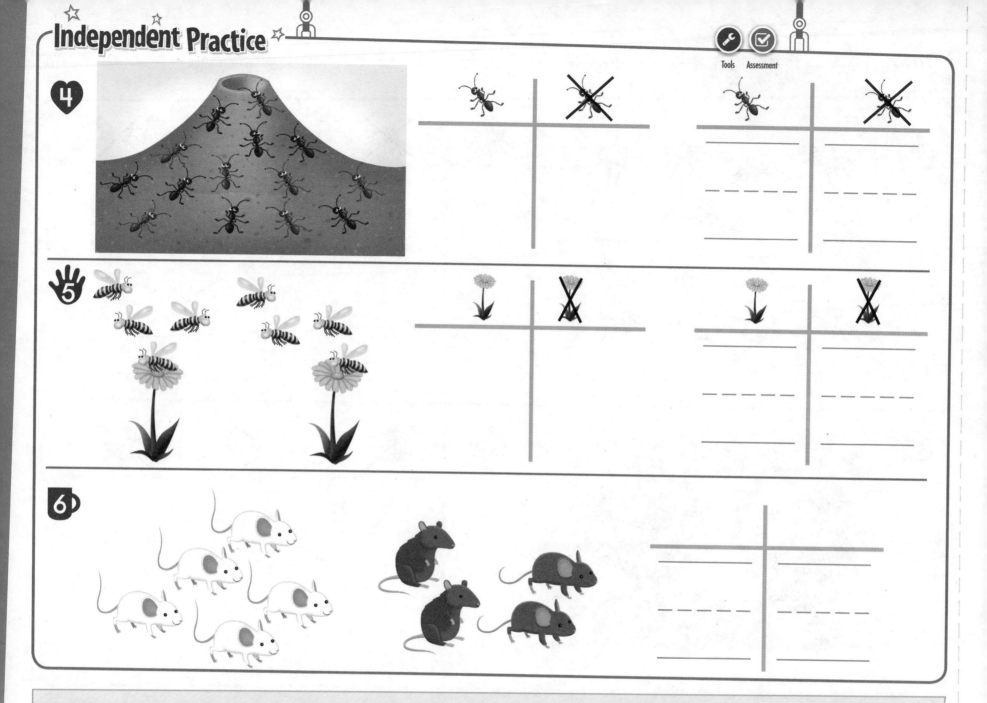

4

5

6

Directions Have students: **4** draw lines in the chart as they count the ants that are red and the ants that are NOT red, and then write the numbers to tell how many in another chart; **5** draw lines in the chart as they count the bees that are on flowers and the bees that are NOT on flowers, and then write the numbers to tell how many in another chart. **6 Higher Order Thinking** Say: *These mice are sorted into two categories. How are the mice on the left different than the mice on the right?* Have students draw a picture in the chart to show the categories, and then write the numbers to tell how many mice are in each category.

Topic 5 | Lesson 2

Solve & Share

Name _____

Directions Say: Carlos's kindergarten class has a new playground area. Sort the new playground into toys that have wheels and toys that do NOT have wheels. Count the toys in each category. Write numbers to tell how many. Draw a circle around the category that is greater than the other category. Tell how you know.

I can ...
use counting to compare how many objects are in categories.

Content Standards K.MD.B.3 Also K.CC.C.6, K.CC.C.7 **Mathematical Practices** MP.1, MP.5, and MP.7

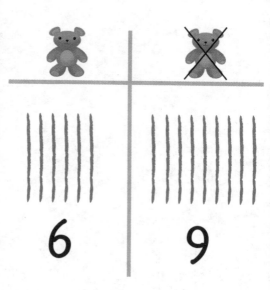

6 | 9

6 9

1 2 3 4 5 6 7 8 9 10

☆ **Guided Practice**

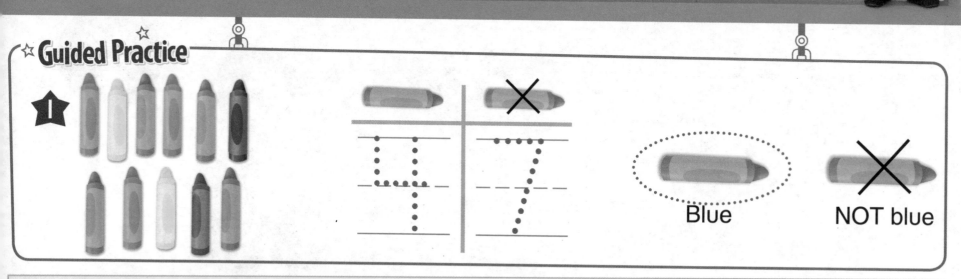

1

Blue   NOT blue

Directions ★ Have students sort the crayons into crayons that are blue and crayons that are NOT blue, count them, and then write numbers in the chart to tell how many. Have students draw a circle around the category that is less in number than the other category and tell how they know.

Name _____

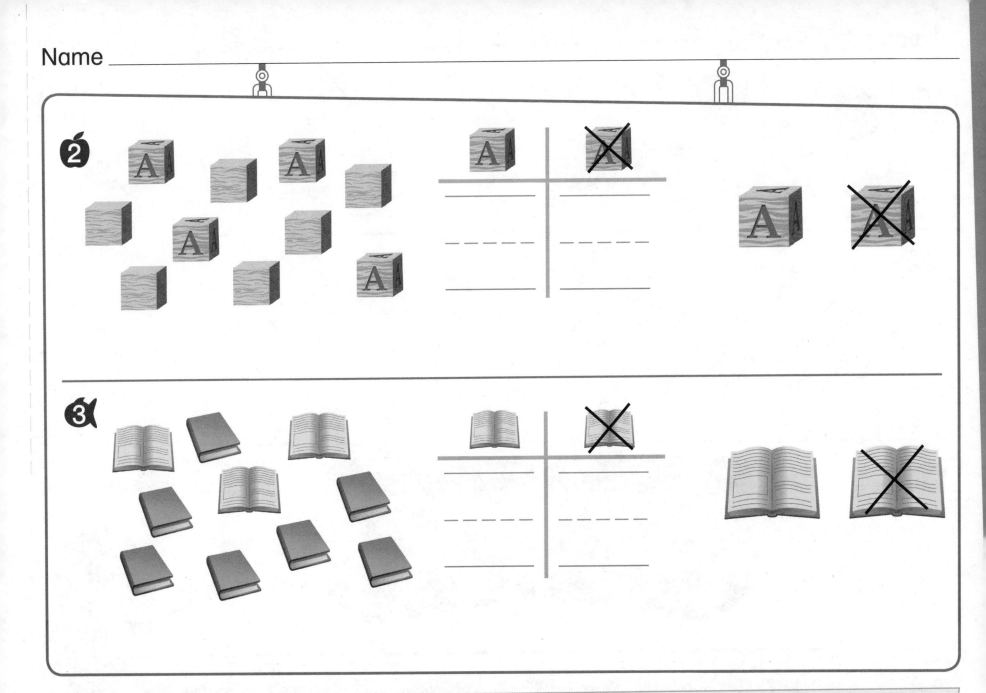

Directions Have students: ❷ sort the blocks into blocks that have letters and blocks that do NOT have letters, count them, and then write numbers in the chart to tell how many. Then have students draw a circle around the category that is greater in number than the other category and tell how they know; ❸ sort the books into books that are open and books that are NOT open, count them, and then write numbers in the chart to tell how many. Then have students draw a circle around the category that is less in number than the other category and tell how they know.

Topic 5 | Lesson 3   one hundred eighty-three **183**

Independent Practice

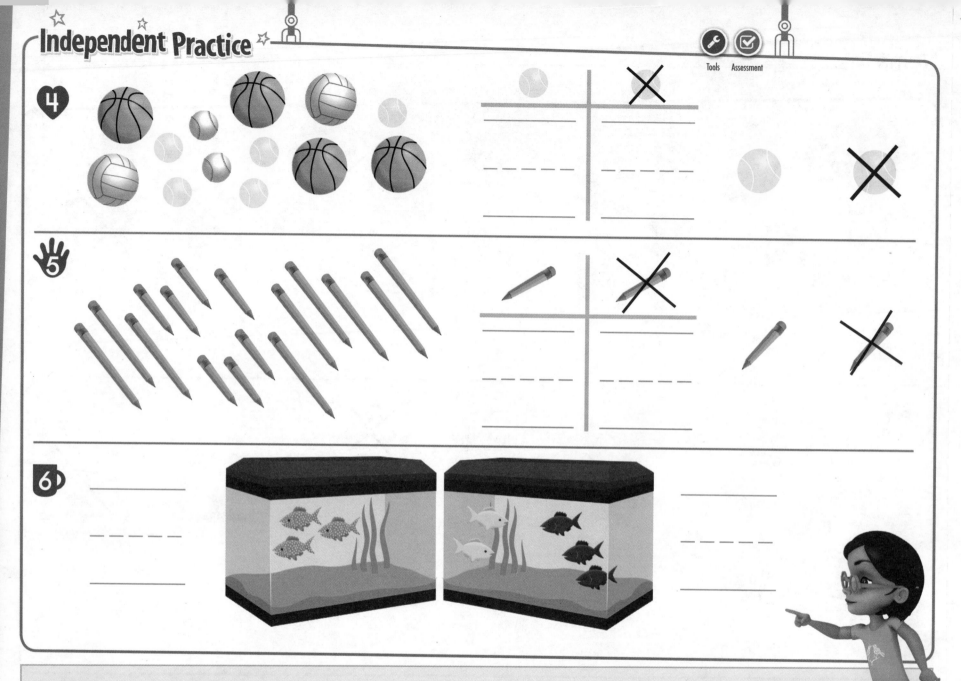

Directions Have students: ❹ sort the balls into balls that are yellow and balls that are NOT yellow, count them, and then write numbers in the chart to tell how many. Then have students draw a circle around the category that is greater in number than the other category and tell how they know; ❺ sort the pencils into pencils that are short and pencils that are NOT short, count them, and then write numbers in the chart to tell how many. Then have students draw a circle around the category that is greater in number than the other category and tell how they know. ❻ **Higher Order Thinking** Say: *The fish are sorted into fish that have spots and fish that do NOT have spots.* Have students draw fish so the categories have an equal number of fish, and then write the number of fish in each category. Ask: *How do you know the categories have an equal number of fish?*

Topic 5 | Lesson 3

Activity

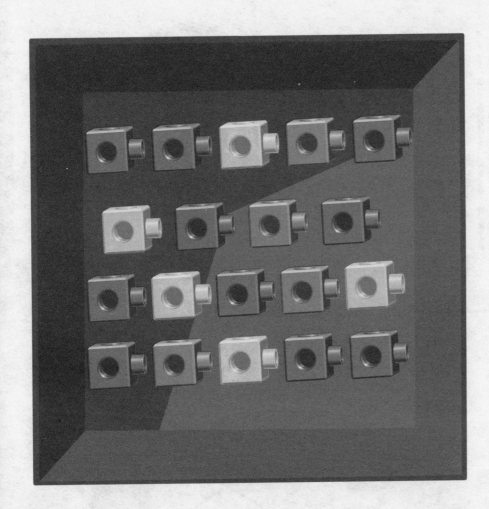

Think.

I can ...
tell whether the way objects
have been sorted, counted,
and compared makes sense.
I can explain how I know.

Directions Say: *Carlos says that the number of blue cubes is equal to the number of cubes that are NOT blue. Does his answer make sense? Use numbers, pictures, or words to explain your answer.*

Ⓒ **Mathematical Practices** MP.3
Also MP.2, MP.6
Content Standards K.MD.B.3
Also K.CC.C.6, K.CC.C.7

Which is correct?

Name __Tucker__

6   5

Name __Olivia__

6   ⑤

1 2 3 4 ⑤ 6 7 8 9 10

Both answers are correct.

☆ Guided Practice

1 yes

no

5

6

Directions ⬆ Say: *Gabbi says that the category of airplanes is greater in number than the category that is NOT airplanes. Does her answer make sense?* Have students draw a circle around *yes* or *no*, and then use the sorting and counting of each category to explain their reasoning.

Topic 5 | Lesson 4

Independent Practice

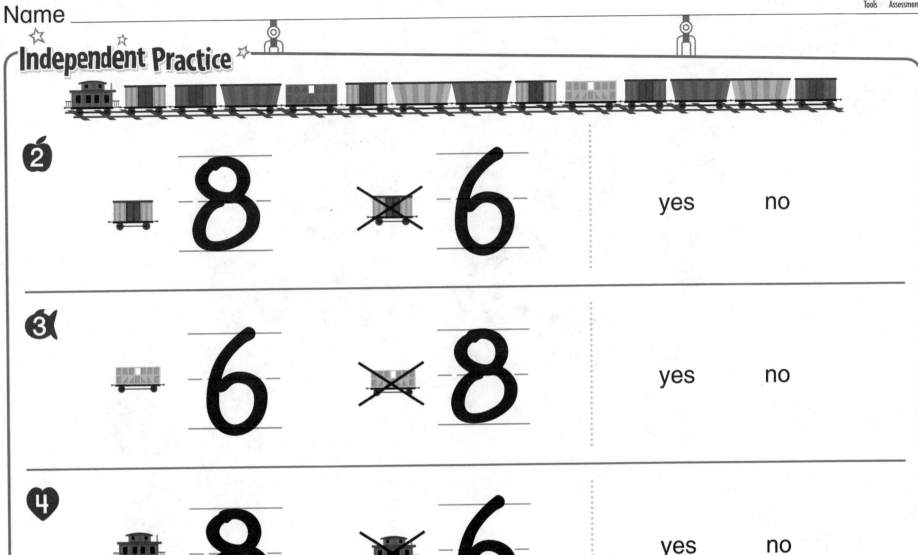

2️⃣ ___ 8   ✗ 6   yes   no

3️⃣ ___ 6   ✗ 8   yes   no

4️⃣ ___ 8   ✗ 6   yes   no

Directions Have students listen to each problem, draw a circle around *yes* or *no*, and then use the sorting and counting of each category to explain their reasoning. 2️⃣ *Damon says that he counted 8 yellow train cars and 6 train cars that are NOT yellow. Does his answer make sense?* 3️⃣ *Malinda says that the category of yellow train cars is less than the category of train cars that are NOT yellow. Does her answer make sense?* 4️⃣ *Aaron says that the category of red train cars is greater than the category of train cars that are NOT red. Does his answer make sense?*

Directions Read the problem aloud. Then have students use multiple problem-solving methods to solve the problem. Say: *Alex says that if there was 1 fewer orange ball, then the category of orange balls would be equal in number to the category of balls that are NOT orange. Does his answer make sense?* 👆 **Reasoning** *Think about it. How many orange balls would there be if there were 1 fewer orange ball? Use numbers, tools, or draw a picture to show how many orange balls there would be.* 👆 **Be Precise** *Is the number of orange balls equal to the number of balls that are NOT orange?* 👆 **Critique Reasoning** *Use the sorting and counting of each category to explain your reasoning.*

Topic 5 | Lesson 4

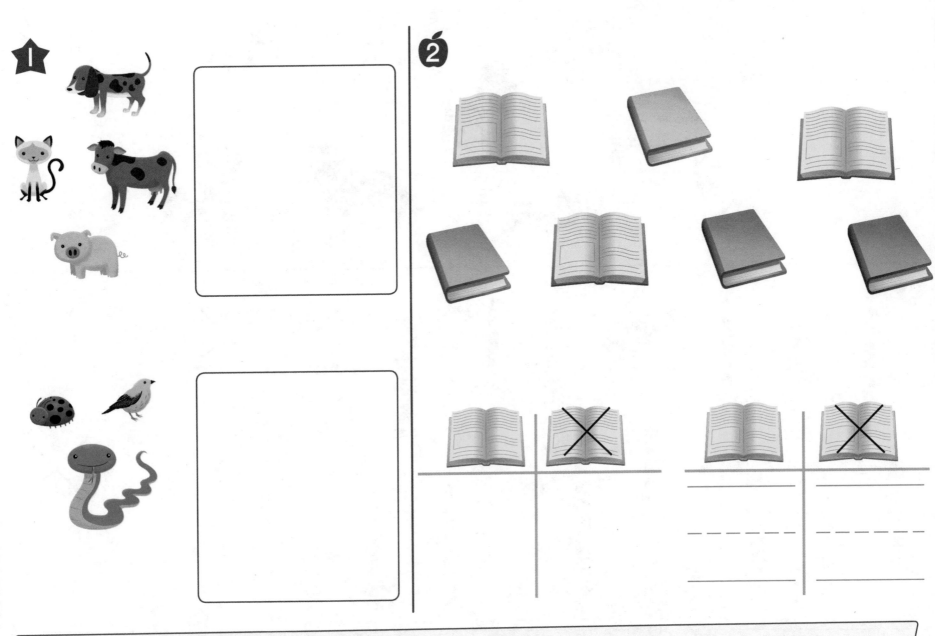

Directions Understand Vocabulary Have students: ⭐ draw an animal that fits each **category**, and then tell how the groups are organized; ② sort books into books that are open and books that are NOT open. Have them draw **tally marks** in the chart as they count, and then write the number in another chart.

③

④

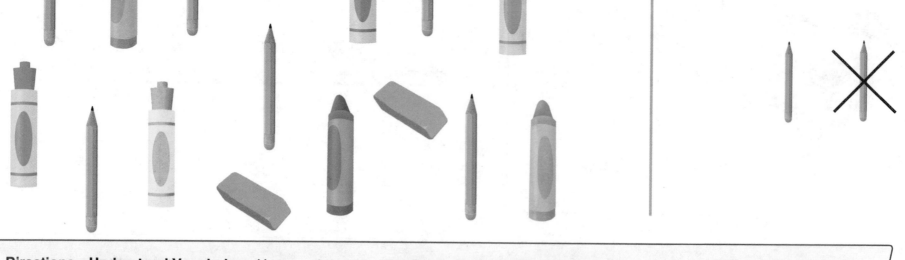

Directions **Understand Vocabulary** Have students: ③ **classify** the dogs by drawing circles and marking Xs, and then explain how they organized them; ④ draw lines in the **chart** to show how many in each group, and then draw a circle around the group that is greater in number than the other group.

Topic 5 | Vocabulary Review

Name _____

Set A

Set B

2 4

Directions Have students: ⭐ draw a circle around the animals that walk on 2 legs, and then mark an X on the animals that do NOT walk on 2 legs; 🍎 draw lines in the chart as they count the toys that are on the rug and the toys that are NOT on the rug. Then have them write the numbers to tell how many are in each group in another chart.

7   ✕

6

Ⓧ   ✕

③

✕

4

❤

(yes)

5   ✕ 3

no

yes

4   ✕ 6

no

Directions ③ Have students sort the balls into balls that are white and balls that are NOT white, and then write numbers in the chart to tell how many. Then have students draw a circle around the group that is greater in number than the other group and tell how they know. ④ Say: *Malik says that the group of airplanes is greater than the group that is NOT airplanes. Does his answer make sense?* Have students draw a circle around *yes* or *no*, and then use the sorting and counting of each category to explain their reasoning.

Name _____

1

A. 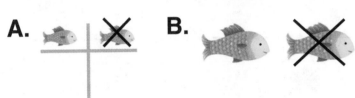 B.

3

A.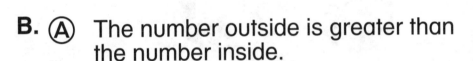

☐ ☐ ☐ ☐

2

B. Ⓐ The number outside is greater than the number inside.

Ⓑ The number inside is less than the number outside.

Ⓒ The number inside is equal to the number outside.

Ⓓ The number outside is less than the number inside.

Directions Have students: **1** A. draw lines in the chart as they count the fish that are yellow and the fish that are NOT yellow; **B.** compare the number of fish that are yellow to the number of fish that are **NOT** yellow. Say: *Draw a circle around the category that is less in number;* **2** draw a circle around the animals that fly, and mark an X on the animals that do NOT fly. **3** A. Say: *The animals have been classified into two categories. Mark all the animals that belong in the category of animals inside the circle.* **B.** Then have students compare the number of animals inside the circle with the number of animals outside the circle. Say: *Which statement correctly describes the picture?*

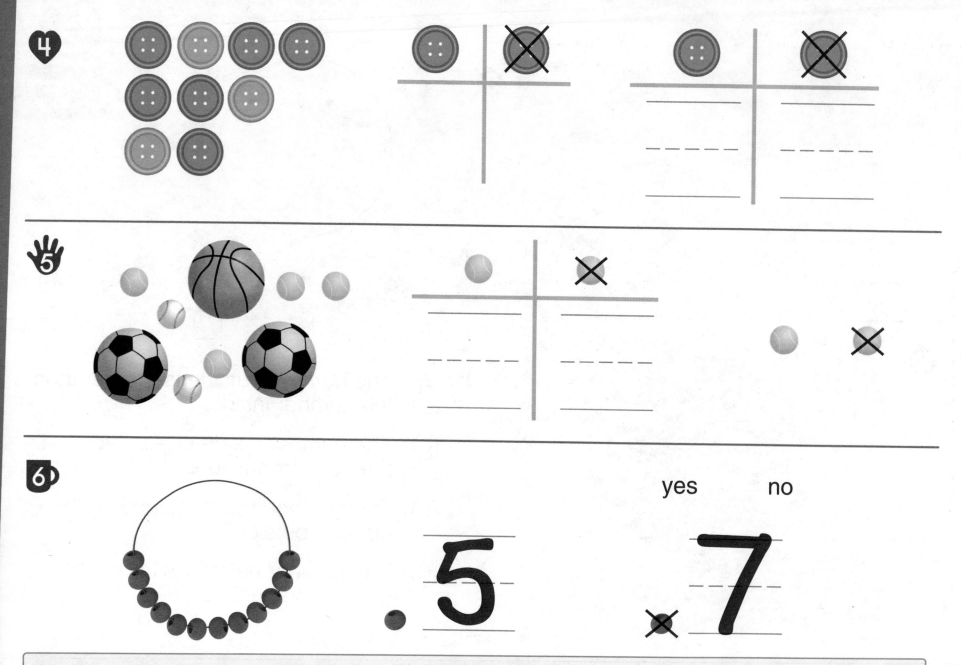

4

5

6

yes   no

. 5

× 7

Directions Have students: **4** draw lines in the chart as they count the buttons that are green and the buttons that are NOT green, and then write the numbers to tell how many in another chart; **5** sort the balls into balls that are tennis balls and balls that are NOT tennis balls, count them, and then write numbers in the chart to tell how many. Then have students draw a circle around the category that is less than the other category. **6** listen to the problem, draw a circle around *yes* or *no*, and then use numbers, pictures, or words to explain how they know whether the answer makes sense. Say: *Dana says that the category of blue beads is greater than the category of beads that are NOT blue. Does her answer make sense?*

Topic 5 | Assessment Practice

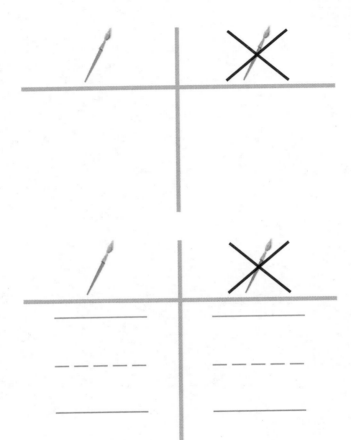

Directions **Works of Art** Say: *A kindergarten class uses paintbrushes and paint to draw pictures.* Have students: ⭐ draw a circle around the little paintbrushes, and then mark an X over the paintbrushes that are NOT little; 🍎 draw lines in the first chart as they count the paintbrushes that are little and the paintbrushes that are NOT little. Then have them write the number to tell how many are in each group in the second chart, and draw a circle around the number of the group that is less than the number of the other group.

3

4   yes   no

Topic 5 | Performance Task

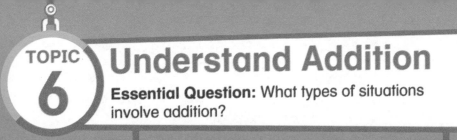

TOPIC 6

Understand Addition

Essential Question: What types of situations involve addition?

Babies

Cats can have kittens.

ënVision STEM Project: Baby Animals

Directions Read the character speech bubbles to students. **Find Out!** Have students explore the difference between animals and non-living things. Say: *Animals can have babies. Non-living things cannot have babies. Talk to friends and relatives about different animals and their babies.* **Journal: Make a Poster** Have students make a poster. Have them draw a cat with 5 kittens, circle the mother cat and the kittens to join them into one group, and then tell a joining story about how many cats there are in all.

Name _____

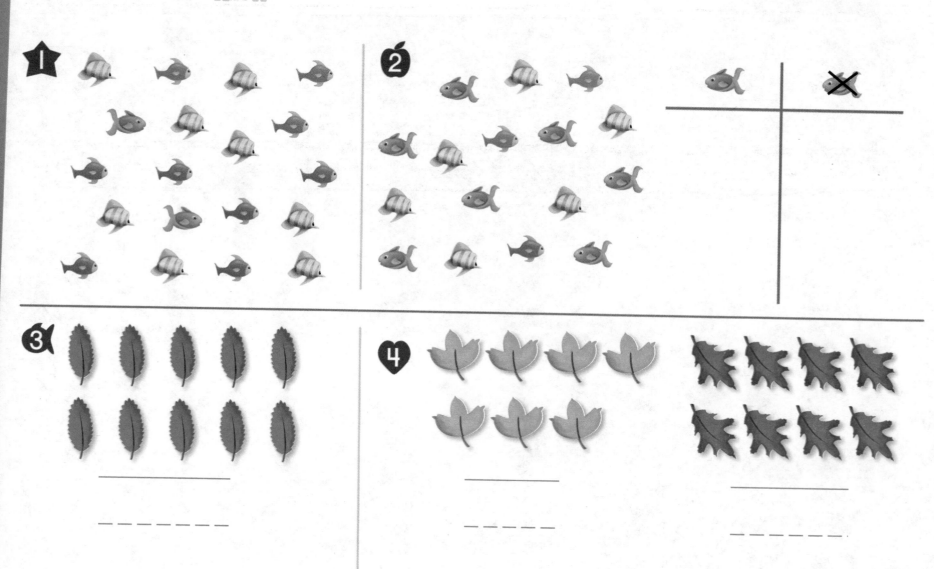

1

2 ✕

3

_ _ _ _ _ _ _ _

4

_ _ _ _ _ _ _ _   _ _ _ _ _ _ _ _

Directions Have students: **1** draw a circle around the fish that are purple, and then mark an X on the fish that are NOT purple; **2** draw lines in the chart as they count the fish that are blue and the fish that are NOT blue. Then have them draw a circle around the picture at the top of the chart of the group that is greater than the other; **3** count the leaves, and then write the number to tell how many; **4** count the leaves, write the numbers to tell how many, and then draw a circle around the number that is less than the other number.

Topic 6

Name _____

A

B

Directions Say: *You will choose one of these projects. Look at picture* **A.** *Think about this question: Do you like baby animals? If you choose Project A, you will make a baby animals booklet. Look at picture* **B.** *Think about this question: How do you get to school? If you choose Project B, you will use a town plan to tell a story about riding the bus to school.*

Directions Say: *Look at picture* **C.** *Think about this question: What fun can you have on the playground? If you choose Project C, you will create a playground and play a hiding game. Look at picture* **D.** *Think about this question: What do you do at school all day? If you choose Project D, you will make a timeline and use it to act out your school day.*

Topic 6 | Pick a Project

Solve & Share

Directions Say: Carlos is thinking about some flowers he picked. Use counters to show how many pink and purple flowers he picked. How many flowers did he pick in all? Think about the problem. Write the number that tells how many. Then use your fingers to show how you know.

I can ...
show numbers in many ways.

Content Standards K.OA.A.1, K.OA.A.2 Also K.CC.A.3, K.CC.B.5 **Mathematical Practices** MP.3, MP.4, and MP.6

Visual Learning Bridge

☆ Guided Practice

1.

2 and **3** is **5** in all.

Directions ⭐ Have students listen to the story, and then do all of the following to show each part and find how many in all: clap and knock, hold up fingers, and give an explanation of a mental image. Ask them to show how many of each color crayon, and then write the number to tell how many in all. *Parker has 2 orange crayons. He has 3 purple crayons. How many crayons does he have in all?*

2

$$3 \text{ and } 1 \text{ is } \underline{\quad} \text{ in all.}$$

3

$$1 \text{ and } 5 \text{ is } \underline{\quad} \text{ in all.}$$

Directions Have students listen to the story, and then do all of the following to show each part and find how many in all: clap and knock, hold up fingers, and give an explanation of a mental image. Ask them to color the number of each part, and then write the number to tell how many in all. **2** *Cami has 3 green crayons. She has 1 blue crayon. How many crayons does she have in all?* **3** *Sammy has 1 brown crayon. He has 5 purple crayons. How many crayons does he have in all?*

Tools   Assessment

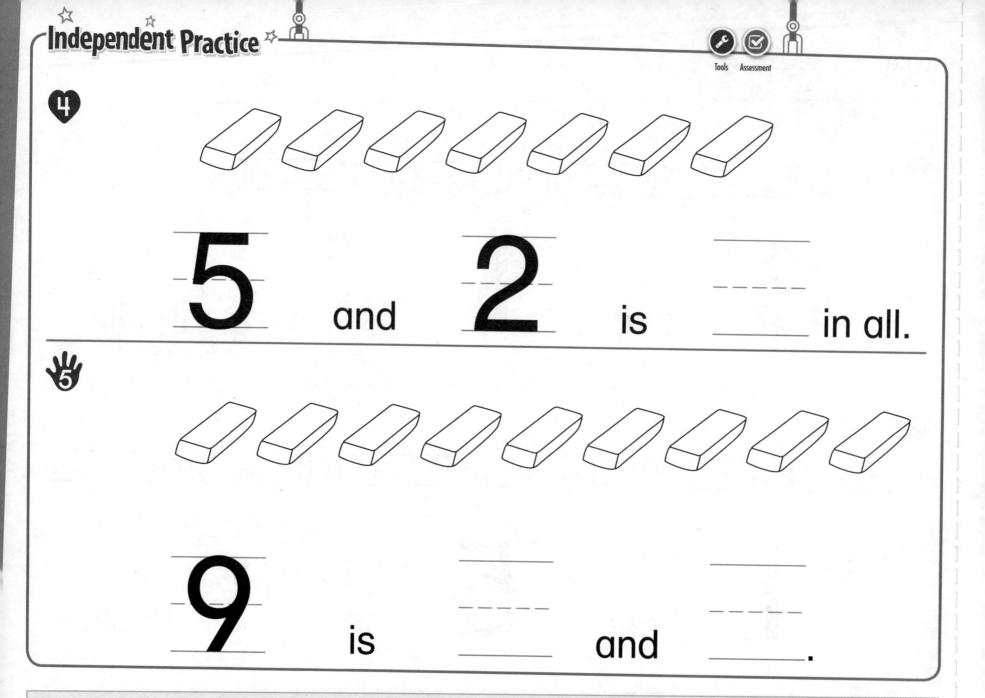

♥ 4

5 and 2 is _____ in all.

✋ 5

9 is _____ and _____.

Topic 6 | Lesson 1

Name _____

Activity

Lesson 6-2

Represent Addition as Adding To

Directions Say: *Daniel sees 2 boats on the water. Then 2 more boats go out on the water. Use red and blue cubes to show how many boats are in each group. How many boats are there in all? Think about the problem. Use your cubes or draw a picture to show how you know.*

I can ...
represent addition as adding to a number.

© **Content Standards** K.OA.A.1 Also K.CC.A.3, K.OA.A.2 **Mathematical Practices** MP.1, MP.2, and MP.5

1 and 2 is 3.

☆ Guided Practice

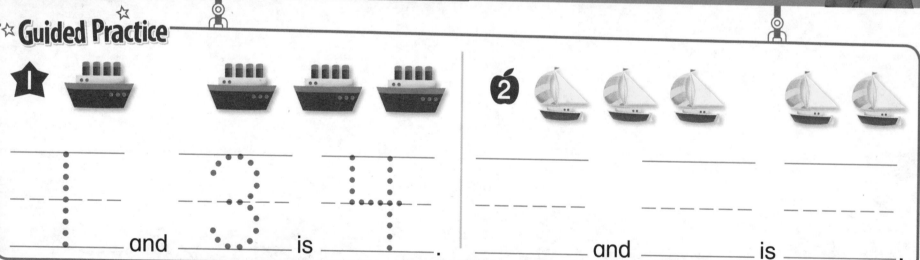

1 _____ and _____ is _____.

2 _____ and _____ is _____.

Directions 1 and 2 Have students use connecting cubes to model adding to the group when more boats come, and then write an addition sentence to tell how many in all.

3

_____ _____ _____

- - - - - -   - - - - - -   - - - - - -

_____ and _____ is _____ .

4

_____ _____ _____

- - - - - -   - - - - - -   - - - - - -

_____ and _____ is _____ .

5

_____ _____ _____

- - - - - -   - - - - - -   - - - - - -

_____ and _____ is _____ .

6

_____ _____ _____

- - - - - -   - - - - - -   - - - - - -

_____ and _____ is _____ .

Directions **3**–**6** Have students use connecting cubes to model adding to the group when more boats come, and then write an addition sentence to tell how many in all.

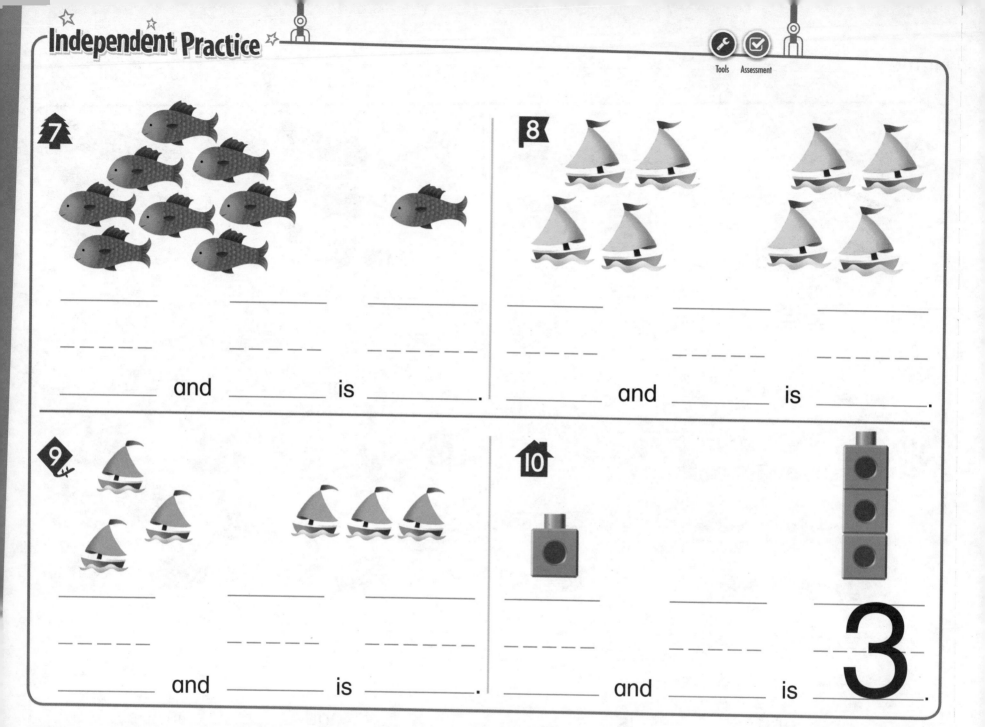

7

_____　_____

_____　_____

_____ and _____ is _____.

8

_____　_____

_____　_____

_____ and _____ is _____.

9

_____　_____

_____　_____

_____ and _____ is _____.

10

_____　_____

_____　_____

_____ and _____ is _____.

3

Directions 7–9 Have students use counters to model adding to the group when more fish or boats come, and then write an addition sentence to tell how many in all. 10 **Higher Order Thinking** Have students draw the number of green connecting cubes to add to the given connecting cube to make 3 connecting cubes in all, and then complete the addition sentence.

Topic 6 | Lesson 2

Name _____

Directions Say: *Daniel sees two tomato plants. One has 2 green tomatoes. The other has 3 red tomatoes. Use counters to show the tomatoes on each plant. Write the number of tomatoes under each plant. How many tomatoes are there in all? Write the number and use counters to show how you know.*

I can ...
represent addition as putting two or more numbers together.

© **Content Standards** K.OA.A.1
Also K.CC.A.3, K.OA.A.2
Mathematical Practices MP.2, MP.4, and MP.8

2 and 4 is 6.

☆ Guided Practice

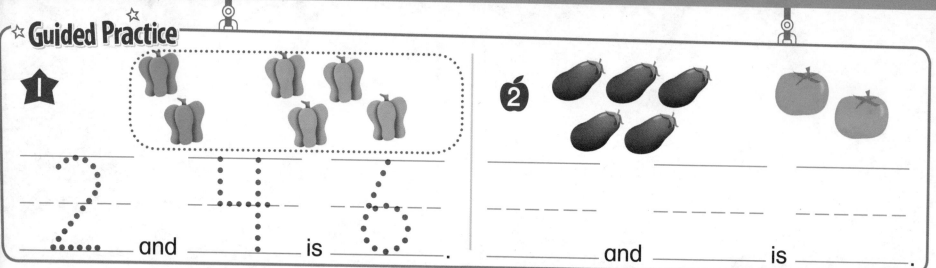

1 ___2___ and ___4___ is ___6___.

2 _____ and _____ is _____.

Directions ★ and ❷ Have students use counters to model putting together the groups, draw a circle around the groups to put them together, and then write an addition sentence to tell how many in all.

Topic 6 | Lesson 3

Name _____

3

_____ _____ _____

_ _ _ _ _ _ _ _ _ _ _ _ _ _

_____ and _____ is _____ .

4

_____ _____ _____

_ _ _ _ _ _ _ _ _ _ _ _ _ _

_____ and _____ is _____ .

5

_____ _____

_ _ _ _ _ _ _ _ _ _ _ _ _ _

_____ and _____ is _____ .

6

_____ _____

_ _ _ _ _ _ _ _ _ _ _ _ _ _

_____ and _____ is _____ .

Directions ❸ **Vocabulary** Have students draw a circle around the groups to put them together, write an **addition sentence** to tell how many in all, and then say the sentence aloud. ❹–❻ Have students use counters to model putting together the groups, draw a circle around the groups to put them together, and then write an addition sentence to tell how many in all.

Topic 6 | Lesson 3

two hundred eleven **211**

Independent Practice

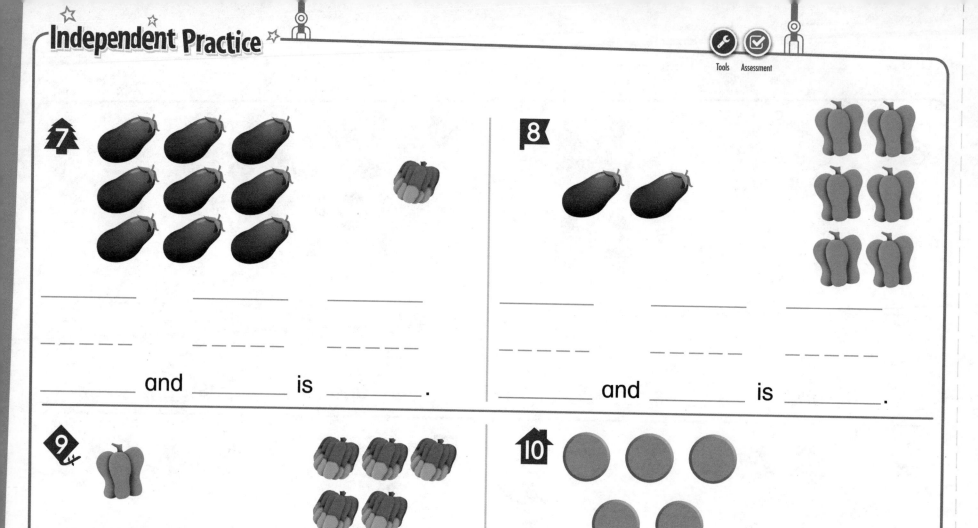

7 _____ _____ _____

_ _ _ _ _ _ and _ _ _ _ _ _ is _ _ _ _ _ _ .

8 _____ _____ _____

_ _ _ _ _ _ and _ _ _ _ _ _ is _ _ _ _ _ _ .

9 _____ _____ _____

_ _ _ _ _ _ and _ _ _ _ _ _ is _ _ _ _ _ _ .

10 _____ _____ _____

_ _ _ _ _ _ and _ _ _ _ _ _ is _ _ _ _ _ _ .

8

Directions 🌲 **enVision®** STEM Say: *What do plants need to grow?* Have students name the vegetables, draw a circle around the groups to put them together, and then write an addition sentence to tell how many in all. **8** and **9** Have students use counters as a model to put together the groups, draw a circle around the groups to put them together, and then write an addition sentence to tell how many in all. **10 Higher Order Thinking** Have students draw the other group of counters, draw a circle around the groups to put them together, and then complete the addition sentence.

     Topic 6 | Lesson 3

Solve & Share

Directions Say: *Daniel counts 4 drums in a parade. Then he sees 1 more drum. What numbers do you add to find how many drums he sees in all? How can you show the adding?*

I can ...
write an equation to show addition.

© **Content Standards** K.OA.A.1 Also K.CC.A.3, K.OA.A.2 **Mathematical Practices** MP.2, MP.3, and MP.6

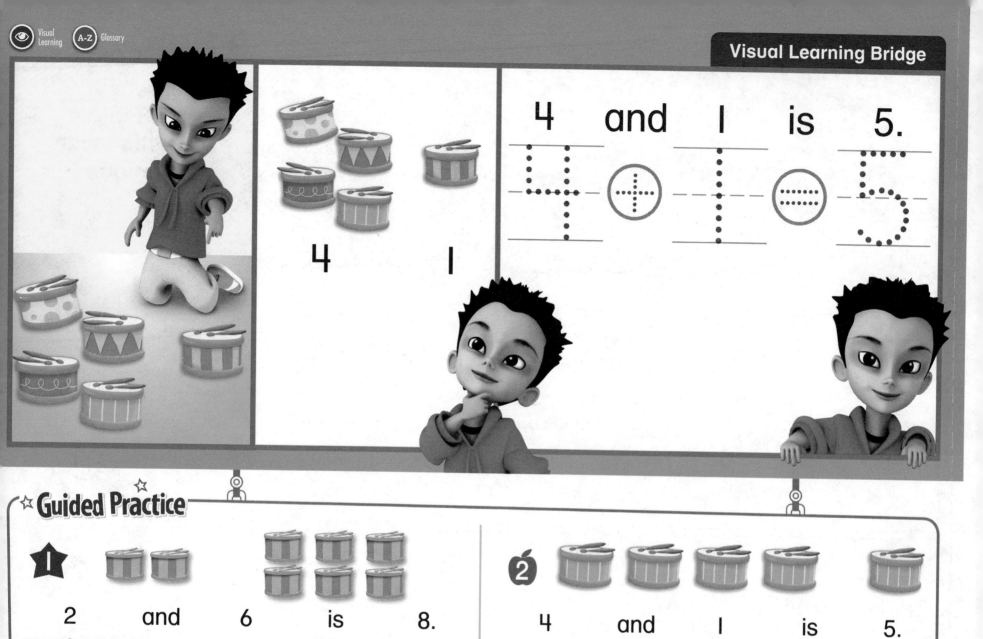

4 and 1 is 5.

4 ⊕ 1 ⊜ 5

☆ Guided Practice

1 2 and 6 is 8.

2 ⊕ 6 ⊜ 8

2 4 and 1 is 5.

Directions 🔼 and ② Have students add the groups to find the sum, and then write an equation to show the addition.

Name _____

3

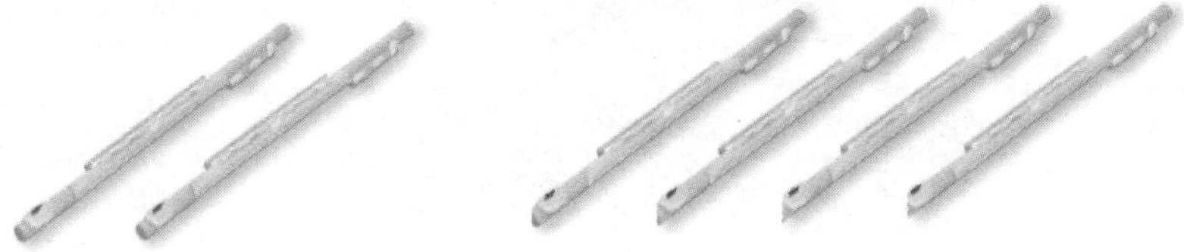

2 and 4 is 6.

___ ◯ ___ ◯ ___

4

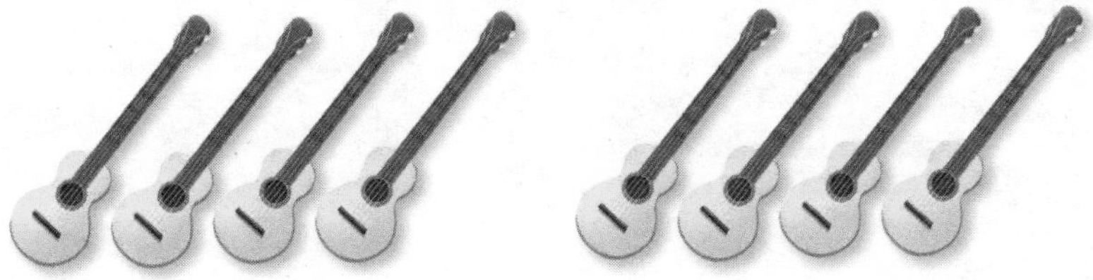

4 and 4 is 8.

___ ◯ ___ ◯ ___

5

6 and 1 is 7.

___ ◯ ___ ◯ ___

6

3 and 4 is 7.

___ ◯ ___ ◯ ___

Directions ❸–❻ Have students add the groups to find the sum, and then write an equation to show the addition.

Independent Practice

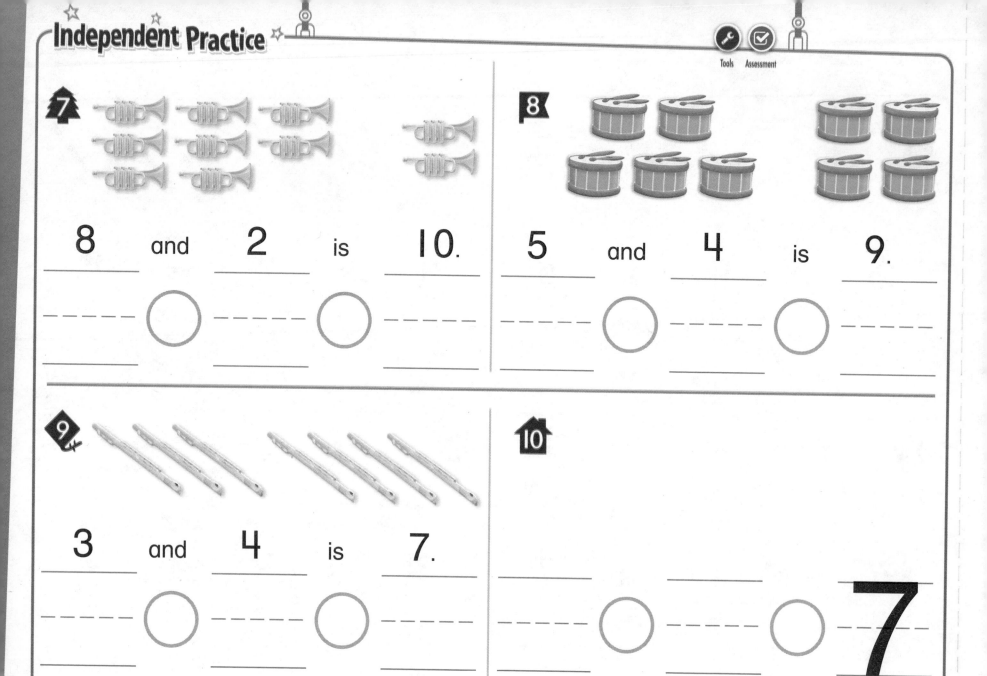

7

8   and   2   is   10.

◯   ◯

8

5   and   4   is   9.

◯   ◯

9

3   and   4   is   7.

◯   ◯

10

◯   ◯   7

Directions ✿–✿ Have students add the groups to find the sum, and then write an equation to show the addition. 🏠 **Higher Order Thinking** Have students listen to the story, draw the groups and add to find the sum, and then complete the equation. *There are some counters on the page. Emily puts 3 more on the page. There are now 7 counters in all.*

Topic 6 | Lesson 4

Solve & Share

Directions Say: *4 squirrels are eating lunch at the squirrel feeder. 2 more join them. How many are eating at the feeder now? Show how you know in two ways, and then explain how you know.*

I can ...
solve addition problems.

© **Content Standards** K.OA.A.2
Also K.OA.A.1
Mathematical Practices MP.1, MP.3, and MP.4

9 in all

9 in all

$$6 + 3 = 9$$

☆ Guided Practice

1

 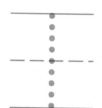 

$$6 \;\oplus\; 1 \;=\; 7$$

Directions Have students listen to the story, draw a picture to show what is happening, and then write the equation. Then have them explain their work. **1** *There are 6 sea stars on the beach. 1 more joins them. How many sea stars are there in all?*

218 two hundred eighteen

Topic 6 | Lesson 5

Name _____

2

_____ ( ) _____ ( ) _____

3

_____ ( ) _____ ( ) _____

4

_____ ( ) _____ ( ) _____

5

_____ ( ) _____ ( ) _____

Directions Have students listen to the story, use counters to show the addition, look at or draw a picture, and then write an equation to tell how many in all. **2** *3 birds are sitting in a tree. 7 more join them. How many birds are sitting in all?* **3** *5 squirrels are looking for food. 4 more join them. How many squirrels are there in all?* **4** *There is 1 turtle on the beach. 5 more walk up. How many turtles are there in all?* **5** *2 turtles swim in the water. 6 more join them. How many turtles are swimming in all?*

Independent Practice

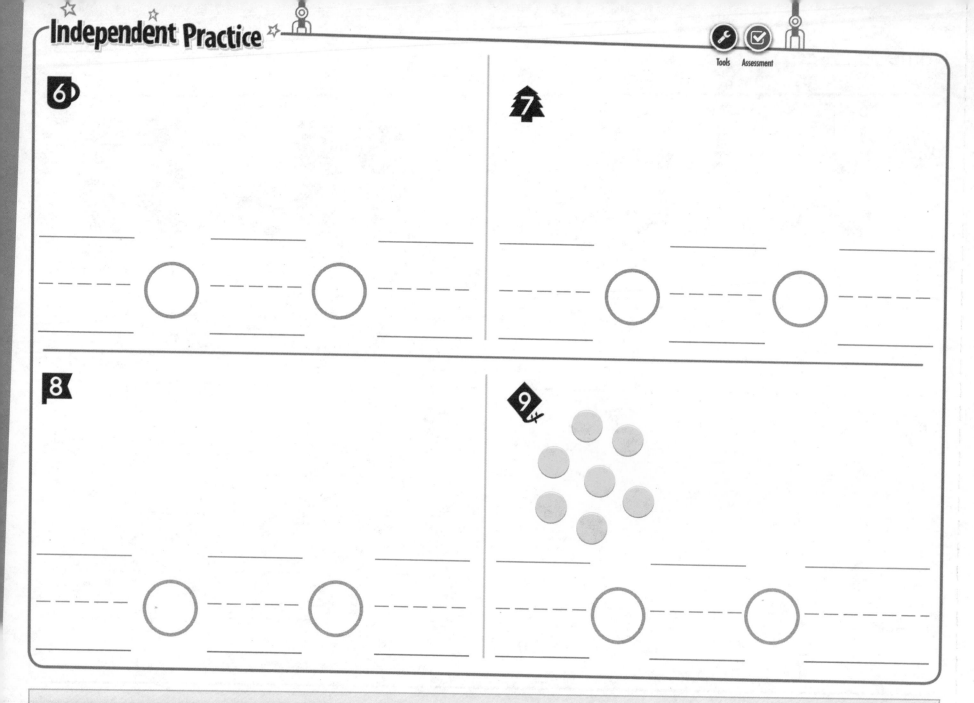

6 ○ _____ ○ _____

7 _____ ○ _____ ○ _____

8 _____ ○ _____ ○ _____

9 _____ ○ _____ ○ _____

Directions Have students listen to the story, use counters to show the addition, draw a picture, and then write an equation to tell how many in all. **6** *4 girls play at the beach. 4 boys join them. How many children are there in all?* **7** *8 children rest on the sand. I girl joins them. How many children are there in all?* **8** *2 boys play in the water. 5 girls join them. How many children are there in all?* **9** **Higher Order Thinking** Have students listen to the story, draw counters to complete the picture, and write an equation. *7 children build a sand castle. Some more help them. There are 10 children building in all. How many more come to help them?*

Solve & Share

Name _____

Directions Say: *Daniel's teacher is making name tags for her students. She makes 3 name tags for boys. She makes 2 more for girls. Now she has 5 name tags. How does Daniel's teacher know that she has made 5 name tags? Explain and then show how you know.*

I can ...
use equations to represent
and explain addition.

Content Standards K.OA.A.2
Also K.OA.A.1
Mathematical Practices MP.3,
MP.4

7 in all

4

3

4 ... 5 6 7

7 in all

$4 + 3 = 7$

☆ Guided Practice

1

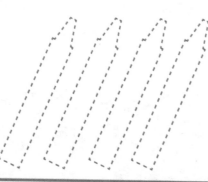

2 ⊕ 4 ◯ 6

Directions 🏠 Have students listen to the story, draw a picture to show what is happening, and then write an equation. Then have them explain their work. *Daniel puts 2 red crayons and 4 blue crayons on the table. Now there are 6 crayons in all. How can Daniel tell there are 6 crayons?*

222 two hundred twenty-two

Topic 6 | Lesson 6

2

3

4

5

Directions Have students listen to each story, use counters to show the addition, look at or draw a picture, and then write an equation to tell how many in all. Then have them explain their work. **2** *Jorge puts 4 blue paint jars and 3 red paint jars in the art room. How many paint jars are there in all?* **3** *Maya has 3 green crayons and 2 orange crayons. How many crayons are there in all?* **4** *Rex has 1 sheet of blue paper and 8 sheets of yellow paper. How many sheets of paper does he have in all?* **5** *Reagan has 4 green blocks and 4 yellow blocks. How many blocks does she have in all?*

Independent Practice

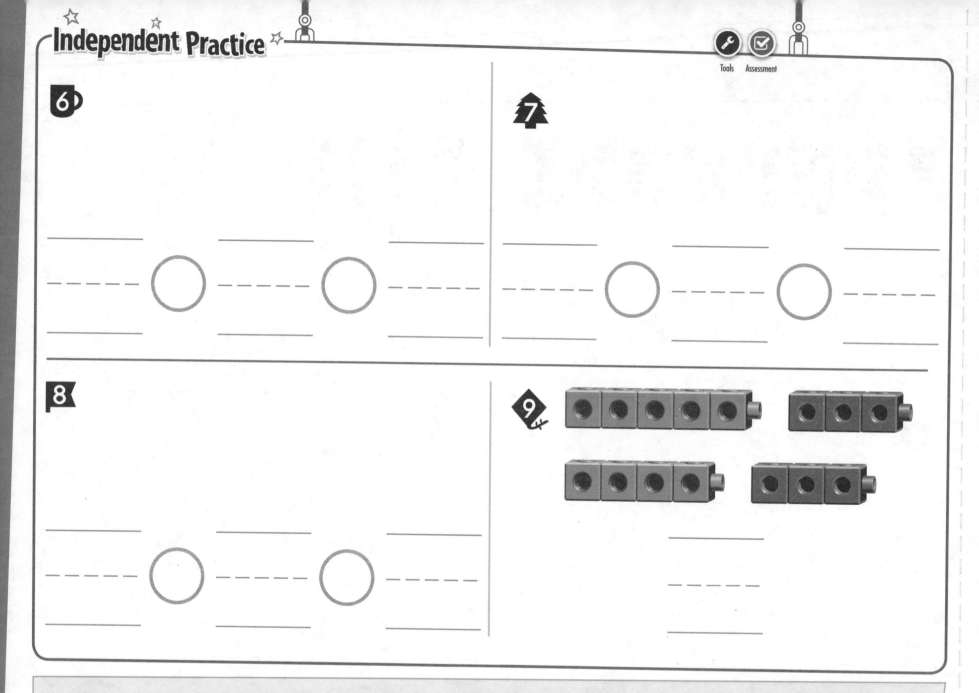

6

7

8

9

Directions Have students listen to each story, draw a picture to show what is happening, and then write an equation. **6** *Benny puts 5 bananas in a bowl and 4 bananas on a plate. How many bananas does he have in all?* **7** *Kris eats 2 grapes at lunch and 6 grapes for her snack. How many grapes does she eat in all?* **8** *There are 4 girls and 2 boys on a train ride. How many children ride the train in all?* **9** **Higher Order Thinking** Have students listen to the story, circle the connecting cubes that show the story and tell why the other cubes do not show the story, and then write the number to tell how many in all. Say: *Jimmy picks 5 raspberries. Then he picks 3 more. How many raspberries does he have in all?*

224 two hundred twenty-four

Solve & Share

Name _____

Activity

Directions Say: *Use blue and red cubes to make stacks of 3 cubes. How many different ways can you make a stack of 3 cubes? Write equations to describe your stacks. Use a blue crayon to tell how many blue cubes and a red crayon to tell how many red cubes.*

I can ...
use patterns to add numbers together.

Ⓒ **Content Standards** K.OA.A.5 Also K.OA.A.1 **Mathematical Practices** MP.1, MP.4, and MP.7

$5 + 0 = 5$

$4 + 1 = 5$

$3 + 2 = 5$

$2 + 3 = 5$

$1 + 4 = 5$

$0 + 5 = 5$

$5 + 0 = 5$

$0 + 5 = 5$

$1 + 4 = 5$

$4 + 1 = 5$

$3 + 2 = 5$

$2 + 3 = 5$

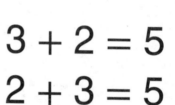 Patterns to make 5

☆ Guided Practice

    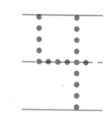

Directions ☆ Have students color a way to make 4, and then write an equation to match the boxes.

Topic 6 | Lesson 7

Name _____

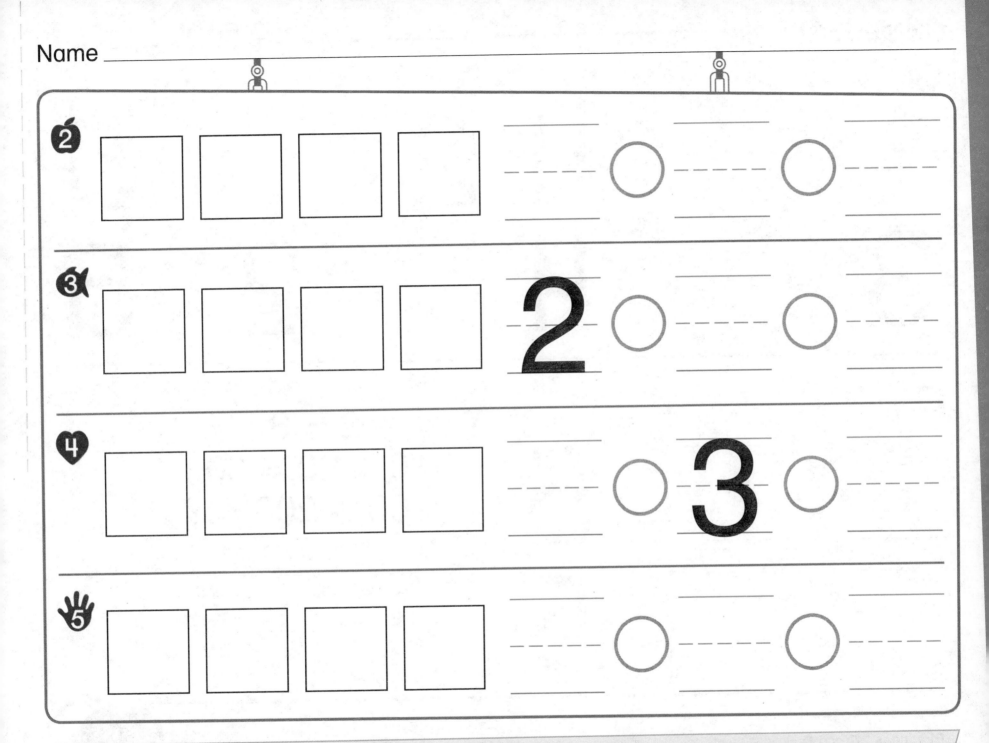

2 〇 〇

3 [ ] [ ] [ ] [ ] **2** 〇 〇

4 [ ] [ ] [ ] [ ] 〇 **3** 〇

5 [ ] [ ] [ ] [ ] 〇 〇

Directions ❷–✋ Have students color the boxes to complete the pattern of ways to make 4 started on the previous page, and then write an equation to match the boxes.

Tools   Assessment

6 ☕

1

_____ ◯ _____ ◯ 4

3 ◯ _____ ◯ _____

7 🌲

4 2 ◯ _____ ◯ 5

_____ ◯ 2 ◯ 5

8 🚩

_____ ◯ _____ ◯ 5

_____ ◯ _____ ◯ 5

9 ✏️

$1 + 2 = 3$
$10 + 20 = 30$
$100 + 200 = ?$

_____

_____

_____

Directions **6** and **7** Have students complete the pair of equations to show a pattern. **8 Higher Order Thinking** Have students write a pair of equations that both equal 5 in a pattern. **9 Higher Order Thinking** Have students listen to the story: $1 + 2 = 3$, and $10 + 20 = 30$. *What does* $100 + 200$ *equal?* Have them write the number.

Name _____

Activity

Think.

Directions Say: *Daniel sees a group of 3 fluffy, white clouds in the sky. Marta sees 1 gray cloud. How many clouds do they see in all? Draw a picture to show what is happening, and then write an equation to tell how many clouds in all. Explain how you know.*

I can ...
model adding different numbers together by drawing, counting, or writing equations.

© **Mathematical Practices** MP.4
Also MP.2, MP.3
Content Standards K.OA.A.2
Also K.OA.A.1

Visual Learning Bridge

$3 + 3$

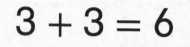

$3 + 3 = 6$

6 fish

How can I show it?

Draw.

Count.

☆ Guided Practice

1

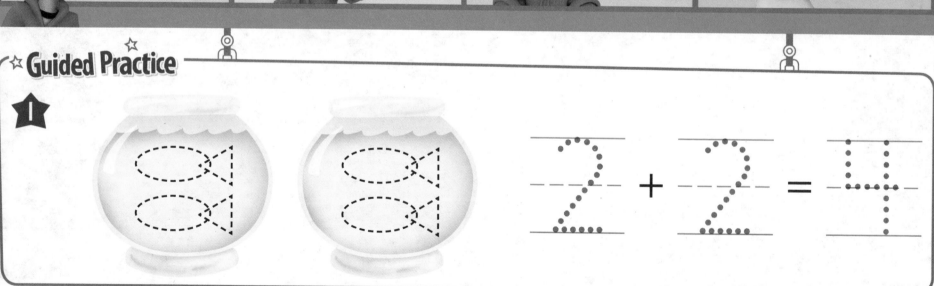

$2 + 2 = 4$

Directions ★ Have students listen to the story, and then draw a picture to model what is happening. Then have them write an equation and explain their answer. *Daniel sees 2 fish in one bowl and 2 fish in another bowl. How many fish does he see in all?*

Topic 6 | Lesson 8

Independent Practice

 2

_____   _____   _____

- - - - - - - - **+** - - - - - - - **=** - - - - - - -

_____   _____   _____

 3

_____   _____   _____

- - - - - - - - **+** - - - - - - - **=** - - - - - - -

_____   _____   _____

 4

_____   _____   _____

- - - - - - - - **+** - - - - - - - **=** - - - - - - -

_____   _____   _____

 5

_____   _____   _____

- - - - - - - - **+** - - - - - - - **=** - - - - - - -

_____   _____   _____

Directions Have students listen to each story, and then draw a picture to model what is happening. Then have them write an equation and explain their answer. **2** *Julie sees 5 stones in one pail and 3 stones in another pail. How many stones does she see in all?* **3** *A hen laid 2 eggs one day and 3 eggs the next day. How many eggs did she lay in all?* **4** *Maria threw a baseball 5 times in one inning and 2 times in the next inning. How many times did she throw the baseball in all?* **5** *Zak scored 2 goals during a soccer game, and then he scored 4 more goals during another soccer game. How many goals did he score in all?*

Problem Solving

$$2 + \underline{\hspace{3cm}} = \underline{\hspace{3cm}}$$

$$2 + 1 = \underline{\hspace{2cm}} \qquad \underline{\hspace{2cm}} + \underline{\hspace{2cm}} = \underline{\hspace{2cm}}$$

Directions Read the problem aloud. Then have students use multiple problem-solving methods to solve the problem. Say: *There are 2 rabbits in a hole. The same number of rabbits come in to join them. How many rabbits are there in all?* ❻ **Reasoning** *What can you answer? How many rabbits join the group?* ❼ **Explain** *Emily says that the answer is 3 rabbits. Is she right or wrong? Explain how you know.* ❽ **Model** *Use cubes, draw pictures, or use numbers to show how many rabbits in all. Then write the equation.*

$$2 \bigcirc 7$$

$$4 + 3 \bigcirc \underline{\quad\quad}$$

Directions **Understand Vocabulary** Have students: write the **plus sign** to show addition; write the **equal sign,** and then complete the equation; listen to the story, draw a picture to show what is happening, and then write an **equation** to match the story. *Max has 5 yellow cups and 5 orange cups. How many cups does he have in all?*

4

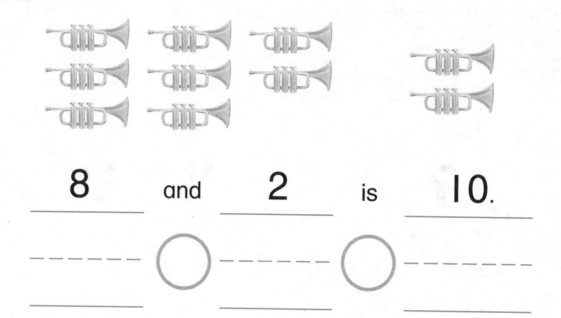

8 and 2 is 10.

_____ ◯ _____ ◯ _____

_____ ◯ _____ ◯ _____

Directions **Understand Vocabulary** Have students: ❹ **add** the groups to find the sum, and then write an equation to show the addition; ✋ listen to the story, draw a picture to show what is happening, and then write an equation. Have them draw a circle around the **sum**. *Bailey sees 3 apples in the tree. Then she sees 5 more. How many apples does she see in all?*

 Topic 6 | Vocabulary Review

Set A

★1

2 and 1 is 3 in all.

0 and 4 is _____ in all.

Set B

2 and 3 is 5.

2

_____ and _____ is _____.

Directions Have students: ★ listen to the story, color the number of each part, and then write the number to tell how many in all. *Margo has 0 red crayons. She has 4 blue crayons. How many crayons does she have in all?* ② add to the first group of instruments, and then write an addition sentence to tell how many in all.

2 and 3 is 5.

_____   _____   _____

_ _ _ _ _ _ _   _ _ _ _ _ _ _   _ _ _ _ _ _ _

_____ and _____ is _____.

Set D

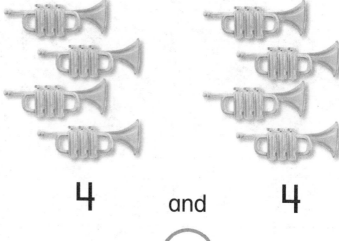

4   4

4   (+)   4

2   and   4

___   ___

_ _ _ _   ( )   _ _ _ _

___   ___

Name _____

_____

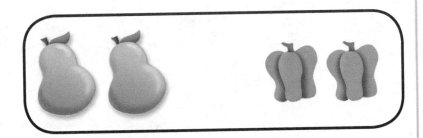

$$2 + 2 = 4$$

○ ─── ○

_____

$$4 + 3 = 7$$

_____ + _____ = _____

Directions Have students: ✋ listen to the story, use counters to show the addition, draw a circle around the groups to put them together, and then write an equation to match the story. *Marta picks 3 vegetables. Then she picks 3 more vegetables. How many vegetables does she have in all?* ☕ listen to the story, use counters to show the addition, draw a picture, and then write an equation to tell how many in all. *Mark has 3 flowers. He picks 2 more flowers. How many flowers does he have in all?*

$$6 + 3 = 9$$

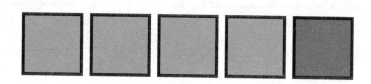

$$4 + 1 = 5$$

Directions Have students: 🌲 listen to each story, draw a picture to show what is happening, and then write an equation. *Karina puts 4 red balls and 4 purple balls into the toy bin. How many balls are there in all?* 🚩 color a way to make 6, and then write an equation to match the boxes.

Name _____

 1

Ⓐ 1 in all;
    1 + 0 = 1

Ⓒ 4 in all;
    2 + 2 = 4

Ⓑ 6 in all;
    4 + 2 = 6

Ⓓ 8 in all;
    4 + 4 = 8

 2

Ⓐ 1 and 4 is 5.
    1 + 4 = 5

Ⓒ 1 and 6 is 7.
    1 + 6 = 7

Ⓑ 1 and 5 is 6.
    1 + 5 = 6

Ⓓ 1 and 3 is 4.
    1 + 3 = 4

 3

Ⓐ 2 and 2 is 4

Ⓒ 2 and 4 is 6

Ⓑ 2 and 6 is 8

Ⓓ 2 and 5 is 7

 4

Ⓐ 3 + 4

Ⓒ 3 + 1

Ⓑ 4 + 0

Ⓓ 4 + 1

Directions Have students mark the best answer. **1** *Jen puts 2 teddy bears on her bed. Then she puts 2 more teddy bears on her bed. Which tells how many teddy bears she puts on her bed in all?* **2** *Hayden sees 1 scarecrow, and then he sees 3 more. Which number sentence tells how many scarecrows Hayden sees in all?* **3** Have students look at the picture and find the sentence that tells about adding the groups of tambourines. Say: *How many tambourines are added to the first group of tambourines to find how many in all?* **4** *Which addition expression tells about the picture?*

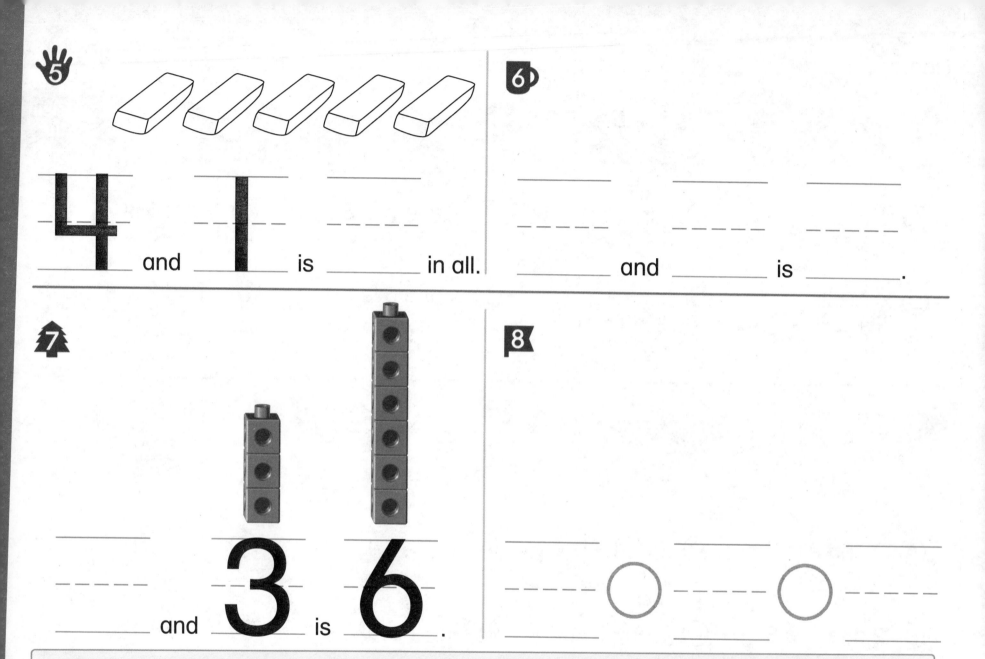

5 ____ 4 ____ and ____ 1 ____ is _____ in all.

6) _____ _____ and _____ is _____ .

7 _____ and **3** is **6** .

8 _____ ◯ _____ ◯ _____

Directions ✋ Have students listen to the story, and then do all of the following to show each part to find how many in all: clap and knock, hold up fingers, and give an explanation of a mental image. Ask them to color the number of each part, and then write the number to tell how many in all. *Ming buys 4 yellow erasers. She buys 1 purple eraser. How many erasers does she buy in all?* **6)** Have students draw two groups of carrots to show 8 in all, and then write a number sentence to match the drawing. **7** Have students draw the number of cubes needed to make 6 cubes in all, and then complete the number sentence. **8** Have students listen to the story, use counters to model putting together the groups, draw the counters to show what is happening, and then write an equation for the story. *There are 6 brown bunnies in a garden and 3 white bunnies in the garden. How many bunnies are there in all?*

Topic 6 | Assessment Practice

Name _____

8

5 + 2 = 7

4 + 4 = 8

1 + 7 = 8

Directions Have students: 🔟 look at the number card, and then draw a circle to put together the groups that show how many in all; 🔟 match each picture with the equation that shows the correct parts and how many in all.

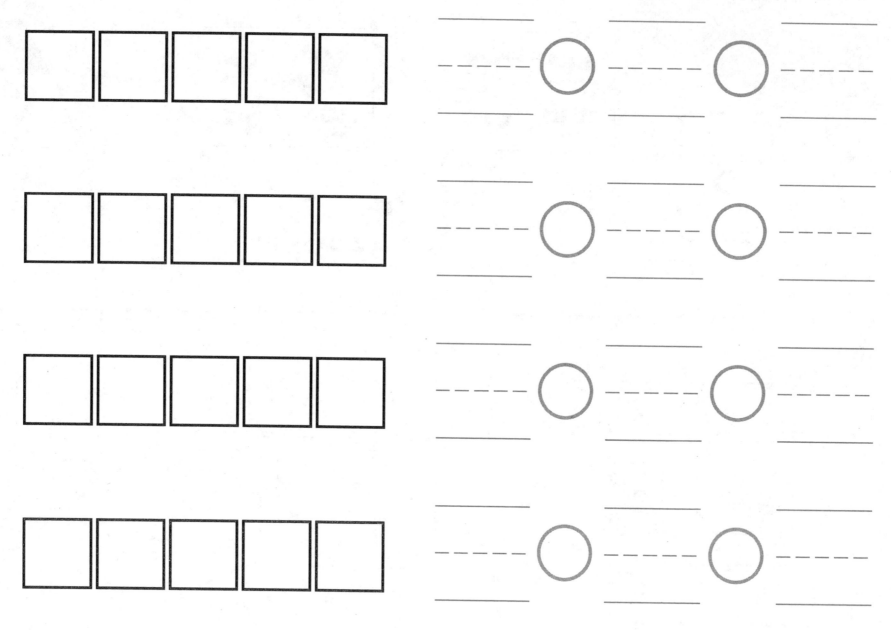

Topic 6 | Assessment Practice

Name _____

1

_____   _____

_ _ _ _ _ _ _ _ _   _ _ _ _ _ _ _ _ _

_____ and _____ is _____.

2

_____   _____   _____

_ _ _ _ _ + _ _ _ _ _ = _ _ _ _ _

_____   _____   _____

Directions **Music Time** Say: *Students play many different instruments in music class.* ⭐ Say: *How many horns are there?* Have students count on to find the number of horns, and then write an addition sentence to tell how many in all. 🍎 Have students add one group of horns to the other group of horns, and then write an equation to find the sum.

□ □ □

_ _ _ _ _ _ _ + _ _ _ _ _ _ = _ _ _ _ _ _

□ □ □

_ _ _ _ _ _ _ + _ _ _ _ _ _ = _ _ _ _ _ _

□ □ □

_ _ _ _ _ + _ _ _ _ _ = _ _ _ _ _

□ □ □

_ _ _ _ _ + _ _ _ _ _ = _ _ _ _ _

❤4

_ _ _ _ _ _ _ + _ _ _ _ _ = _ _ _ _ _

_ _ _ _ _ _ _ + _ _ _ _ _ = _ _ _ _ _

✋5

_ _ _ _ _ + _ _ _ _ _ = _ _ _ _ _

Directions ❸ Say: _The music teacher puts 3 flutes on the shelves._ Have students color the boxes to complete a pattern to show the different ways she could put the flutes on the shelves. ❹ Say: _The bells on the shelves show one way to make 4._ Have students write an equation to show the way, and then use the same numbers to make 4 another way. ✋ Say: _6 drums are on the shelf. Then Luisa puts more drums on the shelf. Now there are 8 drums on the shelf. How many drums did Luisa put on the shelf?_ Have students draw counters to show what is happening, and then complete the equation.

 Topic 6 | Performance Task

Understand Subtraction

Essential Question: How can representing taking apart and taking from in different ways help you learn about subtraction?

Food

Animals need food and water.

enVision STEM Project: Animal Needs

Directions Read the character speech bubbles to students. **Find Out!** Have students find out about how plants, animals, and humans use their environment to meet basic needs such as food, water, nutrients, sunlight, space, and shelter. Say: *Different organisms need different things. Talk to friends and relatives about the different needs of plants, animals, and humans, and how different organisms meet those needs.* **Journal: Make a Poster** Have students make a poster. Ask them to draw as many as 5 pictures of a human's needs and as many as 5 pictures of an animal's needs. Have them cross out the needs that are the same for humans and animals, and then write how many are left.

Name _____

Review What You Know

 1

$$3 + 6 = 9$$

2

$$4 + 1 = 5$$

3

$$2 + 5 = 7$$

 4

_____ + _____ = _____

5

_____ + _____ = _____

6

_____ + _____ = _____

Directions Have students: **1** draw a circle around the plus sign; **2** draw a circle around the equal sign; **3** draw a circle around the sum; **4–6** count the objects in each group, and then write the equation to tell how many in all.

Name _____

A

B

C

Directions Say: *You will choose one of these projects. Look at picture* **A.** *Think about this question: What jobs can you do? If you choose Project A, you will make a jobs chart. Look at picture* **B.** *Think about this question: If you had a garden, how many flowers would you plant? If you choose Project B, you will sing a song about flowers. Look at picture* **C.** *Think about this question: Do stars have different colors? If you choose Project C, you will draw a picture of different-colored stars and tell a number story.*

Video

Math Modeling

Fruit Salad

I will have one of everything!

Directions Read the robot's speech bubble to students. **Generate Interest** Ask students what fruits they enjoy most. Say: *What is your favorite fruit? What fruit do you like least?* Have your class make a tally chart and then decide what the perfect fruit salad for your class would be.

I can ...
model with math to add and subtract to solve a problem.

ⓒ **Mathematical Practices** MP.4
Also MP.1, MP.2
Content Standards K.OA.A.1
Also K.CC.A.2, K.CC.A.3, K.OA.A.2

Solve & Share

Activity

Directions Say: *Marta sees 5 goldfish in the pond. 1 swims away. How many fish are left? Think about the problem in your head. Then act out the story with your fingers. Use counters to show how many are left. Write numbers to explain.*

I can ...
show numbers in many ways.

© **Content Standards** K.OA.A.1, K.OA.A.2 Also K.CC.A.3, K.CC.B.5 **Mathematical Practices** MP.2, MP.3, and MP.4

6 in all

6 in all

6 in all

6 in all

5 are left.

5 are left.

5 are left.

5 are left.

☆ Guided Practice

1 **8** in all

 ___ are left.

2 **5** in all

___ are left.

Directions Have students listen to the story, and then do all of the following to find how many are left: give an explanation of a mental image, use objects to act it out, and hold up fingers. Have them mark Xs on how many birds fly away, and then write the number to tell how many are left.
1 *8 eagles sit on a branch. 2 fly away. How many eagles are left?* **2** *5 blue jays hop on the ground. 1 flies away. How many blue jays are left?*

250 two hundred fifty

Name _____

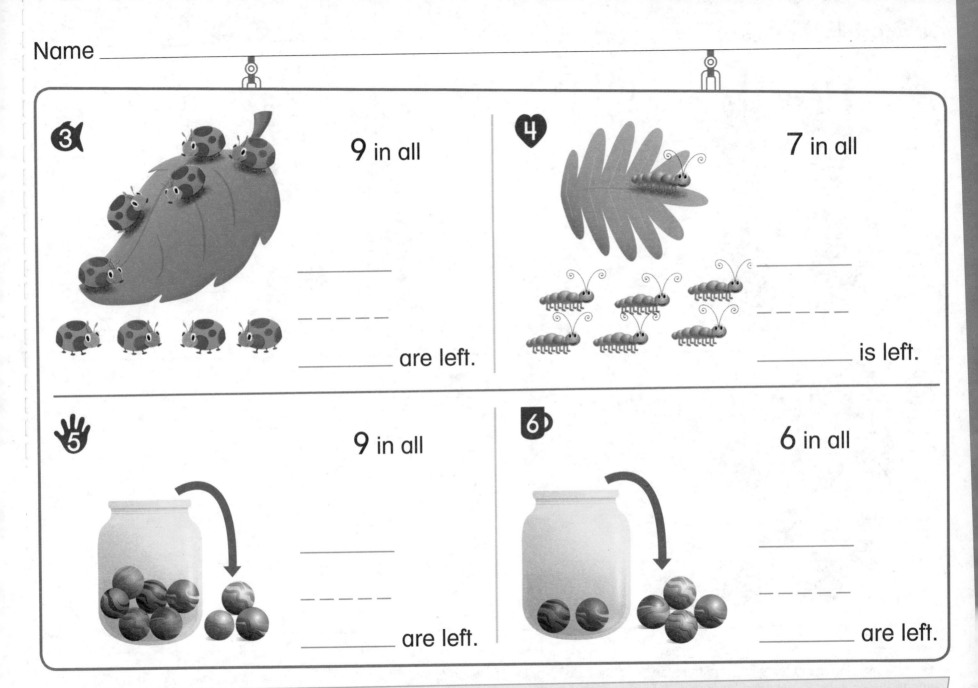

3 9 in all

_____

- - - - -

_____ are left.

4 7 in all

_____

- - - - -

_____ is left.

5 9 in all

_____

- - - - -

_____ are left.

6 6 in all

_____

- - - - -

_____ are left.

Directions Have students listen to the story, and then do all of the following to find how many are left: give an explanation of a mental image, use objects to act it out, and hold up fingers. Have them mark Xs on how many walk away or are taken out, and then write the number to tell how many are left. **3** *9 ladybugs are on a leaf. 4 walk away. How many ladybugs are left?* **4** *7 caterpillars are on a leaf. 6 walk away. How many caterpillars are left?* **5** *9 marbles are in a jar. 3 are taken out. How many marbles are left?* **6** *6 marbles are in a jar. 4 are taken out. How many marbles are left?*

Independent Practice

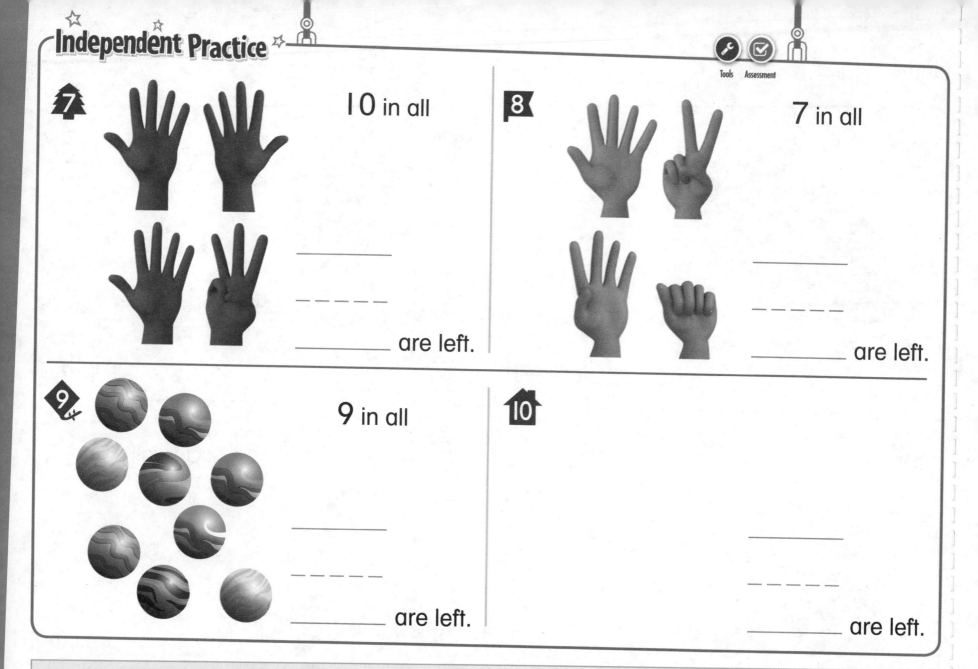

7 | 10 in all

_____
_ _ _ _ _
_____ are left.

8 | 7 in all

_____
_ _ _ _ _
_____ are left.

9 | 9 in all

_____
_ _ _ _ _
_____ are left.

10

_____
_ _ _ _ _
_____ are left.

Directions Have students listen to the story, and then do all of the following to find how many are left: give an explanation of a mental image, use objects to act it out, and hold up fingers. Ask them to write the number to tell how many are left. **7** *10 fingers are in the air. 2 are put down. How many fingers are left?* **8** *7 fingers are in the air. 3 are put down. How many fingers are left?* **9** Have students listen to the story, and then do all of the following to find how many are left: give an explanation of a mental image, use objects to act it out, and then mark Xs on how many are taken away. Ask them to write the number to tell how many are left. *There are 9 marbles. 6 are taken away. How many marbles are left?* **10** **Higher Order Thinking** Have students draw 10 marbles. Have them mark Xs on some of them, and then write the number to tell how many marbles are left.

252 two hundred fifty-two

Topic 7 | Lesson 1

Solve & Share

Name _____

Directions Say: *Alex picks 7 apples. Some apples are red, and some are yellow. Alex wants to put the red apples in one basket and the yellow in the other. How many red apples and how many yellow apples can there be? Use counters to show the red and yellow apples, and write the numbers to tell how many of each. Draw pictures to show your answer.*

I can ...
take apart a number and tell the parts.

© **Content Standards** K.OA.A.1 Also K.CC.A.3, K.OA.A.2 **Mathematical Practices** MP.2, MP.3, and MP.4

Take apart 7.

Take apart 7.

Take apart 7.

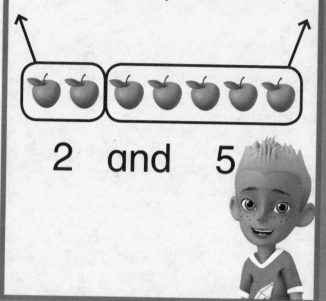

2   and   5

☆ Guided Practice

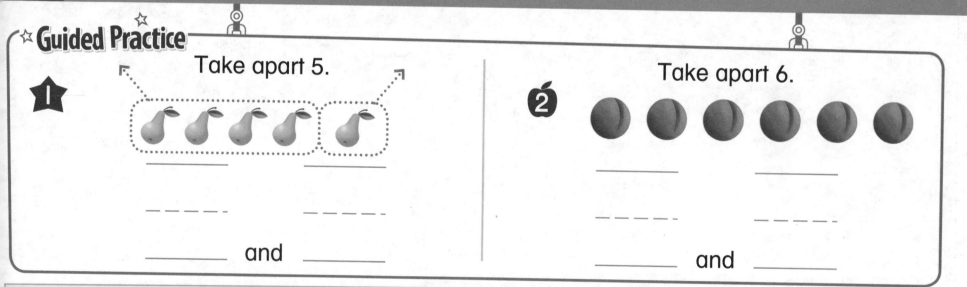

1 Take apart 5.

_____ _____

_____ and _____

2 Take apart 6.

_____ _____

_____ and _____

Name _____

3   Take apart 4.

_____   _____

_ _ _ _ _   _ _ _ _ _

_____ and _____

4   Take apart 10.

_____   _____

_ _ _ _ _   _ _ _ _ _

_____ and _____

5   Take apart 3.

_____   _____

_ _ _ _ _   _ _ _ _ _

_____ and _____

6   Take apart 8.

_____   _____

_ _ _ _ _   _ _ _ _ _

_____ and _____

Directions   **3–6** Have students take apart the group of fruit. Then have them draw a circle around the parts they made, and then write the numbers to tell the parts.

Topic 7 | Lesson 2   two hundred fifty-five   **255**

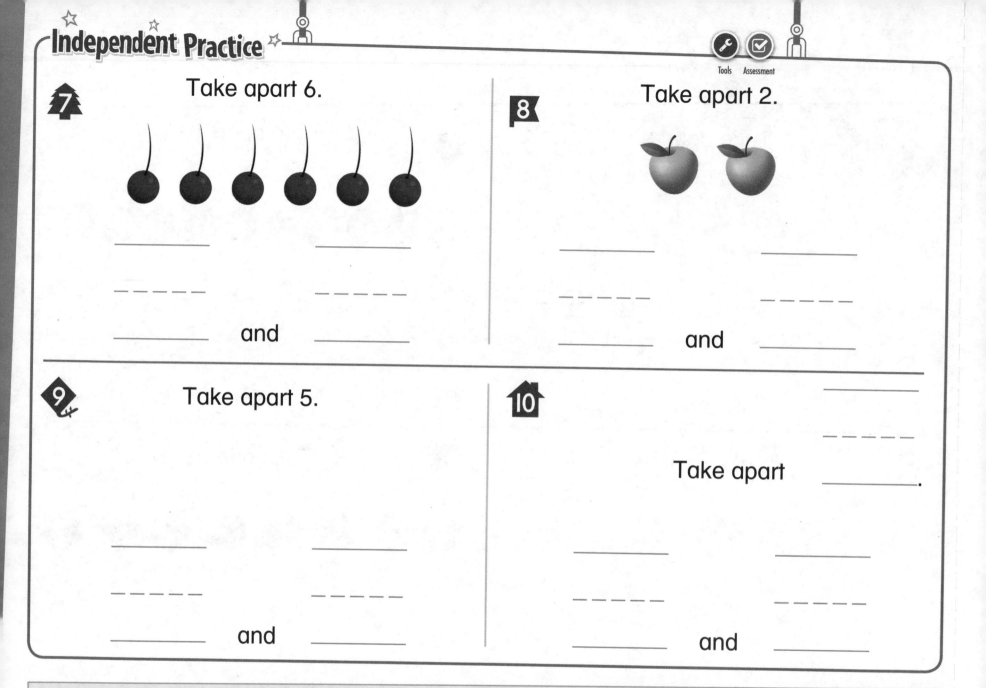

7 Take apart 6.

_____ _____

_ _ _ _ _   _ _ _ _ _

_____ and _____

8 Take apart 2.

_____ _____

_ _ _ _ _   _ _ _ _ _

_____ and _____

9 Take apart 5.

_____ _____

_ _ _ _ _   _ _ _ _ _

_____ and _____

10

_____

_ _ _ _ _

Take apart

_____ .

_____ _____

_ _ _ _ _   _ _ _ _ _

_____ and _____

Directions **7** and **8** Have students take apart the group of fruit. Then have them draw a circle around the parts they made, and then write the numbers to tell the parts. **9** **Higher Order Thinking** Have students draw counters to show a group of 5. Then have them take apart the group of counters, draw a circle around the parts they made, and then write the numbers to tell the parts. **10** **Higher Order Thinking** Have students choose any number between 2 and 10, write that number on the top line, and then draw a group of counters to show that number. Have them take apart the group of counters, draw a circle around the parts they made, and then write the numbers to tell the parts.

Topic 7 | Lesson 2

Solve & Share

Name _____

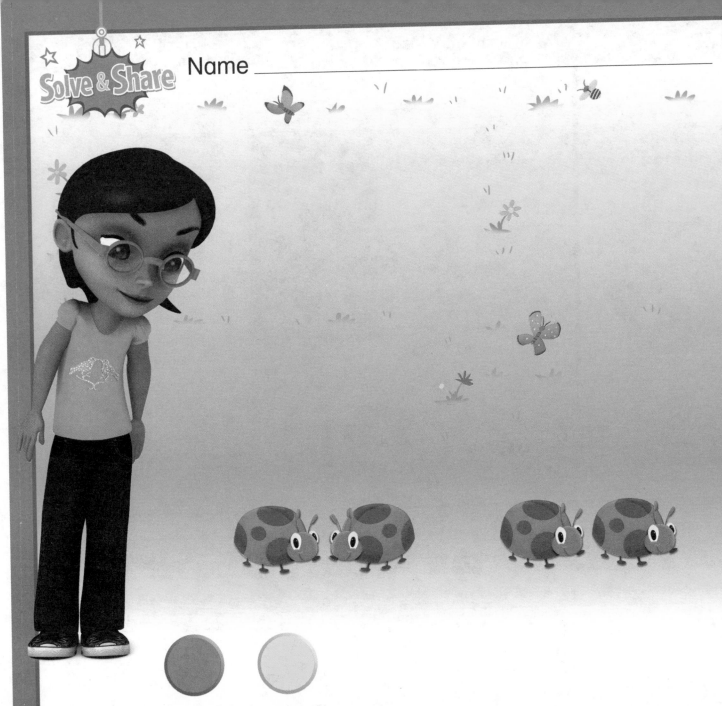

Directions Say: *Marta is watching bugs. She sees 4 ladybugs together in a group. Then some crawl away. Look at the picture and decide how many are left. Use counters to show what you think happens in the story. Then write numbers to tell how many ladybugs are left in the group.*

I can ... represent subtraction as taking away from a whole.

Content Standards K.OA.A.1, K.OA.A.2 Also K.CC.A.3 **Mathematical Practices** MP.2, MP.3, and MP.4

3 take away 1 is 2.

☆ Guided Practice

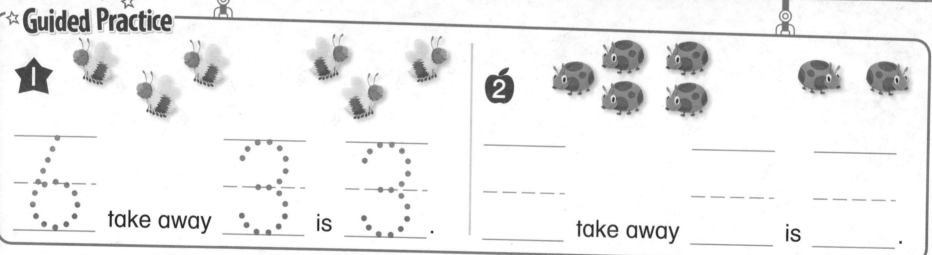

1 _____ take away _____ is _____ .

2 _____ take away _____ is _____ .

Directions Have students listen to each story, and then complete the sentence to tell how many bugs are left. ★ *Marta sees 6 bumblebees. 3 leave. How many bumblebees are left?* **2** *Marta sees 7 ladybugs. 2 leave. How many ladybugs are left?*

Topic 7 | Lesson 3

Name _____

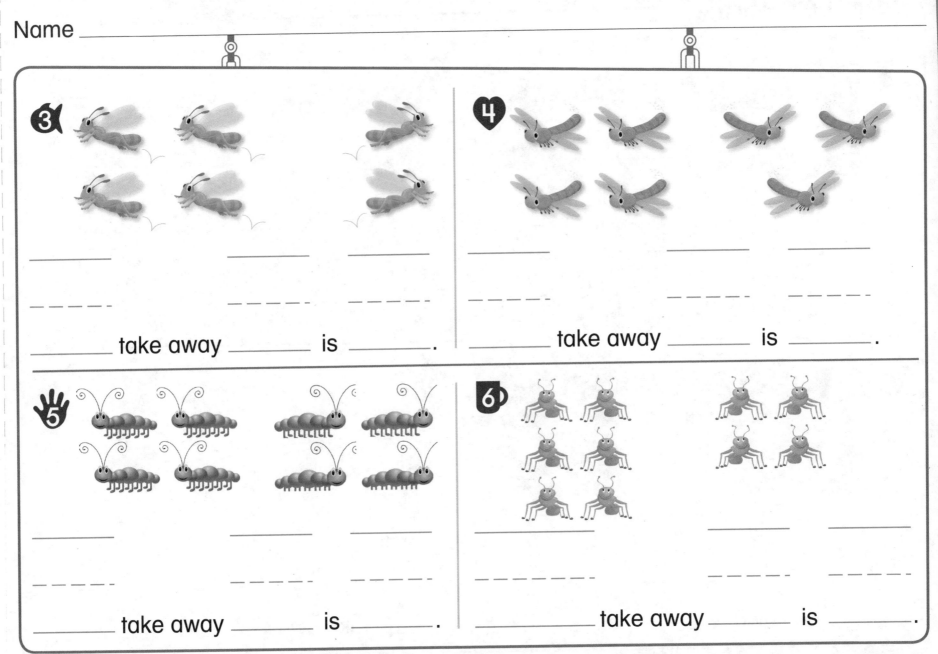

3 _____ take away _____ is _____ .

4 _____ take away _____ is _____ .

5 _____ take away _____ is _____ .

6 _____ take away _____ is _____ .

Directions Have students listen to each story, and then complete the sentence to tell how many bugs are left. 3 *Emily sees 6 grasshoppers on the table. 2 hop away. How many grasshoppers are left?* 4 *Emily sees 7 dragonflies. 3 fly away. How many dragonflies are left?* 5 *Emily sees 8 caterpillars resting on a branch. 4 crawl away. How many caterpillars are left?* 6 **enVision®** STEM Say: *Ants can move material much bigger than themselves. Emily sees 10 ants on a picnic blanket. 4 walk away. How many ants are left?*

Independent Practice

7

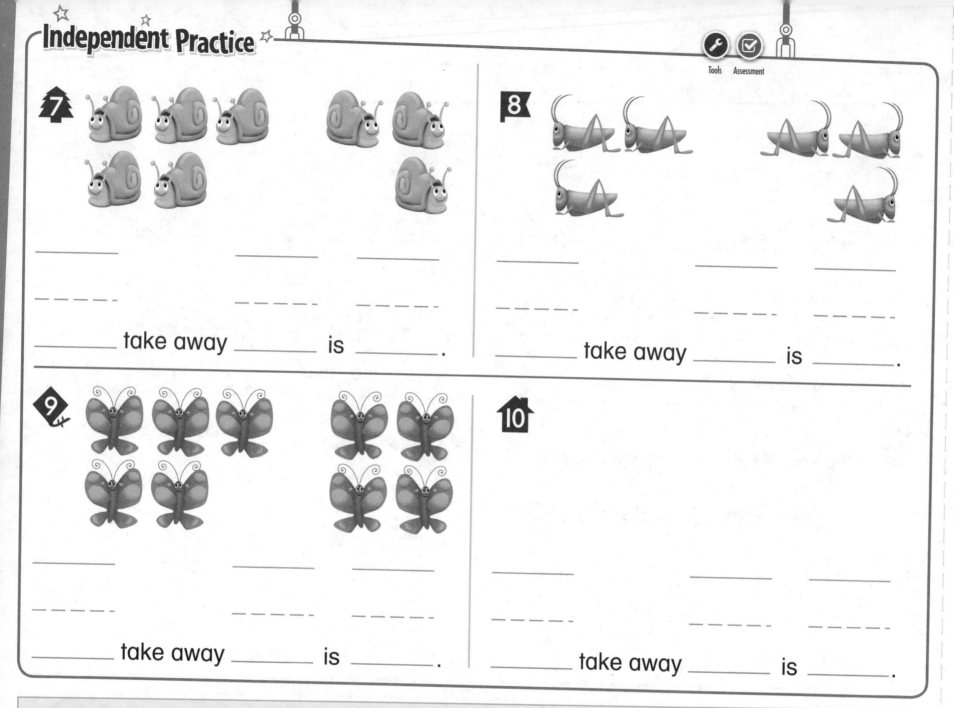

_____ take away _____ is _____.

8

_____ take away _____ is _____.

9

_____ take away _____ is _____.

10

_____ take away _____ is _____.

Directions Have students listen to each story, and then complete the sentence to tell how many are left. **7** Jerome sees 8 snails on the sidewalk. 3 slink away. How many snails are left? **8** Jerome sees 6 grasshoppers in the grass. 3 hop away. How many grasshoppers are left? **9** Jerome sees 9 butterflies in the garden. 4 flutter away. How many butterflies are left? **10** **Higher Order Thinking** Have students listen to the story, draw a picture to show the story, and then complete the sentence to tell how many are left. Jerome sees 7 inchworms on a tree. 4 crawl away. How many inchworms are left?

260 two hundred sixty

Topic 7 | Lesson 3

Solve & Share

Name _____

Activity

Directions Have students listen to the story and use counters to show what happens. Say: *There are 6 fire hats. Firefighters take 3 away. What numbers do you subtract to find how many hats are left? How can you show the subtraction?*

I can ...
write an equation to show subtraction.

© **Content Standards** K.OA.A.1 Also K.CC.A.3, K.OA.A.2 **Mathematical Practices** MP.4, MP.6

Visual Learning Bridge

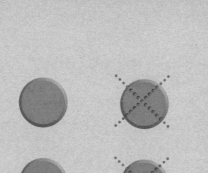

6 take away **3** is **3**.

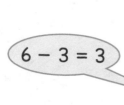

6 − 3 = 3

☆ Guided Practice

1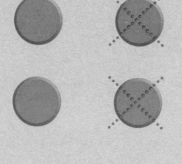

5 take away **4** is **1**.

2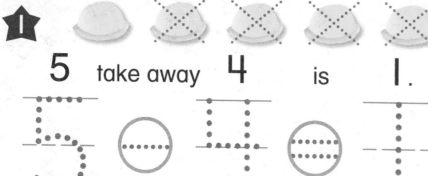

7 take away **5** is **2**.

Directions **1** and **2** Have students use counters to model the problem, mark Xs to subtract, and then write a subtraction equation to find the difference.

262 two hundred sixty-two

Topic 7 | Lesson 4

Name _____

③

8 take away 2 is 6.

_____ ◯ _____ ◯ _____

_____

4

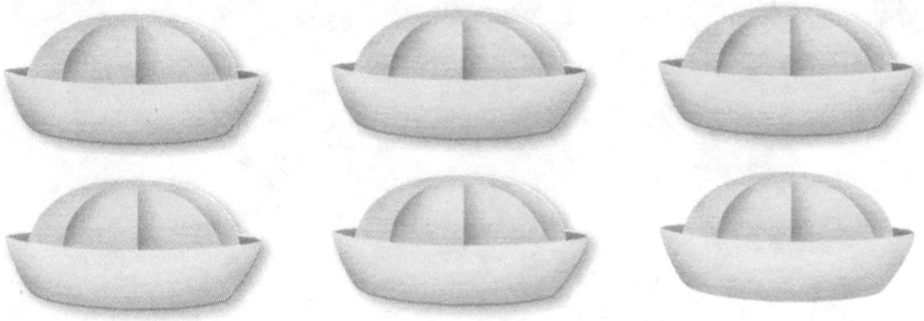

6 take away 5 is 1.

_____ ◯ _____ ◯ _____

5

9 take away 5 is 4.

_____ ◯ _____ ◯ _____

6

7 take away 2 is 5.

_____ ◯ _____ ◯ _____

Directions ③–⑥ Have students use counters to model the problem, mark Xs to subtract, and then write an equation to find the difference.

Tools Assessment

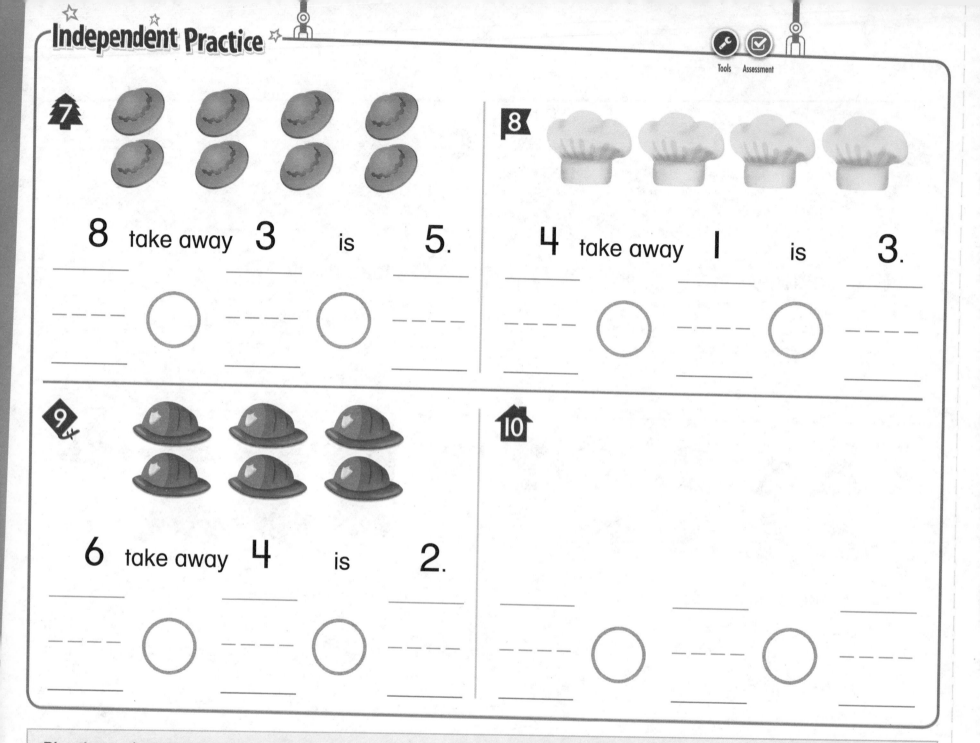

7 8 take away 3 is 5.

◯ ◯

8 4 take away 1 is 3.

◯ ◯

9 6 take away 4 is 2.

◯ ◯

10

◯ ◯

Topic 7 | Lesson 4

Name _____

 Activity

Lesson 7-5

Solve
Subtraction
Word Problems:
Taking From
and Apart

Directions Say: *Marta's dog, Spot, loves to eat doggie biscuits. Marta put 6 biscuits in a bag. One day, Spot ate 4 biscuits. Now there are only 2 left. How does Marta know there are 2 biscuits left? Use counters, pictures, or numbers to explain and show your work.*

I can ...
find the difference of
two numbers.

Content Standards K.OA.A.2
Also K.OA.A.1
Mathematical Practices MP.1,
MP.2, and MP.3

Visual Learning Bridge

 2

 3

2 are left.

 1
 2
 3
 4
 5

2 are left.

$$5 - 3 = 2$$

☆ Guided Practice

 1

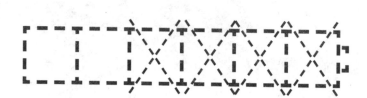

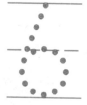  

Directions ⭐ Have students listen to the story, draw a picture to show what is happening, and then write a subtraction equation. Then have them explain their work aloud. Say: *Marta has 6 kittens. She gives them a big bowl of water to drink. But there is only room for 4 kittens to drink at the same time. How does Marta know that 2 kittens have to wait?*

Topic 7 | Lesson 5

Name _____

2

ねぬぬぬぬぬぬぬ

＿＿＿ ◯ ＿＿＿ ◯ ＿＿＿

3

🦜🦜🦜🦜🦜🦜🦜

＿＿＿ ◯ ＿＿＿ ◯ ＿＿＿

4

＿＿＿ ◯ ＿＿＿ ◯ ＿＿＿

5

＿＿＿ ◯ ＿＿＿ ◯ ＿＿＿

Directions Have students listen to each story, use or draw a picture to show what is happening, and then write an equation. Then have them explain their work aloud. **2** *Emily sees 8 rabbits in a pet store. Someone buys 3 of them. How many rabbits are left?* **3** *Emily sees 7 birds in a cage. The pet store owner opens the cage door and 3 fly out. How many birds are left?* **4** *Emily sees 8 puppies in the store. 6 of them are sold. How many puppies are left?* **5** *Emily sees 5 hamsters sleeping. 1 goes away to eat. How many hamsters are left?*

Independent Practice

6

7

8

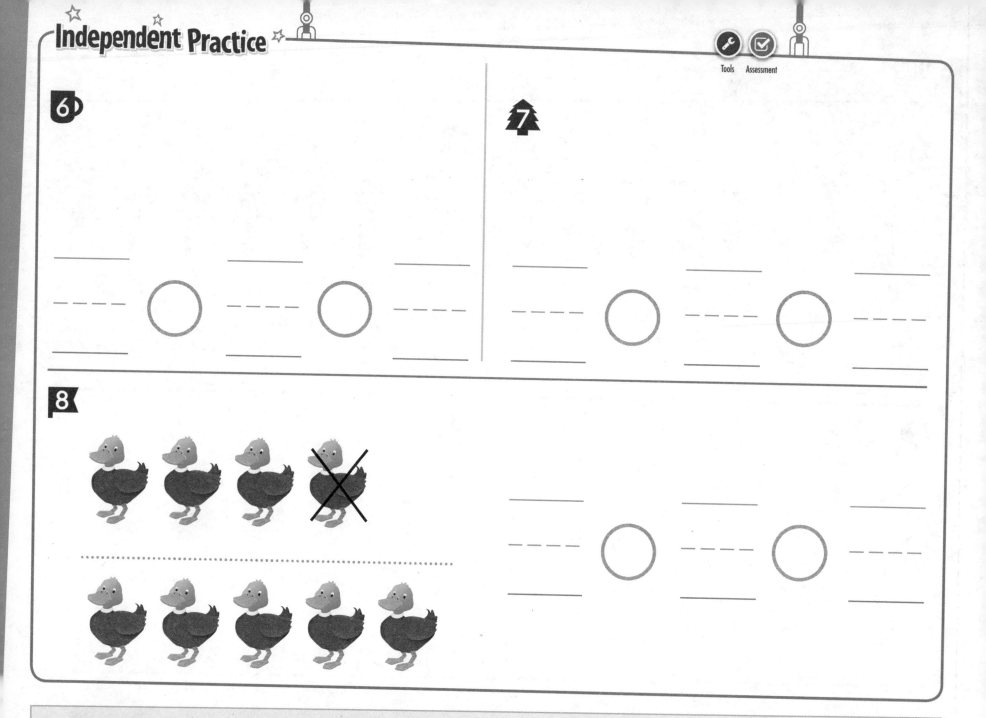

Directions Have students listen to each story, draw a picture to show what is happening, and then write an equation. **6** *There are 6 birds in a birdbath. 4 fly away. How many birds are left?* **7** *There are 5 acorns under a tree. A squirrel takes 3 of them. How many acorns are left?* **8** **Higher Order Thinking** Have students listen to the story, draw a circle around the picture that shows the story and tell why the other picture does NOT show the story, and then write an equation. *There are 4 ducks in a pond. 1 leaves. How many ducks are left?*

Topic 7 | Lesson 5

| 0 | 1 | 2 | 3 |

$5 - \boxed{} = 2$

$5 - \boxed{} = 3$

$5 - \boxed{} = \underline{}$

$5 - \boxed{} = \underline{}$

Directions Say: *Look at the first equation. Write the number from the number card that completes the equation on the orange space. Repeat for the next equation. Finish the pattern by placing the other number cards on the orange spaces, and then write the numbers to complete the equations. What patterns do you see?*

I can ...
find patterns in subtraction equations.

© **Content Standards** K.OA.A.5 Also K.OA.A.1
Mathematical Practices MP.4, MP.7, and MP.8

Visual Learning Bridge

$$5 - 0 = 5$$
$$5 - 1 = 4$$
$$5 - 2 = 3$$
$$5 - 3 = 2$$
$$5 - 4 = 1$$
$$5 - 5 = 0$$

$$5 - 0 = 5$$
$$5 - 5 = 0$$

$$5 - 1 = 4$$
$$5 - 4 = 1$$

$$5 - 2 = 3$$
$$5 - 3 = 2$$

Patterns

☆ Guided Practice

 1 $4 - 0 = $ _____

$4 - 1 = $ _____

$4 - 2 = $ _____

$4 - 3 = $ _____

Directions ⭐ Have students complete each equation to find the pattern, and then explain the pattern they see.

270 two hundred seventy

Topic 7 | Lesson 6

Name ______________________

2

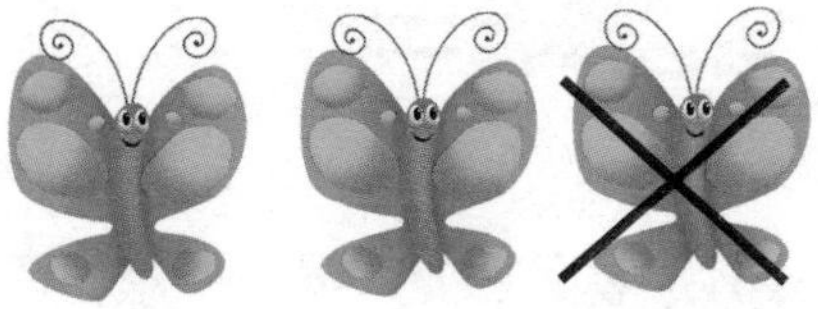

3 − ______ = ______

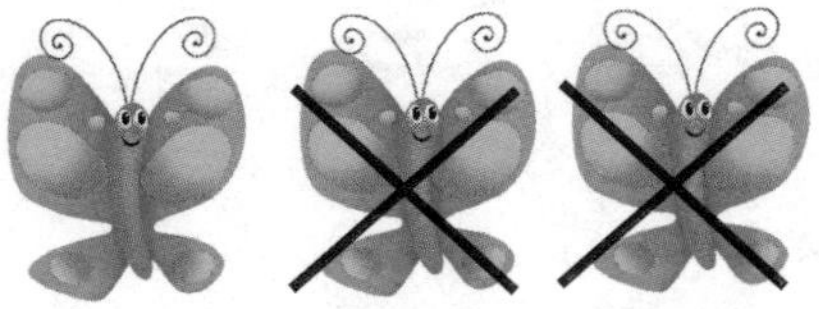

3 − ______ = ______

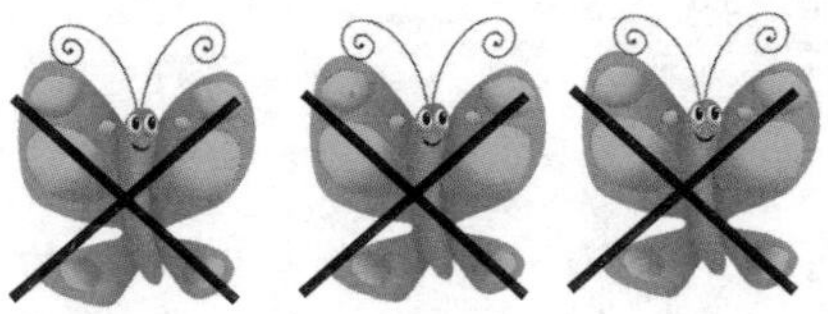

3 − ______ = ______

3

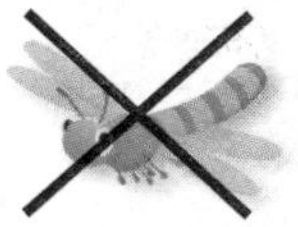

1 − ______ = ______

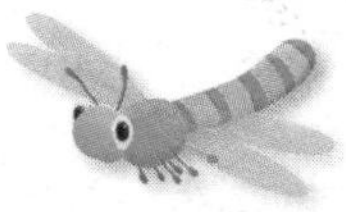

1 − ______ = ______

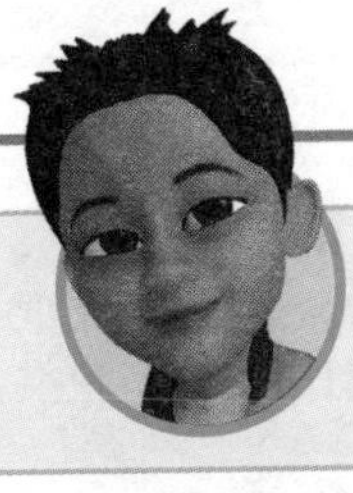

Directions 2 and 3 Have students look for a pattern, explain the pattern they see, and then write an equation for each row of insects.

❹

2 − _ _ _ _ _ = _ _ _ _ _

2 − _ _ _ _ _ = _ _ _ _ _

2 − _ _ _ _ _ = _ _ _ _ _

✋❺ 10 − 6 = 4

10 − 4 = _ _ _ _ _

☕❻ 5 − 1 = 4

5 − _ _ _ _ _ = 1

Directions ❹ **Algebra** Have students mark Xs to complete the pattern, explain the pattern they see, and then write an equation for each row of flowers. ✋ **Higher Order Thinking** Have students find the pattern, and then complete the equation. ☕ **Higher Order Thinking** Have students find the pattern, and then write the missing number in the equation.

Think.

_____ _____   _____

_ _ _ _ ◯ _ _ _ _ = _ _ _ _

_____   _____

Directions Say: *Alex has a food bar with 8 pieces of food for the flamingos at the lake. He takes apart 2 pieces of the bar to feed the flamingos. How many pieces does he have left on his bar? Use one of the tools you have to help solve the problem. Draw a picture of what you did, and then write the equation.*

I can ...
use tools to
subtract numbers.

© **Mathematical Practices** MP.5
Also MP.1, MP.6
Content Standards K.OA.A.2
Also K.OA.A.1

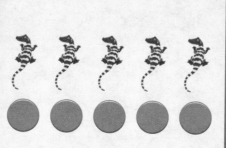

$$5 \quad \bigcirc \quad 3 = 2$$

+ or − ?

☆ Guided Practice

1

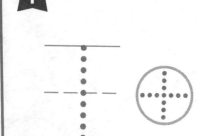

$$1 \quad \bigoplus \quad 8 = 9$$

2

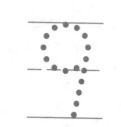

$$\_\_\_ \quad \bigodot \quad \_\_\_ = \_\_\_$$

274 two hundred seventy-four

☆ ☆
☆ Independent Practice ☆

3 🐟

_____ ⃝ _____ = _____

4 ♥

_____ ⃝ _____ = _____

5 ✋

_____ ⃝ _____ = _____

6 ☕

_____ ⃝ _____ = _____

Directions Have students listen to each story, use a tool to help them solve the problem, and then write the equation. Then have them tell which tool they chose and whether or not it helped to solve the problem. **3** *There are 3 raccoons in a tree. 3 more climb the tree to join them. How many raccoons are there in all?* **4** *Marta sees 9 turtles swimming in a pond. 5 dive under the water. How many turtles are left?* **5** *There are 7 beavers in the water. 4 swim away. How many beavers are left?* **6** *Marta see 6 ducks in the lake. 2 more join them. How many ducks are there in all?*

Problem Solving

Directions Read the problem aloud. Then have students use multiple problem-solving methods to solve the problem. Say: *Carlos collects stamps. He has 9 stamps in all. He puts 1 stamp on the cover. He puts the rest inside the book. How many stamps does Carlos put inside his stamp book?* ✿ **Make Sense** *What are you trying to find out? Will you use addition or subtraction to solve the problem?* ✦ **Use Tools** *What tool can you use to help solve the problem? Tell a partner and explain why.* ✦ **Be Precise** *Did you write the equation correctly? Explain what the numbers and the symbols mean in the equation.*

276 two hundred seventy-six

Name _____

$$7 \bigcirc 5$$

$$9 - 6 = 3$$

_____ _____

- - - - - - - - - - - - - - - -

8 take away _____ is _____.

_____

- - - - - - - - - -

_____

_____

- - - - - - - - - -

_____

Directions   **Understand Vocabulary** Have students: ★ write the **minus sign** to show subtraction; ② draw a circle around the number that tells how many are **left**; ③ complete the **subtraction sentence**; ④ **separate** the tower into 2 parts, draw each part, and then write the numbers to tell the parts.

$$8 - 3 = 5$$

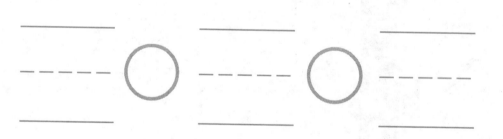

Topic 7 | Vocabulary Review

Set A

★ 1

_____

_ _ _ _ _

_____ are left.

2 are left.

Set B

Take apart 7.

★ 2

Take apart 7.

2 and **5**

_____   _____

_ _ _ _ _   _ _ _ _ _

_____ and _____

Directions Have students: ★1 count the bees, tell how many are NOT on the flower, and then write the number to tell how many are left on the flower; ★2 take apart the group of apples. Have them draw a circle around the parts they made, and then write the numbers to tell the parts.

8 take away 4 is 4.

_____   _____   _____

- - - - -   - - - - -   - - - - -

_____ take away _____ is _____.

6 take away 2 is 4.

6 – 2 = 4

4 take away 1 is 3.

_____   _____

- - - - - ◯ - - - - - ◯ - - - - -

Directions Have students: ❸ listen to the story, and then complete the sentence to tell how many are left. *Javi sees 9 dragonflies. 4 fly away. How many dragonflies are left?* ❹ use counters to model the problem, mark Xs to subtract, and then write an equation to find the difference.

Name _____

$$7 - 5 = 2$$

_____ ⃝ _____ ⃝ _____

$$4 - 1 = 3$$

_____ ⃝ _____ ⃝ _____

Directions Have students: ✋ use counters to model the problem, and then write an equation to tell how many are left; ☕ listen to the story, draw a picture to show what is happening, and then write an equation to match the story. *Lidia has 5 balloons. 2 balloons pop. How many balloons does she have left?*

$$4 - 3 = 1$$
$$4 - 2 = 2$$
$$4 - 1 = 3$$

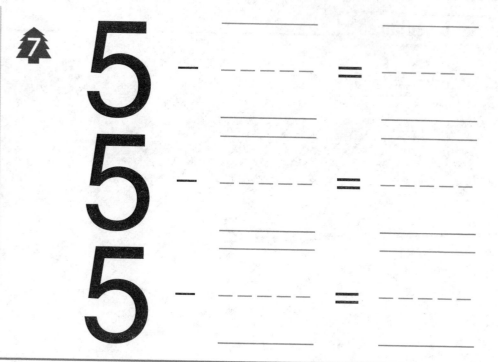

$$6 - 3 = 3$$

8

___ ___ ◯ ___ ◯ ___

Name _____

1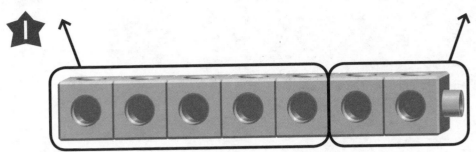

Ⓐ 6 take away 2

Ⓑ 7 take away 2

Ⓒ 4 take away 2

Ⓓ 5 take away 3

2

Ⓐ 4 take away 2 is 2. $8 - 2 = 6$

Ⓑ 4 take away 3 is 1. $4 - 3 = 1$

Ⓒ 3 take away 1 is 2. $3 - 1 = 2$

Ⓓ 5 take away 3 is 2. $5 - 3 = 2$

3

Ⓐ $5 - 3 = 2$

Ⓑ $5 - 2 = 3$

Ⓒ $7 - 3 = 4$

Ⓓ $7 - 2 = 5$

Directions Have students mark the best answer. ⭐ Say: *Which expression matches the picture and tells the number of cubes in all and a part that is taken away?* **2** Say: *There are some animals in a group. Then some animals leave. Which sentence and subtraction equation match the picture and tell how many animals are left?* **3** *Which equation matches the picture and tells how many ducks are left?*

4

_____   _____   _____

- - - - -   - - - - - - - -

_____ take away _____ is _____ .

5

_____

- - - - -

_____ are left.

_____   _____   _____

- - - - - - - - **—** - - - - - **=** - - - - -

_____   _____   _____

6

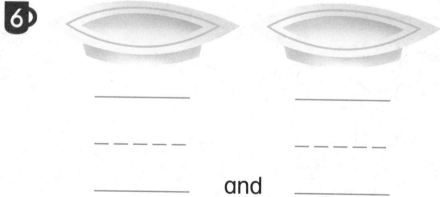

_____   _____

- - - - -   - - - - -

_____ and _____

Directions **4** Have students listen to the story, and then complete the sentence to tell how many are left. _Kyle sees 10 turtles at the zoo. 2 turtles crawl away. Write a number sentence that tells how many are left._ **5** Have students count the fish. Then have them mark Xs on some of the fish that swim away, write the number to tell how many are left, and write a matching equation. **6** Say: _Ramona has 7 apples. She puts the apples on 2 plates. Draw apples to show how many Ramona could put on each plate. Then write the numbers to tell the parts._

Topic 7 | Assessment Practice

7

$$4 - 1 = \underline{}$$

$$4 - 2 = \underline{}$$

$$\underline{} - \underline{} = \underline{}$$

8

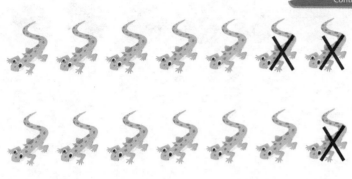

$$\underline{} \bigcirc \underline{} \bigcirc \underline{}$$

9

(A) $6 - 2 = 4$ (B) $5 - 4 = 1$ (C) $9 - 4 = 5$ (D) $4 - 4 = 0$

Directions **7** Have students complete each equation to find the pattern. **8** Have students listen to the story, draw a circle around the picture that shows the story, and then write an equation. *There were 7 lizards in the sand. 1 crawls away. How many are left?* **9** Which equation matches the picture?

Take apart 6.

_____ _____ _____

– – – –   —   – – – –   =   – – – –

_____

– – – –   _____   – – – –   ◯   _____   – – – –

   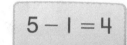 $5 - 1 = 4$

 $5 - 0 = 5$

 $5 - 3 = 2$

 $5 - 4 = 1$

 $5 - 2 = 3$

Directions Have students: 🏠 take apart the group of plums. Have them draw a circle around the parts they made, and then write an equation that matches their picture; 🌼 listen to the story, draw a picture, use counters or other objects to help solve the problem, and then write an equation that matches the story. _Kim collects 9 shells. She gives 6 away. How many shells does Kim have left?_ 12 Have students match each equation with a row of flowers to find the pattern.

286 two hundred eighty-six

Topic 7 | Assessment Practice

Name _____

1

_____ _____

_____ _ _ _ _ _ _ _ _ _

_____ take away _____ is _____ .

_____

2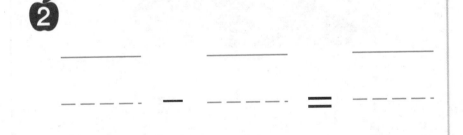

_ _ _ _ _ _ _ — _ _ _ _ = _ _ _ _ _ _

_____

3

5 – _ _ _ _ = _ _ _ _

5 – _ _ _ _ = _ _ _ _

Directions **Puppet Show** Say: *Paco's class uses many puppets for their puppet show.* **1** Have students listen to the story, and then write a subtraction sentence to tell how many duck puppets are left. *Paco has 8 duck puppets at school. He takes 3 home. How many duck puppets are left at school?* **2** Write an equation to tell how many duck puppets Paco has left at school. **3** Say: *The picture shows that Paco put 1 cat puppet in a drawer. How many cat puppets are left?* Have students write an equation for the picture, and then write another equation to complete a pattern.

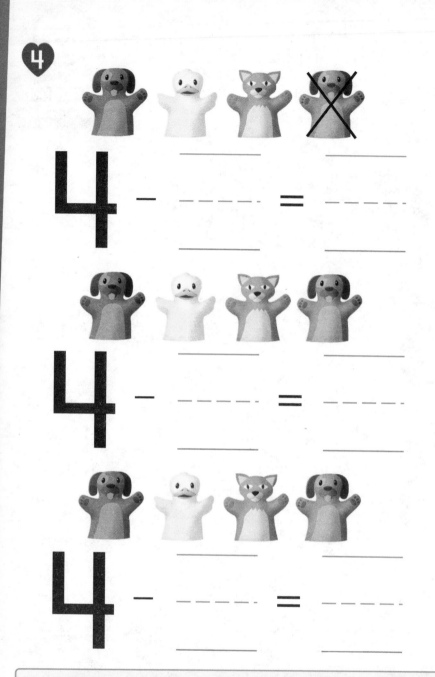

4

4 − _ _ _ _ = _ _ _ _

_ _ _ _

4 − _ _ _ _ = _ _ _ _

_ _ _ _

4 − _ _ _ _ = _ _ _ _

_ _ _ _

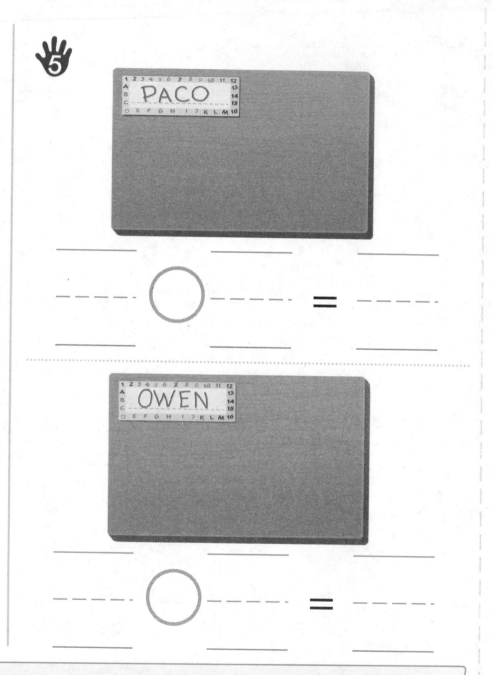

5

_ _ _ _ ◯ _ _ _ _ = _ _ _ _

_ _ _ _

_ _ _ _ ◯ _ _ _ _ = _ _ _ _

_ _ _ _

Directions ❤ Say: *Paco's class puts on a play using 4 puppets. Each scene of the play has 1 more puppet leave the stage than the scene before.* Have students mark Xs to complete the pattern. Then have them write equations to show how many puppets leave each scene. ✋ Have students listen to the story, use counters to help solve each part of the problem, and then write an equation. *Paco has 4 yellow bird puppets and 3 red bird puppets on his desk. How many bird puppets does Paco have in all? Then Paco moves 2 bird puppets to his friend Owen's desk. How many bird puppets are left on Paco's desk?*

 Topic 7 | Performance Task

More Addition and Subtraction

Essential Question: How can solving problems in more than one way help you learn about addition and subtraction?

Digital Resources

Interactive Student Edition | Activity | Visual Learning | Video | Practice

Assessment | Games | Tools | Glossary

Look!

We can recycle.

enVision STEM Project: Recycling

Directions Read the character speech bubbles to students. **Find Out!** Have students find out about the impact of littering and how recycling reduces human impact on the environment. Say: *Talk to friends and relatives about the items they recycle. Ask them how they are helping to protect the environment.* **Journal: Make a Poster** Then have students make a poster. Ask them to draw a playground littered with 4 paper, 3 plastic, and 2 metal recyclables. Have them draw a circle around the papers in green, the plastics in yellow, and the metals in orange. Finally, have students write an equation that adds the 4 paper and 3 plastic recyclables together.

Name _____

Review What You Know

 1

$$7 - 5 = 2$$

2

$$8 - 6 = 2$$

$$3 + 2 = 5$$

3

$$+ \qquad -$$

4

_____

_ _ _ _ _ _ _ _

5

_____

_ _ _ _ _ _ _ _

6

_ _ _ _ _ _   _ _ _ _ _ _

Directions Have students: **1** draw a circle around the difference; **2** draw a circle around the subtraction equation and mark an X on the addition equation; **3** draw a circle around the minus sign; **4** and **5** count the counters, and then write the number to tell how many; **6** count the counters, and then write the numbers to tell the parts.

Topic 8

Name _____

A

B

Directions Say: *You will choose one of these projects. Look at picture* **A.** *Think about this question: How many eggs do hens lay? If you choose Project A, you will act out egg collecting. Look at picture* **B.** *Think about this question: Are flowers the only plants you can grow in a garden? If you choose Project B, you will make a garden poster.*

Directions Say: *You will choose one of these projects. Look at picture* **C.** *Think about this question: What do you see in the sky at night? If you choose Project C, you will create a star drawing. Look at picture* **D.** *Think about this question: Would you like to live in this house? If you choose Project D, you will draw a tree house.*

 Topic 8 | Pick a Project

Name _____

Activity

5 = ? + ?

$$5 = \underline{\quad\quad} + \underline{\quad\quad}$$

Directions Say: *Alex plants 5 daisies in a flowerpot. Some are yellow. Some are red. Use counters to show one way to break apart a group of 5 daisies. Draw your counters on the flowerpot. Color the daisies. Complete the equation to show how many red and how many yellow daisies.*

I can ...
write equations to show parts of 5 and solve problems.

ⒸContent Standards K.OA.A.2, K.OA.A.3 Also K.OA.A.I **Mathematical Practices** MP.5, MP.7, and MP.8

$$5 = \boxed{} + \boxed{}$$

 ## Guided Practice

1

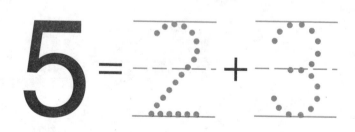

$$5 = 2 + 3$$

Directions ⭐ Have students listen to the story, use and draw counters, color the flowers, and complete the equation to model another way to break apart 5. *Alex plants 5 daisies. Some are yellow. Some are red. How many are yellow and how many are red?*

Topic 8 | Lesson 1

Name _____

2

$5 =$ _____ $+$ _____

3

$5 =$ _____ $+$ _____

Directions **2** and **3** Have students listen to the story, use and draw counters, color the flowers, and complete the equation to model other ways to break apart 5. Say: *Marta plants 5 flowers. Some are yellow. Some are red. How many are yellow and how many are red?*

Independent Practice

4

$5 = \underline{\hspace{2cm}} + \underline{\hspace{2cm}}$

$5 = \underline{\hspace{2cm}} + \underline{\hspace{2cm}}$

Directions ♥ Have students listen to the story, use and draw counters, color the flowers, and complete the equation to show another way to break apart 5. Say: *Carlos plants 5 flowers. Some are yellow. Some are red. How many are yellow and how many are red?* ✋ **Higher Order Thinking** Have students draw another way to break apart 5 with flowers, and then write an equation to match the story and show the parts that equal 5.

Topic 8 | Lesson 1

Name _____

Activity

$$2 + 2 = 4$$

$$4 - 2 = 2$$

Directions Say: *4 penguins play outside. 2 penguins go in the ice cave. How many penguins are left outside? Draw a circle around the equation that matches the story. Tell how you know.*

I can ...
solve related addition and subtraction equations.

Content Standards K.OA.A.5 Also K.OA.A.1
Mathematical Practices MP.1, MP.2, and MP.6

$$3 + 2 = 5$$

Add.

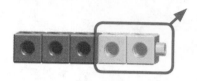

$$5 - 2 = 3$$

Subtract.

⭐ Guided Practice

1

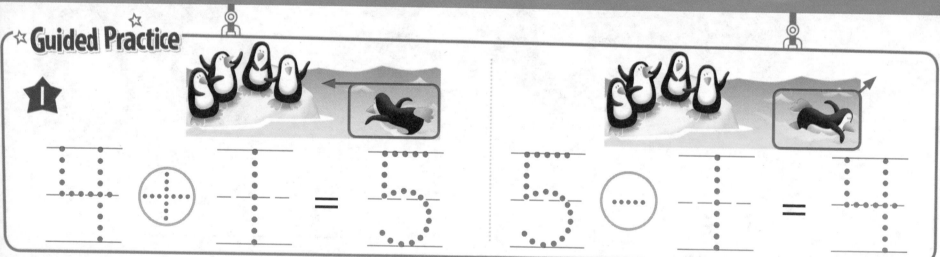

Directions 🏠 **Vocabulary** Have students listen to each story and use connecting cubes to help act out each story to choose an **operation**. Then have students complete the equations to tell the related facts. Say: *4 penguins are in a group. 1 joins them. How many penguins are there in all?* Then say: *5 penguins are in a group. 1 leaves. How many penguins are left?*

Name _____

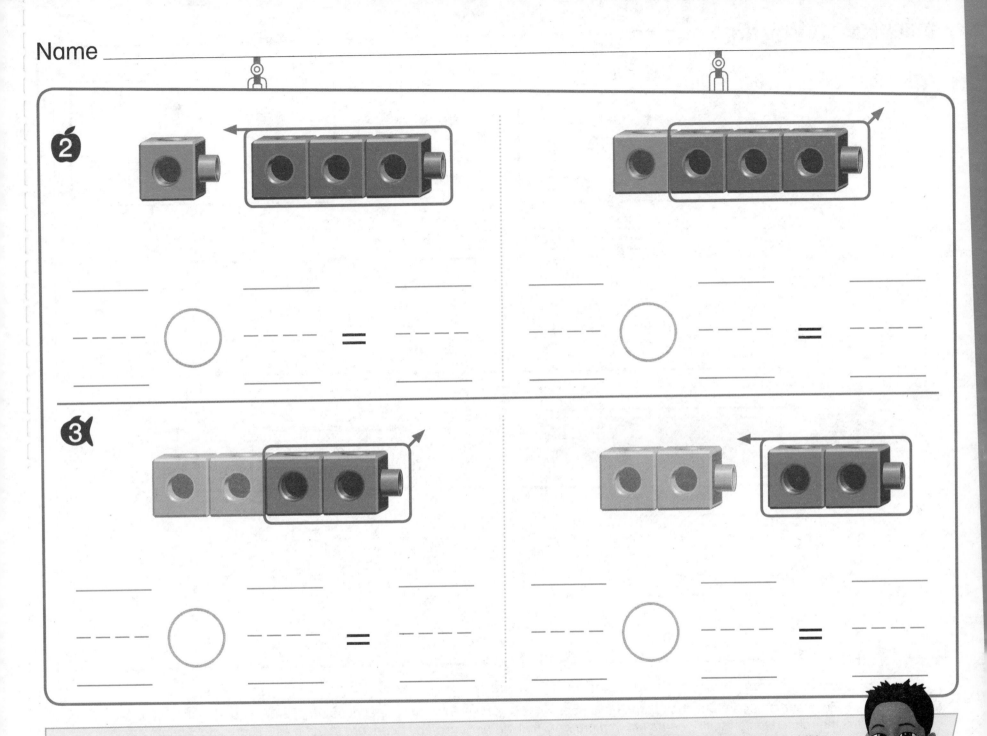

2

_ _ _ _ _ ◯ _ _ _ _ = _ _ _ _

_ _ _ _ _ ◯ _ _ _ _ = _ _ _ _

3

_ _ _ _ _ ◯ _ _ _ _ = _ _ _ _

_ _ _ _ _ ◯ _ _ _ _ = _ _ _ _

Directions **2** and **3** Have students use cubes for these facts with 4. Have them decide whether the cubes show addition or subtraction. Encourage students to make up their own stories to match the cubes. Then have them write equations to tell the related facts.

Independent Practice

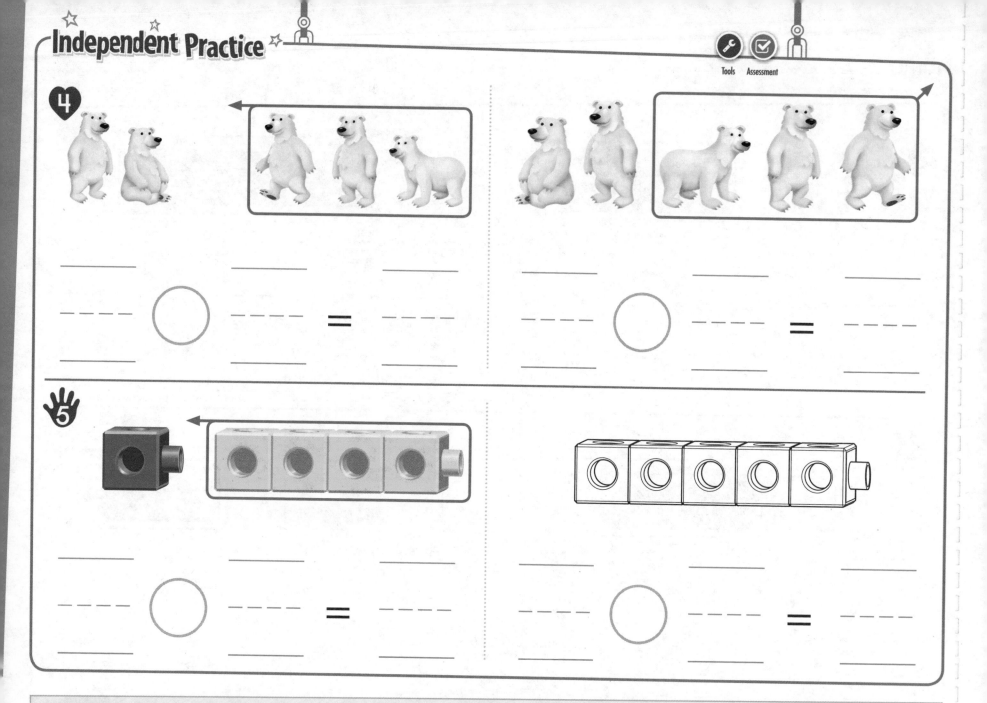

4

_ _ _ _   ◯   _ _ _ _ = _ _ _ _ _   _ _ _ _   ◯   _ _ _ _ = _ _ _ _ _

5

_ _ _ _   ◯   _ _ _ _ = _ _ _ _ _   _ _ _ _   ◯   _ _ _ _ = _ _ _ _ _

Directions 4 Have students listen to each story, use cubes to help act out each story to choose an operation, and then write the equations to tell the related facts. Say: _2 bears are in a group. 3 join them. How many bears are there in all?_ Then say: _5 bears are in a group. 3 leave. How many bears are there now?_ 5 **Higher Order Thinking** Have students decide whether the first set of cubes shows addition or subtraction, and then write an equation to match. For the second set of cubes, students color the cubes using the same numbers as the equation they just wrote, draw an arrow to tell the related fact, and then write the equation to match.

Name _____

$$4 - 3 = 1$$

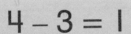

Think.

Directions Say: *Jada and Carlos are at the zoo. Each of them tells a story about an animal in a habitat. How could you tell a story to match the equation shown? Tell your story to a partner. Draw a picture to show your story.*

I can ...

reason about numbers and operations.

© **Mathematical Practices** MP.2
Also MP.4, MP.5
Content Standards K.OA.A.1
Also K.OA.A.5

$$2 + 3 = ?$$

What does the + mean?

$$2 + 3 = 5$$

$$2 + 3 = 5$$

☆ Guided Practice

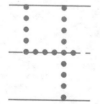  =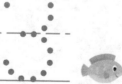

Directions ☆ Have students tell a story for 4 − 1. Then have them draw a picture to illustrate their story and write the equation.

Independent Practice

2

_____ ◯ _____ = _____

3

_____ ◯ _____ = _____

Directions Have students tell a story for: **2** 1 + 3 turtles. Then have them draw a picture to illustrate their story and write the equation; **3** 3 − 2 snakes. Then have them draw a picture to illustrate their story and write the equation.

$$4 + \underline{\quad} = 5$$

Solve & Share

Name _____

Activity

$$0 \quad 1 \quad 2 \quad 3 \quad 4 \quad 5$$

$$1+2=3 \quad 4-2=2$$

Directions Say: *Help Jada write 2 more addition equations and 2 more subtraction equations using the numbers at the top of the page. Explain your equations using counters.*

I can ...
write addition and subtraction equations within 5 and remember them.

© **Content Standards** K.OA.A.5 Also K.OA.A.1
Mathematical Practices MP.1, MP.2, and MP.3

3 + 2 = ?

3 + 2 = 5

3...4, 5

3 − 1 = ?

3 − 1 = 2

3 − 1 = 2

Guided Practice

1

$$4 + 1 = 5$$

2

$$5 - 1 = \underline{\quad\quad}$$

Directions **1** and **2** Have students solve the equation any way they choose, and then tell how they solved the problem.

Topic 8 | Lesson 4

Name _____

3 🐟

$$2 + 1 = \text{-----}$$

4 ❤️

$$3 - 1 = \text{-----}$$

5 ✋

$$2 - 2 = \text{-----}$$

6 ☕

$$1 + 4 = \text{-----}$$

7 🌲

$$4 + 0 = \text{-----}$$

8 🚩

$$4 - 2 = \text{-----}$$

Directions **3**–**8** Have students solve the equation any way they choose, and then tell how they solved the problem.

Independent Practice

9

$$4 - 1 = \underline{\hspace{3cm}}$$

10

$$3 + 1 = \underline{\hspace{3cm}}$$

11

$$3 - 2 = \underline{\hspace{3cm}}$$

12

$$1 + 0 = \underline{\hspace{3cm}}$$

13

$$5 - 2 = \underline{\hspace{3cm}}$$

14

$$5 - \underline{\hspace{2cm}} = 5$$

Directions 9–13 Have students solve the equation any way they choose, and then tell how they solved the problem. 14 **Higher Order Thinking** Have students solve for the missing number in the equation any way they choose, and then tell how they solved the problem.

Solve & Share

Name _____

6 = ? + ?

Directions Say: Jada has 6 books she wants to break apart into 2 groups and place on her book shelves. Draw one way she could put her books away, and then write the numbers to tell how many books you drew on each shelf. Write an equation to match what you drew. Explain why your answer is correct.

I can ...
write equations to show parts of 6 and 7 and solve problems.

 Content Standards K.OA.A.2, K.OA.A.3 Also K.OA.A.1 **Mathematical Practices** MP.2, MP.3, and MP.4

Visual Learning Bridge

7

1   6

$7 = ? + ?$

$7 = 1 + 6$

$7 = \boxed{6} + \boxed{1}$

Directions ⬆ Have students listen to the story, use the cubes to tell how many flowers are in each vase, and then complete the equation to match the cubes. Say: *Jada has 7 flowers. She puts some in a blue vase and some in a red vase. How many flowers did she put in each vase?*

Topic 8 | Lesson 5

Name _____

2

$$7 = \text{\_\_\_\_\_} + \text{\_\_\_\_\_}$$

3

$$7 = \text{\_\_\_\_\_} + \text{\_\_\_\_\_}$$

4

$$7 = \text{\_\_\_\_\_} + \text{\_\_\_\_\_}$$

Directions 2–4 Have students listen to the story, use and color cubes to show 3 different ways you can break apart the flowers and put them in the vases, and then complete the equations to match each way. Say: *Carlos has 7 flowers. He wants to put some in a red vase and some in a blue vase. How many flowers can he put in each vase?*

Independent Practice

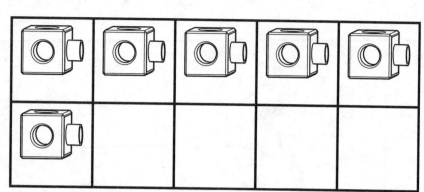

$6 =$ 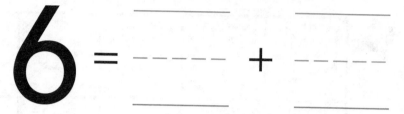 ____ + ____

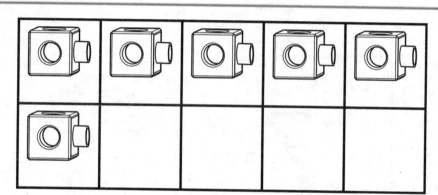

$6 =$ 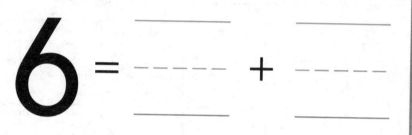 ____ + ____

____ = ____ + ____

Directions 👋 and ☕ Have students listen to the story, use and color cubes to show different ways you can break apart the flowers and put them in the vases, and then complete the equations to match each way. Say: *Daniel has 6 flowers. He puts some in a red vase and some in a blue vase. How many flowers could he put in each vase?* 🌲 **Higher Order Thinking** Have students draw cubes to show another way to solve the problem, and then write an equation to match.

       Topic 8 | Lesson 5

Solve & Share

Name _____

Activity

$$8 = \underline{} + \underline{}$$

8 = ? + ?

Directions Say: *8 children are going rafting. They need life jackets. Some of the life jackets are red. Some are blue. How many of each color will they need if everyone has a life jacket? Use cubes to model one way to break apart 8 and show how many are red and how many are blue. Complete the equation to match the cubes.*

I can ...
write equations to show parts of 8 and 9 and solve problems.

© **Content Standards** K.OA.A.2, K.OA.A.3 Also K.OA.A.1 **Mathematical Practices** MP.2, MP.4, and MP.6

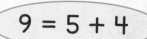
Visual Learning Bridge

One Way

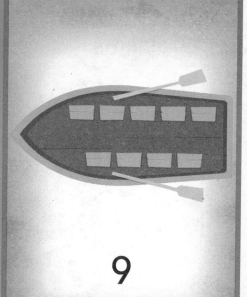

9

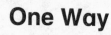

5
4

Another Way

9 = ? + ?

$9 = 5 + 4$

☆ **Guided Practice**

1

$9 = 8 + 1$

Directions ★ Have students listen to the story, use and color cubes to tell how many of each color, and then complete the equation to show another way to break apart 9. Say: *9 children are going to ride a boat. They need life jackets. Some of the jackets are red and some are blue. How many of each color will they need if everyone has a life jacket?*

314 three hundred fourteen

Topic 8 | Lesson 6

2

$$8 = \text{\underline{\hspace{2cm}}} + \text{\underline{\hspace{2cm}}}$$

3

$$8 = \text{\underline{\hspace{2cm}}} + \text{\underline{\hspace{2cm}}}$$

4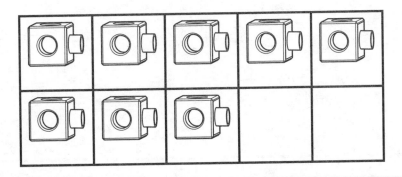

$$8 = \text{\underline{\hspace{2cm}}} + \text{\underline{\hspace{2cm}}}$$

Directions **2–4** Have students listen to the story, use and color cubes to tell how many of each color, and then complete the equations to match the cubes and model 3 more ways to break apart 8. Say: *8 children are going to ride a boat. They need life jackets. Some of the jackets are red and some are blue. How many of each jacket will they need if everyone has a life jacket?*

Independent Practice

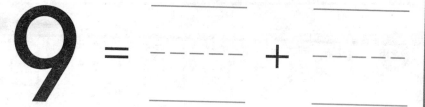

$$9 = \underline{} + \underline{}$$

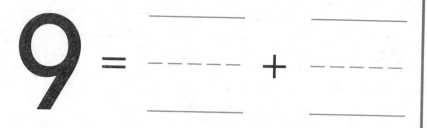

$$9 = \underline{} + \underline{}$$

$$\underline{} = \underline{} + \underline{}$$

Directions and Have students listen to the story. Then have them use and color cubes to tell how many of each color. Then have them complete the equations to model 2 more ways to break apart 9. Say: *9 children are going to ride a boat. They need life jackets. Some of the jackets are red and some are blue. How many of each color could they have, if everyone has a life jacket?* **Higher Order Thinking** Have students draw cubes to show another way to solve the problem, and then write an equation to match.

Topic 8 | Lesson 6

Directions Say: Jackson puts 10 watering cans on a shelf in the garden store. Use counters to show how Jackson could place the 10 watering cans. Then use different numbers of red and yellow counters to show other ways the cans could be placed on the shelf. Color the counters in the ten-frame red and yellow to show your favorite way.

I can ...
show how to make a group of 10.

© **Content Standards** K.OA.A.1 Also K.CC.A.3 **Mathematical Practices** MP.1, MP.7, and MP.8

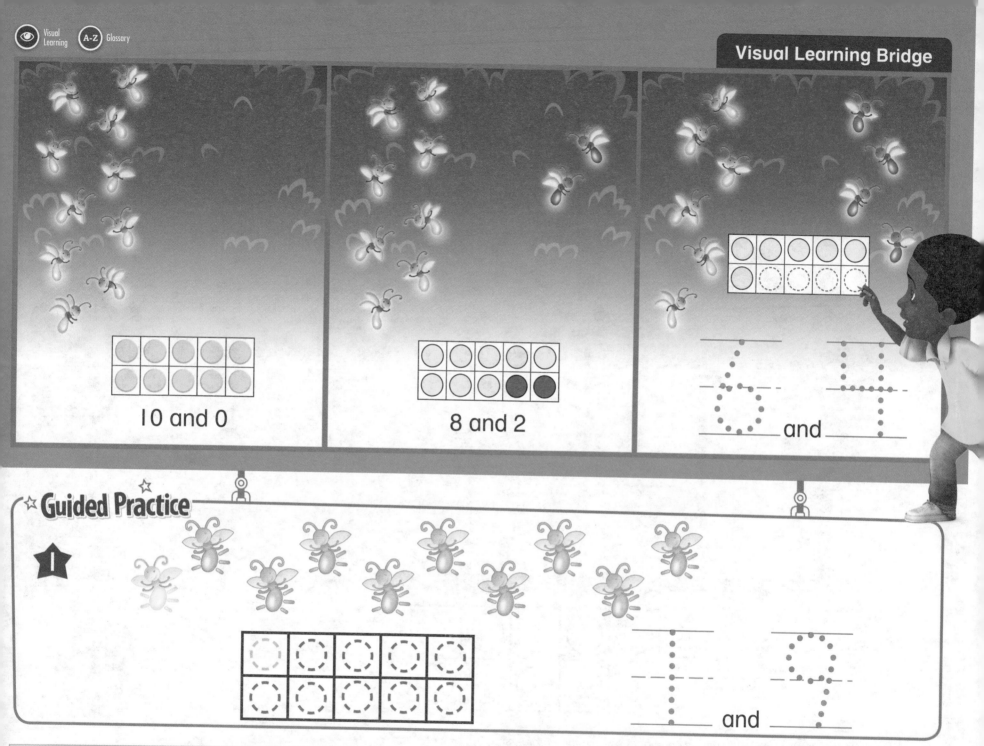

10 and 0

8 and 2

_____ and _____

☆ Guided Practice

1

_____ and _____

Directions ★ Have students draw and color counters red and yellow to show one way to make 10, color the fireflies red and yellow to show that way, and then write the numbers.

318 three hundred eighteen

Name _____

2

[ten-frame grid]

_____

_ _ _ _ _   _ _ _ _ _

_____ and _____

3

[ten-frame grid]

_____

_ _ _ _ _   _ _ _ _ _

_____ and _____

4

[ten-frame grid]

_____

_ _ _ _ _   _ _ _ _ _

_____ and _____

Directions ❷–❹ Have students draw and color counters red and yellow to show one way to make 10, color the insects red and yellow to show each way, and then write the numbers.

Topic 8 | Lesson 7

three hundred nineteen   319

Independent Practice

5

_____   _____

– – – – –   – – – – –

_____ and _____

6

_____   _____

– – – – –   – – – – –

_____ and _____

7

_____   _____

– – – – –   – – – – –

_____ and _____

Directions ✋ and **6** Have students draw and color counters red and yellow to show one way to make 10, color the insects red and yellow to show each way, and then write the numbers. **7 Higher Order Thinking** Have students draw a way to make 10, and then write the numbers.

Topic 8 | Lesson 7

Solve & Share

Name _____

Activity

10 = ? + ?

$10 =$ _____ $+$ _____

Directions Say: *10 children are going on a bus for a field trip. Each child will wear either a red or a yellow shirt because those are the school colors. Use counters to model a way to break 10 into two parts and show what color shirt each child wears. Then write an equation to match the counters.*

I can ...
write equations to show parts of 10 and solve problems.

Content Standards K.OA.A.2, K.OA.A.3 Also K.OA.A.1 **Mathematical Practices** MP.2, MP.7

10

$$10 = ? + ?$$

$$10 = 7 + 3$$

☆ Guided Practice

 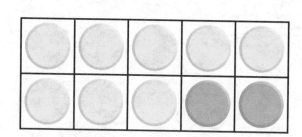

$$10 = 3 + 2$$

Directions ★ Have students listen to the story, use the counters to tell how many of each color, and then complete the equation to show the way 10 is separated into two parts. Say: *10 children are going on a field trip. Each child will wear either a red or a yellow shirt. How many of each color shirt will there be?*

Topic 8 | Lesson 8

2

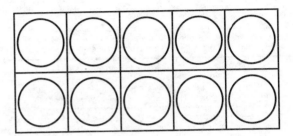

$10 = \underline{\hspace{2cm}} + \underline{\hspace{2cm}}$

3

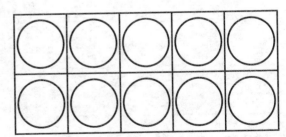

$10 = \underline{\hspace{2cm}} + \underline{\hspace{2cm}}$

4

$10 = \underline{\hspace{2cm}} + \underline{\hspace{2cm}}$

Directions 2–4 Have students listen to the story again, use and color counters to show 3 different ways to break apart 10 and tell how many of each color shirt, and then complete the equations to match their answers.

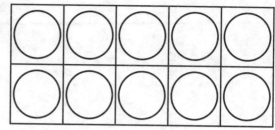

$$10 = \underline{\hspace{3em}} + \underline{\hspace{3em}}$$

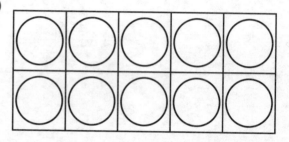

$$10 = \underline{\hspace{3em}} + \underline{\hspace{3em}}$$

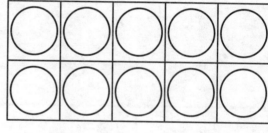

$$10 = 2 + 8$$

$$\underline{\hspace{3em}} = \underline{\hspace{3em}} + \underline{\hspace{3em}}$$

Directions ✋ and ☕ Have students use and color counters to show 2 more different ways to break apart 10 and tell how many of each color shirt for the field trip story. Then have them complete the equations to match each way. 🌲 **Higher Order Thinking** Have students color yellow and red counters in the top ten-frame to show the equation. Then have students write the related fact to the given equation, and then color yellow and red counters in the bottom ten-frame to match the equation they wrote. Have students tell how the equations are alike and different.

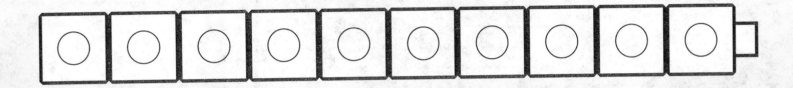

_____
_____ + _____ = **10**
_____

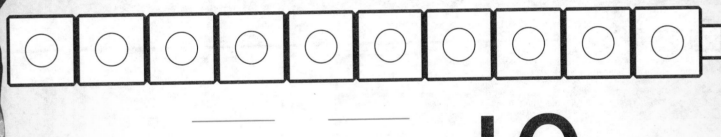

_____
_____ + _____ = **10**
_____

Directions Say: *Use red and blue cubes to make two different trains. Each train should have 10 cubes. Use blue and red crayons to color the cube trains you made. Then write the missing numbers in the equation for each cube train.*

I can ...
find number partners for 10.

© **Content Standards** K.OA.A.4
Also K.CC.A.3, K.OA.A.3
Mathematical Practices MP.2, MP.4, and MP.8

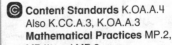

$$3 + \boxed{?} = 10$$

10 in all

$$3 + 7 = 10$$

☆ Guided Practice

1 $5 + 5 = 10$

2 $9 + \underline{\quad} = 10$

Directions Have students: **1** count the red cubes to find one part of 10, use blue cubes to find the number under the cover, and then write the missing number in the equation to tell the parts of 10; **2** count the blue cubes to find one part of 10, use red cubes to find the number under the cover, and then write the missing number in the equation to tell the parts of 10.

Name _____

3 $7 + \text{\_\_\_\_} = 10$

4 $2 + \text{\_\_\_\_} = 10$

5 $6 + \text{\_\_\_\_} = 10$

6 $5 + \text{\_\_\_\_} = 10$

7

$$4 + \underline{\quad\quad} = 10$$

8

$$8 + \underline{\quad\quad} = 10$$

9

$$1 + \underline{\quad\quad} = 10$$

10

$$\underline{\quad\quad} + \underline{\quad\quad} = 10$$

Directions ❼–❾ Have students draw a picture to show the parts of 10, and then write the missing number in the equation to tell the parts of 10. ❿ **Higher Order Thinking** Say: *A child is holding up 3 fingers to show how old she is. What part of 10 is she showing? Use that number to write the missing numbers in the equation to tell the parts of 10.*

328 three hundred twenty-eight

Solve & Share

Directions Say: *Jada visits a farm. The owner says there are 10 goats on the farm. Jada only sees 8 goats. How many are inside the barn? Use counters or draw pictures to show the goats that are in the barn, and then tell how you know.*

I can ...
find a missing part to make 10.

© **Content Standards** K.OA.A.4
Also K.CC.A.3, K.OA.A.3
Mathematical Practices MP.4, MP.7, and MP.8

Visual Learning Bridge

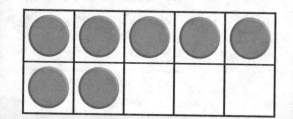

$$7 + ? = 10$$

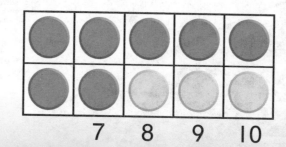

7   8   9   10

3 yellow counters

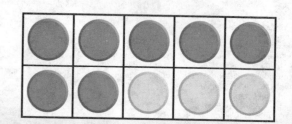

$$7 + 3 = 10$$

☆ Guided Practice

1

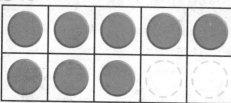

$$8 + 2 = 10$$

2

$$5 + \underline{\quad\quad} = 10$$

Directions 1–2 Have students draw yellow counters in the ten-frame to find the missing part of 10, and then write the missing number in the equation.

Topic 8 | Lesson 10

Name _____

3 $9 + \underline{} = 10$

4 $4 + \underline{} = 10$

5 $2 + \underline{} = 10$

6 $1 + \underline{} = 10$

Directions **3**–**6** **Algebra** Have students draw yellow counters in the ten-frame to find the missing part of 10, and then write the missing number in the equation.

Tools Assessment

 7 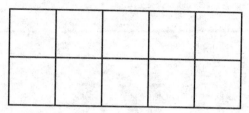 $3 + \underline{\hspace{2cm}} = 10$

8 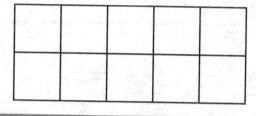 $5 + \underline{\hspace{2cm}} = 10$

9 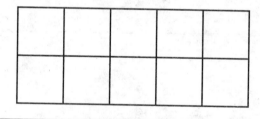 $0 + \underline{\hspace{2cm}} = 10$

10

$$5 + 5 = 10 \qquad 5 + 6 = 10 \qquad 9 + 2 = 10 \qquad 9 + 1 = 10$$

Directions 7–9 Have students draw counters in the ten-frame to show the part that they know, and then draw yellow counters in the empty spaces in the ten-frame and count to find the missing part of 10. Then have students write the missing number in the equation.
10 Higher Order Thinking Have students mark an X on the two equations that are NOT true. Then have them explain how they know which equations are true and which are NOT true.

Topic 8 | Lesson 10

1

1 + 2	5 – 2	4 – 1	3 + 0	3 – 0
5 – 3	4 + 1	0 + 3	2 + 2	1 + 0
2 – 1	5 – 4	5 – 2	0 + 0	1 + 4
3 + 2	3 – 1	4 – 1	5 – 1	4 – 0
3 – 3	2 + 0	2 + 1	2 + 3	1 + 1

2

_____

_ _ _ _ _

_____

I can ...
add and subtract fluently to 5.

© **Content Standard** K.OA.A.5
Mathematical Practices MP.3, MP.6, MP.7, and MP.8

Directions Have students: **1** color each box that has a sum or difference that is equal to 3; **2** write the letter that they see.

1

$$10 - 5 = 5$$

2

$$6 + 3 = 9$$

3

$$8 \bigcirc 7 = \underline{}$$

 4

 **9** = _ _ _ _ _ _ $\bigcirc$ _ _ _ _ _ _

Directions **Understand Vocabulary** Have students: **1** draw a circle around the **minus sign**; **2** draw a circle around the **sum**; **3** complete the number sentence and find the **difference**; **4** show a way to make the number by drawing one part in the box and one part outside the box. Then have them write the numbers of the parts and fill in the **operation** to complete the equation.

334 three hundred thirty-four

Name _____

Set A

⭐ 1

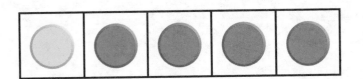

$$5 = 1 + 4$$

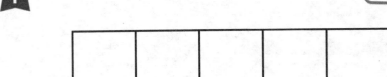

$$5 = \rule{1cm}{0.4pt} + \rule{1cm}{0.4pt}$$

Set B

🍎 2

$$2 + 1 = 3$$

$$\rule{2cm}{0.4pt} \bigcirc \rule{2cm}{0.4pt} = \rule{1cm}{0.4pt}$$

Directions Have students: ⭐ listen to the story then use and draw counters to model another way to break apart 5, and complete the equation to match the counters. Say: *Emily plants 5 roses. Some are yellow. Some are red. How many are yellow and how many are red?* 🍎 listen to the story, and then use connecting cubes to help act out the story to choose an operation. Then have students complete the equation to show the related fact for 2 + 1 = 3. *3 penguins are in a group. 1 leaves. How many penguins are left?*

$$4 + 1 = 5$$

$$\underline{\hspace{3em}} \quad \underline{\hspace{3em}} \quad \underline{\hspace{2em}}$$

$$\underline{\hspace{1.5em}} \bigcirc \underline{\hspace{1.5em}} = \underline{\hspace{1.5em}}$$

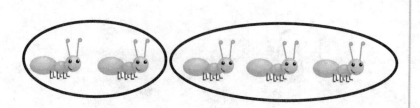

$$5 - 3 = 2$$

♥ 4

$$3 + 1 = \underline{\hspace{3em}}$$

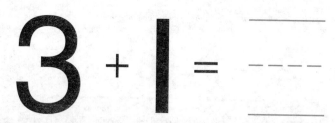

Directions Have students: ❸ tell a story for 4 – 3. Then have them draw a picture to illustrate their story and write the equation.
❹ solve the equation in any way they choose, and then tell how they solved the problem.

Name _____

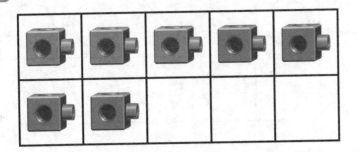

$$7 = 3 + 4$$

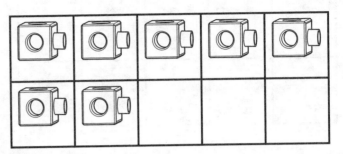

$$7 = \underline{} + \underline{}$$

$$9 = 6 + 3$$

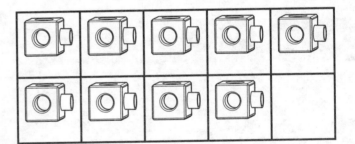

$$9 = \underline{} + \underline{}$$

Directions Have students: listen to each story, use and color cubes to model other ways to break apart 7 and 9 and tell how many of each color, and then complete the equation to match the cubes. ✋ Say: *Jada has 7 flowers. She puts some in a red vase and some in a blue vase. How many flowers will be in each vase?* ☕ Say: *9 children are going to ride a boat. They need life jackets. Some of the jackets are orange and some are red. How many of each color will they need if everyone has a life jacket?*

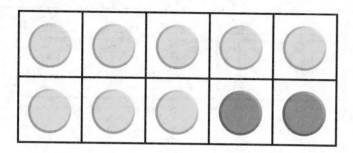

$$10 = 8 + 2$$

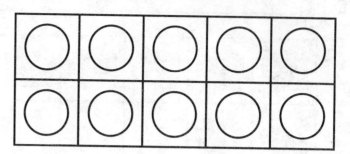

7

$$10 = \text{\_\_\_\_} + \text{\_\_\_\_}$$

$$1 + 9 = 10$$

8

$$6 + \text{\_\_\_\_} = 10$$

Directions Have students: 7 draw and color counters red and yellow to show another way to break 10 into two parts. Then complete the equation to match the counters; 8 count the green cubes to find one part of 10, use yellow cubes to find the number under the cover, and then complete the equation to show the parts of 10.

Topic 8 | Reteaching

Name _____

1

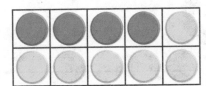

$$10 = \underline{\quad\quad} + \underline{\quad\quad}$$

2

_____

_____ fruits

3

(A) $5 + 4 = 9$ and $9 - 4 = 5$

(B) $5 + 2 = 7$ and $7 - 2 = 5$

(C) $5 + 3 = 8$ and $8 - 5 = 3$

(D) $5 + 1 = 6$ and $6 - 1 = 5$

4

☐ $2 + 6 = 8$ ☐ $2 + 7 = 9$

☐ $3 + 6 = 9$ ☐ $6 + 3 = 9$

☐ $6 + 4 = 10$

Directions Have students: **1** write an equation that shows how the red and yellow counters are used to show the parts that make 10. **2** count the fruits, draw counters to show how many more fruits are needed to make 10, and write the number that tells how many. **3** look at the picture and mark the best answer. Say: *What pair of addition and subtraction equations can be used to model a story about the apples?* **4** listen to the story, and then mark all the equations that show possible ways to break apart 9. *Valentina buys 9 beads to make a bracelet. Some beads are blue and some are purple. How many beads of each color could Valentina use to make a bracelet that has exactly 9 beads?*

5

$$5 = \underline{\quad\quad} + \underline{\quad\quad}$$

 6

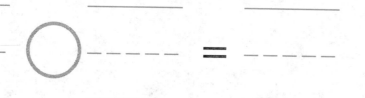 ⬭ = _____　　　　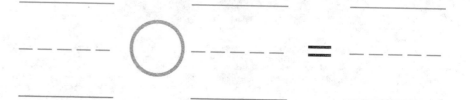 ⬭ = _____

 7

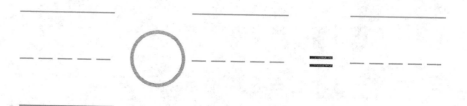 ⬭ = _____

Directions Have students: use yellow and red counters to show a way the 5 snails can be separated into 2 groups, draw circles around two groups of snails to show a number pair that matches the counters, and then complete the equation to show the way to make 5; look at the pictures as they listen to each story, use connecting cubes to act out each story and choose an operation, and then write the equations to show the related facts. Say: *2 penguins are in a group. 3 join them. How many penguins are there in all?* Then say: *5 penguins are in a group. 3 leave. How many penguins are left?* tell a story for 5 − 4. Then have them draw a picture to illustrate their story and write the equation.

Topic 8 | Assessment Practice

Name _____

8  $6 =$ _____ $+$ _____

9  $8 =$ _____ $+$ _____

10  $5 =$ _____ $+$ _____

Directions Have students: **8** draw a circle around two groups of cars to show number pairs for 6, and then complete the equation to match the picture and show the way to make 6; **9** draw a circle around two groups of onions to show number pairs for 8, and then complete the equation to match the picture and show the way to make 8; **10** look at the picture and listen to the story, draw circles to show how to break apart 5 flowers, and then write the numbers in the equation to match the circled groups of flowers in the picture. *Marco has 5 flowers. He gives some to his mom and some to his grandmother. How many flowers does he give to his mom? How many does he give to his grandmother?*

_____ + _____ = 10

_____

12

10 = _____ + _____

_____

13

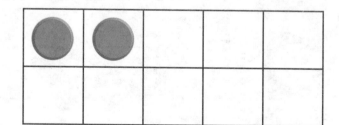

2 + _____ = 10

_____

Directions Have students: count the red cubes to find one part of 10, use blue cubes to find the number under the cover, and then complete the equation to show the parts of 10; 12 use red and blue crayons to color the cube train to show a way 10 can be separated into parts. Then have them complete the equation to match their picture and show each part of 10; 13 draw yellow counters in the ten-frame to show the missing part of 10. Then have them complete the equation to match the picture.

Topic 8 | Assessment Practice

Name _____

⭐ 1

$$7 = \text{-----} + \text{-----}$$

$$7 = \text{-----} + \text{-----}$$

🍎 2

$$\text{-----} = \text{-----} + \text{-----}$$

⭐ 3

$$\text{-----} + \text{-----} = 5$$

$$\text{-----} + \text{-----} = 5$$

$$5 - \text{-----} = \text{-----}$$

$$5 - \text{-----} = \text{-----}$$

Directions **Fern's Farmstand** Say: *Fern sells different fruits and vegetables at her farmstand.* Have students look at the: ⭐ carrots and cucumbers Fern has at her farmstand, and then write two equations to describe them; 🍎 lettuce and radishes Fern has at her farmstand, and then write an equation to describe them; ⭐ red and green peppers that Fern is selling at her farmstand. Have students tell a story about them, and then write the missing numbers in the equation for their story. Then have students write the missing numbers in the other three equations.

$9 = \text{---} + \text{---}$ $9 = \text{---} + \text{---}$

$4 + \text{---} = 10$

Directions Have students: ♥ listen to the story, draw pictures to show two ways to break apart 9 and solve the problem, and then complete the equations to match. *Fern grows tomatoes for her farmstand. She grows red tomatoes and yellow tomatoes. How many tomatoes of each color should she put in her farmstand so that she has exactly 9 tomatoes in her farmstand?* 🖐 listen to the story, draw counters to complete the model, and then write an equation to solve the problem. *Fern has 10 onions in her farmstand. 4 of them are on one side of the farmstand. How many are on the other side?*

   Topic 8 | Performance Task

Glossary

A

above

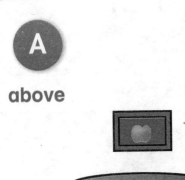

add

$$3 + 2 = 5$$

addition sentence

3 and 5 is 8.

attribute

B

balance scale

behind

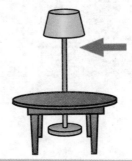

below

beside

break apart

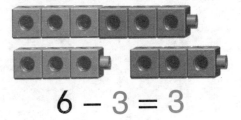

$$6 - 3 = 3$$

capacity

category

| II | III |

chart

| II | III |

circle

classify

column

I	2	3	4	5
II	12	13	14	15
21	22	23	24	25
31	32	33	34	35

compare

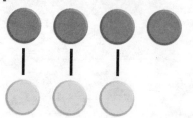

cone

count

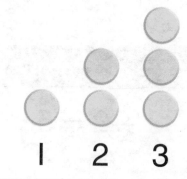

| I | 2 | 3 |

cube

cylinder

decade

1	2	3	4	5	6	7	8	9	10
11	12	13	14	15	16	17	18	19	20
21	22	23	24	25	26	27	28	29	30
31	32	33	34	35	36	37	38	39	40
41	42	43	44	45	46	47	48	49	50
51	52	53	54	55	56	57	58	59	60
61	62	63	64	65	66	67	68	69	70
71	72	73	74	75	76	77	78	79	80
81	82	83	84	85	86	87	88	89	90
91	92	93	94	95	96	97	98	99	100

difference

$$8 - 3 = 5$$

eight

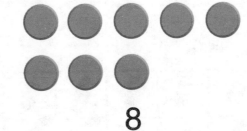

$$8$$

eighteen

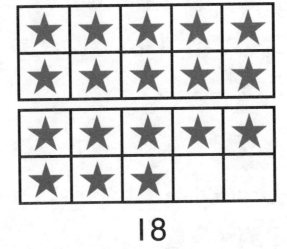

$$18$$

eleven

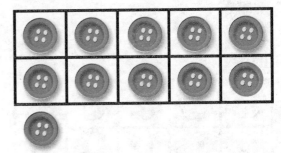

$$11$$

equal

equal sign (=)

$$4 + 3 = 7$$

equation

$$5 + 3 = 8$$

$$8 = 8$$

fifteen

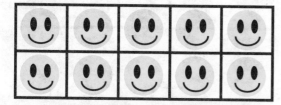

15

five

5

flat surface

four

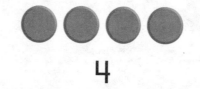

4

fourteen

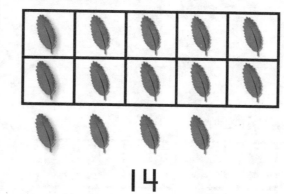

14

G

greater than

group

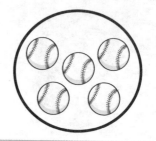

H

heavier

height

hexagon

How many more?

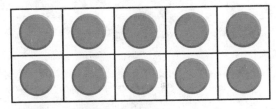

hundred chart

1	2	3	4	5	6	7	8	9	10
11	12	13	14	15	16	17	18	19	20
21	22	23	24	25	26	27	28	29	30
31	32	33	34	35	36	37	38	39	40
41	42	43	44	45	46	47	48	49	50
51	52	53	54	55	56	57	58	59	60
61	62	63	64	65	66	67	68	69	70
71	72	73	74	75	76	77	78	79	80
81	82	83	84	85	86	87	88	89	90
91	92	93	94	95	96	97	98	99	100

column

row →

I

in all

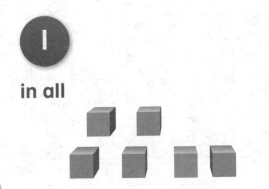

in front of

J

join

L

left

length

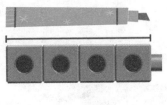

4

less than

4   (3)

lighter

longer

---

minus sign (−)

$$8 - 3 = 5$$

---

model

N

next to

---

nine

9

---

nineteen

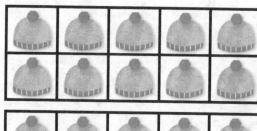

19

---

none

0

---

number

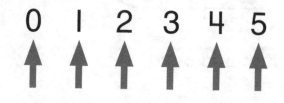

O

one

1

---

ones

5	6	7	8	9	10
15	16	17	18	19	20
25	26	27	28	29	30

operation

$$4 \oplus 2 = 6$$
$$4 \ominus 2 = 2$$

order

$$0 \to 1 \to 2 \to 3 \to 4 \to 5$$

P

part

pattern

10 20 30 40 50

plus sign (+)

$$3 + 1 = 4$$

R

rectangle

roll

row

1	2	3	4	5
11	12	13	14	15
21	22	23	24	25
31	32	33	34	35

S

same number as

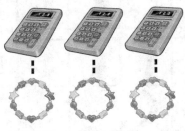

separate

seven

7

seventeen

17

shorter

side

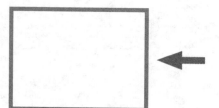

six

6

sixteen

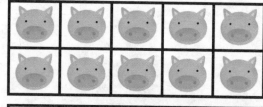

16

slide

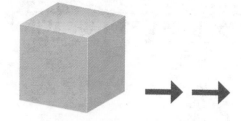

sort

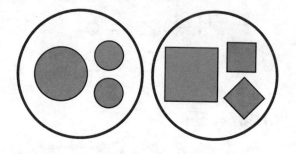

sphere

square

stack

subtract

$$3 - 1 = 2$$

subtraction sentence

4 take away 3 is 1.

sum

$$2 + 3 = 5$$

↑

T

take away

taller

↑

tally mark

 |
II | III

ten

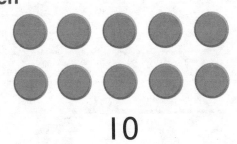

10

tens

5	6	7	8	9	10
15	16	17	18	19	20
25	26	27	28	29	30

thirteen

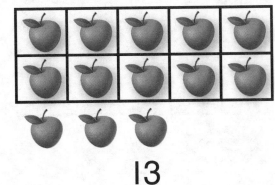

13

three

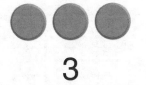

3

three-dimensional shape

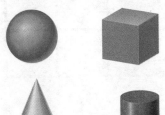

triangle

twelve

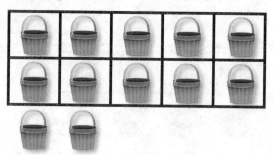

12

twenty

20

two

2

two-dimensional shape

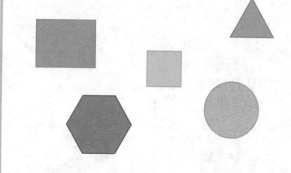

V

vertex/vertices

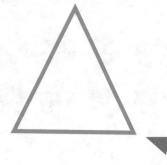

W

weighs

weight

whole

Z

zero

0

enVision® Mathematics
Common Core

Photographs

Every effort has been made to secure permission and provide appropriate credit for photographic material. The publisher deeply regrets any omission and pledges to correct errors called to its attention in subsequent editions.

Unless otherwise acknowledged, all photographs are the property of Savvas Learning Company LLC.

Photo locators denoted as follows: Top (T), Center (C), Bottom (B), Left (L), Right (R), Background (Bkgd)

1 Jorge Salcedo/Shutterstock; **3** (T) Leighton Photography & Imaging/Shutterstock, (C) FatCamera/iStock/Getty Images, (B) Amy Cicconi/Alamy Stock Photo; **4** (Bkgrd) Rawpixel/Shutterstock, (L) Peacorx/Shutterstock, (R) Yulia Sverdlova/Shutterstock; **57** (L) Evgeny Murtola/Shutterstock, (R) 2rut/Shutterstock; **59** (T) Aleksey Stemmer/Shutterstock, (B) Pedro Turrini Neto/Shutterstock; **60** (T) Loan Florin Cnejevici/123RF, (B) KPG_Payless/Shutterstock; **89** Michal Kolodziejczyk/Fotolia; **91** (T) Carterdayne/E+/Getty Images, (C) Ssuaphotos/Shutterstock, (B) Cdwheatley/iStock/Getty Images; **92** (Bkgrd) Owen Franken/Alamy Stock Photo, Evgeny Karandaev/Shutterstock; **137** James Insogna/Fotolia; **139** (T) LightField Studios/Shutterstock, (B) Daniel Reiter/Alamy Stock Photo; **140** (T) Dmitro2009/Shutterstock, (B) Ian Dagnall/Alamy Stock Photo; **169** Christopher Elwell/Shutterstock; **171** (T) Yui/Shutterstock, (C) Monkey Business Images/Shutterstock, (B) Ted Foxx/Alamy Stock Photo; **172** (Bkgrd) Best dog photo/Shutterstock, Creative Stock Exchange/Shutterstock; **197** Tankist276/Shutterstock; **199** (T) Frank Krahmer/Radius Images/Getty Images, (B) Sean Pavone/Shutterstock; **200** (T) Wisanu_nuu/Shutterstock, (B) Phonix_a Pk.sarote/Shutterstock;

245 Somdul/Shutterstock; **247** (T) Helen Marsden christmassowhite/DigitalVision/Getty Images, (C) 21singha/Shutterstock, (B) Engel Ching/Alamy Stock Photo; **248** (Bkgrd) Leonori/Shutterstock, Gts/Shutterstock, Sarawut Aiemsinsuk/Shutterstock; **289** Winai Tepsuttinun/Shutterstock; **291** (T) Chesh/Alamy Stock Photo, (B) Irina Fischer/Shutterstock; **292** (T) Vovan/Shutterstock, (B) Ron Zmiri/Shutterstock; **345** Panda3800/Shutterstock; **347** (T) Pixpack/123RF, (C) Delpixel/Shutterstock, (B) Dobermaraner/Shutterstock; **348** (Bkgrd) 5second/123RF, Elena Zajchikova/Shutterstock; **385** Turbojet/Shutterstock; **387** (T) Oliveromg/Shutterstock (B) Daniel Mortell/123RF; **388** (T) Inna Reznik/Shutterstock (B) Robert F. Leahy/Shutterstock; **429** Andrey Pavlov/Shutterstock; **431** (T) Nattawat Kaewjirasit/Shutterstock, (C) Africa Studio/Shutterstock, (B) Evru/Shutterstock; **432** (Bkgrd) Anatoli Styf/Shutterstock, Romsvetnik/Shutterstock; **461** Eugene Sergeev/Shutterstock; **463** (T) Robert McGouey/Alamy Stock Photo, (B) ESB Professional/Shutterstock; **464** (T) Olga Ezdakova/Shutterstock, (B) Milena Ugrinova/Shutterstock; **505** Michael Flippo/Fotolia; **507** (T) Monkey Business Images/Shutterstock, (C) Africa Studio/Shutterstock, (B) Stanislav Samoylik/Shutterstock; **508** (Bkgrd) Tomertu/123RF, Berke/Shutterstock; **545** Singkham/Shutterstock; **547** (T) Jean-Paul Chassenet/123RF, (B) Guy Bell/REX/Shutterstock; **548** (T) Wavebreakmediamicro/123RF, (B) Giannimarchetti/Shutterstock.